CW00566622

THE ROYAL NAVAL COLLEGE OSBORNE

A History 1903–21

Michael Partridge

SUTTON PUBLISHING

First published in 1999 by
Sutton Publishing Limited · Phoenix Mill
Thrupp · Stroud · Gloucestershire · GL5 2BU
in association with The Royal Naval Museum, Portsmouth

British Library Cataloguing in Publication Data
A catalogue record for this book is available from the British Library

ISBN 0 7509 1969 8

Typeset in 10/13 pt New Baskerville.
Typesetting and origination by
Sutton Publishing Limited.
Printed in Great Britain by
Redwood Books, Trowbridge, Wiltshire.

Contents

The publication of this book has been made possible by the generous support of the Society for Nautical Research

Acknowledgements

The author would like to acknowledge the permission of the Public Record Office to use and quote from the Admiralty and Office of Works correspondence. He would also like to thank the Churchill Archive, Churchill College, Cambridge, for permission to use and quote from papers of Admiral Lord Fisher, Commander J.C.H. Nelson, Captain S.W. Roskill and Admiral Lord Wester Wemyss.

The Lord Fisher, Mr David French and Mrs Helen Nelson kindly gave permission for their family papers to be used. The author would also like to thank the Trustees of the National Maritime Museum, Greenwich, for permission to use and quote from the papers of Admiral Sir Louis Hamilton and Admiral Sir Herbert Richmond.

The author would particularly like to thank the 'survivors' of Osborne Naval College, whose recollections provide the main sources for this work. All of these gentlemen (and their wives) provided him with hospitality as well as historical evidence, and enjoyed being treated as an historical source. Grateful acknowledgement is therefore extended to:

Lieutenant Commander P. Barlow, Commander R. Barrett, Commander H. Barry, Reverend H. Bliss, Commander W. Bradbury, Mr J. Bryans, Lieutenant Commander J. Cobb, Commander H.G.D. de Chair, Captain C. Drake, Reverend A. Ford, Captain G. French, Commander L. Gowlland, Captain J.R. Grindle, Captain E. Hale, Admiral J. Ham, Captain K. Harkness, Commander H. Jenkins, Admiral Sir Charles Madden, Commander E. Morrison, Captain M. Neame, Vice Admiral Sir Arthur Pedder, Brigadier C. Richardson, Vice Admiral J. Salter, Captain E.H. Thomas and Mr J. Worthington.

These interviews were all conducted between August and December 1987 and it is to be regretted that this book has taken so long to appear.

Dr Evan Davies collected the written sources from the Churchill Archive and the National Maritime Museum for his own researches, and I am grateful for his kindness in lending them to me and allowing me to use them here. He also lent copies of *Life on Board HMS Britannia, How to Become a Naval Officer,* and *The Entry and Training of Naval Cadets,* which I have used freely.

The author would also like to thank the Trustees of the Royal Naval Museum, Portsmouth, for permission to use its collections. Particular thanks go to Dr Chris Howard Bailey, Keeper of Collections and Director of Publications, Mr Stephen Courtney, Curator of Photographs, and Mr Alaistair Wilson, editorial consultant.

The author is grateful to Mr John Milner and his family for the use of photographs from an album in his possession. Copying of these was kindly arranged by Captain Peter Hore, RN.

Captain J.L. Williams, RN, organised meetings of the survivors of the College in the 1980s and collected material relating to it, which he kindly lent to the author. He is not alone in hoping that a more complete record of the College's existence might yet be created.

The assistance of the Imperial War Museum in providing the tape recording equipment and arranging the transcription of the interviews conducted by the author is gratefully acknowledged.

Mr Stuart Smith and staff of the Crown Estate Urban Estates Business Group, London, provided useful information on the later history of the College buildings at the author's request and are thanked for doing so.

The author would like to thank Rear Admiral Roger Morris and Lieutenant Commander Lawrence Phillips, and the then Council of the Society for Nautical Research, under whose guidance this project was begun. Rear Admiral Richard Hill has done much to bring it to completion. The Society is pleased to acknowledge the help of the Plessey Corporation and Racal Electronics, both of whom made grants towards the costs of the project.

The author's colleagues at St Mary's, Strawberry Hill, are thanked for their understanding while this work was being completed.

Finally, but not least, the help of Ms Karen Partridge is gratefully acknowledged. She has helped the author in his research, typed (frequently more than once) what he had written in an often barely legible hand, and thereby made this work possible.

Introduction

At the beginning of the twentieth century the Royal Navy faced several serious problems. Not least among these was concern for the recruitment and training of officers. This was not just a question of numbers, but of their specialisation once in the service. There was perceived to be a dangerous shortfall in the quality and quantity of those destined to serve in the engine-rooms of the fleet. Indeed, the social status of engineers was such that they were generally looked down on by 'deck' officers, those of the 'Executive branch' who specialised in Gunnery, Torpedo and Navigation, on the way to command ships and, eventually, fleets. Few of them wished to get involved in the dirty work carried on in engine-rooms. To overcome this general feeling of hostility would be no easy matter. The perceptions of most naval officers would have to be radically altered and more Engineer Officers made available.

However, the Royal Navy possessed at least one energetic administrator who was prepared to tackle this issue – Admiral Sir John Arbuthnot Fisher. Fisher can be seen as the brains behind the 'Selborne scheme' for naval officers. This, and the 'Cawdor Memorandum', which followed it, set out a new recruiting strategy whereby all naval officer cadets would now receive a measure of engineering training, and would specialise in engineering (or one of the Executive branches) only later in their careers. But this change would force others to be made. It meant, in particular, that more time would be needed to educate cadets – this, indeed, went up to four years – and they would have to be recruited earlier, so their training would be completed at what was perceived to be a suitably young age.

All of this meant that there would be more naval cadets being trained than before: but where was this training to take place? The decision had already been taken to close the ships that constituted the naval college HMS Britannia and build a suitable, land-based, establishment at Dartmouth. This, however, would take some time to build, and even when it was finished it would not be large enough to hold all the cadets in training. Hence, it was decided to open a 'junior' college, where cadets would receive their first two years training, before completing their time at Dartmouth. This was the Royal Naval College at Osborne, Isle of Wight, which opened its doors in September 1903 and closed in May 1921.

The primary aims of this present work are to outline the history of the Royal Naval College at Osborne and to try and assess the extent to which it achieved the aims of its founders. It will look at both the official records, where they survive, and at less official ones, to assess the background and motivation of those who went there, and contrast this with official intentions, as well as at other, specific questions. These include an investigation into the process of admission, claims that the Osborne site was unhealthy and the arrangements for, and maintenance of, discipline within the College. Most attention, however, is paid to the daily life of cadets at the College. This includes material on their daily routine – both inside and outside of the classroom – and on its ethos and atmosphere.

An attempt has been made, using the eye-witness accounts of former cadets of the College as well as other, written, records, to recover the story of the establishment from its earliest days to its eventual closure. It did not exist for long, but during its lifetime some 4,000 cadets passed through its doors. Most, if not all, saw service as naval officers (others became army officers, or High Court Judges or served their country in many other ways). This book is their memorial, and a memoir of the life of a now almost forgotten naval training establishment: the Royal Naval College, Osborne.

CHAPTER ONE

The Foundation and Evolution of the College

In 1857 Admiralty circular number 288 had decreed that officer cadets should serve on board a training vessel moored, initially, in Haslar Creek, Portsmouth. In August of that year the two-decker line of battle ship HMS *Illustrious* accepted her first cadets, being replaced two years later by a larger three-decker, HMS *Britannia*. Complaints about the unhealthy site of this vessel (those about the ship herself were ignored) led to her removal, in February 1862, to Portland, where she remained for eighteen months. It was only at the end of September 1863 that she took up moorings in the River Dart by Mill Creek.[1]

For the next thirty years, executive officer cadets – those destined to command ships and fleets – were trained on board vessels moored at this location. In 1864 the two-decker *Hindostan* was moored astern of *Britannia* and the two ships were joined by a walkway. The original *Britannia* was replaced in 1869 by a larger vessel, the three-decker *Prince of Wales*, who took on her name. However, as early as 1875 a committee chaired by Admiral E.B. Rice had reported that it would be better to train the cadets on shore. Another committee, chaired by Admiral G.G. Wellesley, had taken up this suggestion and looked at no less than thirty-two possible sites. In the end they had come to the conclusion that Mount Boone, overlooking the existing training vessels, would be 'admirable . . . in all respects' for this purpose. But, for reasons now lost, nothing came of this proposal. It was only in November 1895 that the Admiralty definitely decided in favour of a land-based training course for cadets. As part of the proposals put forward by the First Lord, G.J. Goschen, in March 1896, it was announced that it was intended to purchase the land on Mount Boone recommended by the Wellesley Committee ten years earlier as the site for a new naval officer training college.[2] This ran into some opposition: 'many adverse comments about sewage, smallpox, scarlet fever and a relaxing and oppressive climate in the summer [complaints remarkably similar to those later levelled at the Osborne site] were all renewed.'[3]

In addition, negotiations to purchase the land did not run smoothly. But Goschen had personally visited and approved the site in September 1897 and, after protracted negotiations, a final settlement was reached in June 1898. The last tenant left Mount Boone Farm in October. The Admiralty engaged the eminent architect Sir Aston Webb to design the new buildings and in April 1900 agreed a contract for their construction with Higgs and Hill, who estimated the work would take three and a half years to complete and would cost £22,600.[4]

Even now not everyone was content. *Truth* magazine informed its readers that:

> if the hideous Admiralty design is carried out, the hills above Dartmouth harbour will be crowned by a building which appears to be a combination of a workhouse and stable.[5]

– an ungenerous assessment.

Work continued on the site throughout 1901, with construction of the sick-quarters speeded up because of a 'flu epidemic, which killed two cadets on the ships. By March 1902, when King Edward VII laid the foundation stone, work on the main building had also commenced.[6] But by September 1903 the College buildings were still incomplete, a fact which was to have some serious repercussions.

While consideration about where to train executive officer cadets had continued, the entry regulations for them had been repeatedly amended. In 1869 it had been decided that prospective cadets would be aged between twelve and thirteen years, would have to take a competitive examination for the seventy-four places available and would have to pass a formal medical examination. Five years later the nature of the examination itself was amended: from now on it was to be a qualifying examination rather than a competitive one. This system lasted only until 1881, when a competitive examination was reintroduced (which from 1887 was administered by the 'neutral' Civil Service Commissioners).[7]

In 1886 a committee chaired by Vice Admiral W.G. Luard proposed that the age at which boys were to be taken on should be raised to between thirteen and fourteen years.[8] Ten years later, in 1896, the Goschen Board of Admiralty again raised the minimum age of entry to between fourteen and a half and fifteen and a half years. They also agreed that these cadets would spend four terms, each of four months duration, at the new land-based College.[9] Boys of this age could receive nominations from serving Admirals and from Captains on their first appointment to a command. Most of the nominations, however, were the result of applications made by the parent or guardian of a boy direct to the Assistant Private Secretary to the First Lord of the Admiralty. If nominated, the boy had to compete in a rather challenging written examination (unless he happened to be the son of one of the six 'gentlemen in the colonies' or seven servicemen whose boys had only to pass a test examination).

The subjects of this examination fell into two classes: Class I, where candidates had to obtain a set aggregate of marks, and Class II, which were available as a source of additional marks. The Class I subjects included mathematics (divided into arithmetic, algebra and geometry and the candidate had to secure pass marks in all three); English, English history, geography and two languages, from a choice of Latin, French and German. A language was also available in Class II (though not if it had been taken in Class I), as was drawing, and 'natural science' (or mechanics with either physics or chemistry, the latter two with practical tests). Candidates who failed the examination had another chance to take it, if they remained within the age limits set down.

It was estimated by one contemporary authority that

the curriculum at any good school is sufficient preparation for boys of average ability, but it is to be borne in mind that a certain percentage of marks *must* be obtained in the subjects of the test examination.

Inattention to these compulsory subjects in the earlier stages of a boy's education renders it necessary in many cases to send him to be specially worked up in them, during the last months before the examination.[10]

– this was, after all, the great age of the naval 'crammer'.

By the turn of the twentieth century, the Royal Navy faced several major problems. Among these were the rise of new rivals, and developments in technology. It was the consequences of the latter developments which were to have the greatest impact on the training of naval officers. The adoption of increasingly sophisticated propulsion machinery in naval vessels meant that larger numbers of more specialised Engineer Officers were required on board ships. These engineers, however, were trained separately from other naval officers, at a special establishment at Keyham. This, the Royal Naval Engineering College, had been opened in July 1880, replacing the training ship HMS *Marlborough*. Cadets for Keyham were taken from older boys who, it would seem, came from a somewhat different background to those who joined *Britannia*. 'There is little doubt that instruction was of a very high order and the products of this institution were able men',[11] who could, when their training was complete, rise through the ranks of naval officer, even becoming Admirals in due time. But they remained as 'Engineers', on a separate list from those officers who had received their training on board the *Britannia*, and who joined the 'Executive' list, and they could not command ships or fleets.

The result of this was a deep division within the ranks of the naval officer corps and a general perception that the Engineer officer was a 'second class citizen'. There was ample evidence to support this view, as knighthoods and other honours flowed more freely in the direction of the Executive Officers than they did to their engineering counterparts. Sir John Fisher, at the time Second Naval Lord and responsible for personnel, had got to the heart of the matter early in 1902:

> All must admit we have been slow to appreciate the alteration in the status of the Engineer consequent on the abolition of masts and sails. The deck officers have no longer what really was an all absorbing task in becoming proficient in handling a ship under sail.

and he put forward a practical suggestion:

> It would be good for our officers as a body to get much more than the present scanty attendance of the midshipmen when the ship is under steam and their entire absence when the maximum propelling power is being exerted which is the most impressive time of instruction.

He went on to detail how he believed the problem of the lowly status of the Engineer Officer could be dealt with:

> This attention in training so essential for the efficiency of the Navy can be readily brought about by following precisely the same method as was employed to make the navigation of His Majesty's Ships more

efficient. . . . The method then pursued . . . was gradually to stop the entry of the old navigating class and increase that of Naval Cadets and for officers so selected (and in view of the advantages and extra pay there has been no lack of candidates) to take up navigating duties as sub-lieutenant . . . following on to the Captain's list and the flag list in the usual course. Such a plan is suggested with a feeling of absolute confidence in its ultimate success in regard to the engineering duties of the Navy. This course is not proposed on account of the present engineering agitation, it is proposed solely in the interests of the service. . . . It is not worthwhile to enter into the grievances put forward by the engineers. . . . The general good and efficiency of the Navy renders it imperative that the entry of engineer students as at present engaged shall be gradually stopped and the entry of Naval Cadets gradually increased in like proportion, and that instruction from the moment of entry should in a large measure, *at least half the time*, be devoted to engineering. That like Gunnery, Torpedo and Navigation officers as at present, there should be Engineer Officers. . . .

To persuade reluctant 'deck' or Executive Officers into the ranks of engineers, Fisher suggested a simple solution - an increase of pay for the latter. He also argued that fewer Engineer Officers would be required if another element in his scheme was taken up: namely, that a class of 'Artificer Engineers' – Warrant Officers – should be trained. These, he pointed out, would form the 'backbone' of the engine room establishment, just as they already did in torpedo work and gunnery.[12]

These ideas formed the basis of a statement of naval policy issued by the First Lord of the Admiralty, the Earl of Selborne, in December 1902. In that month, he produced his famous (or, to some, notorious) memorandum, on the scheme for naval reforms that still bears his name. The key to this new scheme was that all officers, naval and Royal Marine, and Executive and Engineer, 'shall enter the service as naval cadets under exactly the same conditions between the ages of 12 and 13'.[13] They would then spend four years at naval colleges, two at the senior, which was currently under construction at Dartmouth, and two at a junior one, projected for construction at Osborne, on the Isle of Wight. Cadets would attend each college for some thirty-nine weeks of the year: each year would be divided into three terms. While at college, cadets would study a broad-based syllabus, which would include practical subjects such as seamanship and engineering, together with more academic ones like English and history.

On successful completion of this part of the course, cadets would spend eight months in one of two training cruisers (in 1914 these were HMS *Cornwall* and HMS *Cumberland*). This would normally include one six-month, or less frequently, two three-month, cruises. During this time they would continue to receive instruction in seamanship, which would include torpedo and electrical work, engineering and navigation, pilotage and gunnery. When this time was completed, the cadet became a Midshipman, and spent two years and four months in this rank. This was concluded by an examination in Seamanship and Navigation which, if passed, placed him on the Acting Sub-Lieutenant's list. Within six months, he should have passed examinations in gunnery, torpedo and engineering, to become a Sub-Lieutenant. After at least thirteen months at this rank, he was examined for the rank of Lieutenant. Once he had been a commissioned officer (Sub-Lieutenant or Lieutenant) for between one and three years, the officer could choose to specialise in one of five branches of the service: Navigation, Gunnery, Torpedo and – what was new under the Selborne scheme – Engineering or Royal Marines.[14] Thus, one of the cardinal features of the Selborne scheme would be introduced: there would be 'one system of supply, one system of entry, [and] one system of training' for all naval officers, including engineers.[15]

In the event, only those cadets who entered the Navy between the introduction of the Selborne scheme in September 1903 and September 1910, or who joined from 1917 onwards, were able to spend the full four years (or twelve terms) at Osborne and Dartmouth. The outbreak of war with Germany in August 1914 meant the time spent in the Colleges was reduced. Cadets who had entered the service in 1913, 1914 or 1915 reported staying there for ten, rather than twelve, terms.[16] The senior term at Osborne was even, briefly, sent to sea in July 1914:

> The war started and we were sent to the test mobilisation. I was in the *Princess Royal* but the Osborne cadets were sent back to Osborne for one term but the Dartmouth cadets were sent to sea as sea-going cadets and were killed in large numbers, many of whom got Distinguished Service Crosses at the age of fifteen and so on.[17]

By 1916 time spent at the Colleges had been further reduced to nine terms, that at Osborne being cut to four terms, or just over one year:

We were in the middle of the war. The fleet required a large number of midshipmen. They were milked off early at Dartmouth and as the accommodation in Dartmouth became vacant so they took terms away from Osborne rather earlier than normal. We were one of those who were removed early.[18]

At the height of the war, cadets entering in September 1916 and January 1917 spent only three terms at the junior College.[19] Discussions at the Admiralty during 1917 might have cut the land-based training courses still further. The Earl of Selborne recommended in July of that year that to make up for a projected shortfall of officers for the fleet in 1918–19, the land-based course should be cut to six terms only. The Admiralty Board agreed to act on this, and proposed sending the three senior terms to sea in September, while moving the three senior Osborne terms to Dartmouth, and sending the remaining Dartmouth and senior Osborne term to sea at Christmas 1917.[20] This was not taken up, however. As the war ended, cadets reverted to a twelve-term College course, and the practice of sending fifteen-year-old youths to sea as officers in warships ceased.[21]

In 1902 Selborne, as well as Sir John Fisher, had anticipated strong opposition to their proposals; hence, Selborne had detailed a justification for them in his memorandum. The early age of recruiting the boys, he stated, would mean cadets would be no older than twenty at the start of their careers as officers, and this would help the naval policy of 'early homogenous training', and give cadets time to assimilate the 'extra' work that was now being added to their curriculum. In addition, the age of entry was that 'when boys have been most successfully moulded to seamanship' and when most left private preparatory schools. He also noted that many public schools were not training the boys in the way the Navy hoped, but he added a reassurance for parents: the entrance examination would be 'of an elementary kind, and confined to those subjects in which a carefully educated boy has usually been instructed up to the age of 13'.

No other changes to the entry arrangements (medical, etc) were contemplated. The cadets, he concluded, would now be given

elementary instruction in physics and marine engineering, and in the use of tools and machines in connection therewith [as well as a] good grounding in general subjects.[22]

Selborne and Fisher had allies for at least part of their proposals. Captain Herbert Richmond was one who was to become a noteworthy figure in the development of naval education, particularly in the 1920s and 1930s. He quite recognised:

> the difficulty of the Admiralty in the matter of age of entry. Certainly the elementary education of boys is the duty of their parents and not the state. But the difficulty which arises is the amount which has to be done in a certain time by a certain age.
>
> Given a limiting age, older than which we do not want our officers to become Lieuts., given a certain length of time which they should serve at sea before they take that rating . . . and given a length of time in which their teaching can be completed we find we *must* enter them young. . . .

Richmond, not surprisingly, also had very definite ideas of his own about what the young naval cadet should learn, namely,

> such an amount as would place him at sea with a good knowledge of Navigation, the Mathematics necessary for that and sufficient Statics, Dynamics and Hydrostatics as are desirable in an officer. Seamanship, Gunnery, Natural Science, History and Languages, Torpedo, Steam & Construction.
>
> The History should be taught in a manner which will lead to a strategical course. . . . I would insist on every officer knowing one foreign language fluently & if taught properly this can be done. . . .
>
> To send every officer to sea with a good education of this kind I think four years are necessary. There should be no smattering of Gunnery, or the other subjects, but a good knowledge.

At this time, however, Richmond felt the training on shore should be completed after the boy had spent a period of time at sea. Richmond's ideas about naval education to some extent coincided with Fisher's: the curriculum he outlined bore more than a passing resemblance to that adopted at Osborne College. Richmond also recorded his 'undisguised pleasure' when the Selborne scheme announced the reduction in the age of entry,[23] but he was less happy with some of its details.

Others, however, objected to the whole scheme. One retired naval officer summed up the 'navalist' opposition rather well:

It is easy to see that the majority of the . . . executive naval officers, for one reason or another, disliked the new scheme. The sahibs believed that, inevitably, the high standards of what the executive officer should be, and the duties he should perform, would be lowered. The bluff seaman, appreciating the poorness of his theoretical equipment, felt that he, more than ever, would fall into the background; and others, with a strong sense of conservatism which is bound to be the feature of a fighting force, hated change of all sort; hating change merely because it was change.[24]

It was not only serving officers who opposed the measure. When H.O. Arnold Forster, the Secretary of the Admiralty, introduced the Navy estimates for 1903/4 in March 1903, he was strongly attacked in the House of Commons. Gibson Bowles, a staunchly conservative figure and retired naval officer, argued that no change was necessary; the scheme, he declared, was entirely Selborne's and was designed simply to calm the unrest among Engineers. Bowles did not believe Engineers in the Royal Navy needed to be officers – they were only mechanics – and a pay increase was all that was necessary. He also believed that the basic concept of 'interchangeability', which he erroneously believed was being introduced, was unworkable and that the whole measure was simply a means of increasing the Admiralty's patronage. He proposed the entire scheme be reconsidered. He was seconded, in a much more persuasive speech, by Sir John Gorst. Gorst believed the scheme to be 'fundamentally bad' and objected to the new low age for recruits – the Admiralty, after all, did not have a good educational record. He believed that the competitive examination would force boys to 'cram', and wondered what would become of boys who failed the course. He also objected that only rich parents would be able to send their boys to the new College and the Navy would become an even more socially exclusive club than it was already. Other MPs also objected to the new low age of entry, one of them being Sir Henry Campbell Bannerman, the Liberal opposition leader: but when the issue was put to a vote the Government was in a clear majority with 200 votes to 57.[25]

At the same time, Selborne himself came under strong attack in the House of Lords from the Earl of Glasgow, at that time President of the Institute of Naval Architects. Glasgow echoed Bowles' view that the scheme was introduced solely to placate Engineers. It was, he said, unnecessary and unworkable, and that if it did work the quality of naval officers generally would be reduced. On the other hand, Earl Spencer, a former First Lord of the Admiralty, was pleased to see the Admiralty had responded to the need for change, although he was cautious about some elements of the scheme and anxious that poorer boys should not be totally excluded. Selborne's own defence repeated the essence of his memorandum and he successfully weathered this storm.[26]

These debates brought out the sources of opposition to the Selborne scheme that were to persist throughout the next few years and they fall into two broad categories. In the first were those like Bowles and Admiral Lord Charles Beresford, who represented the staunchly conservative point of view. This was that the existing state of affairs was more or less satisfactory and the kind of radical change Selborne was proposing was unnecessary. These men generally sat on the Conservative benches of the House of Commons and drew a considerable amount of support from serving (Executive) officers in the Royal Navy. It seems to have arisen primarily from a diehard opposition to change and found expression in the Parliamentary utterances of several characters who the Government began increasingly to recognise over the years.

The second source of opposition, however, was of a different type. This arose from the view that the changes Selborne was proposing were positively harmful from a social point of view. Some, like Sir John Gorst and E. Robertson, felt that the officer corps of the Royal Navy was simply too socially exclusive already. By closing the Royal Naval Engineering College at Keyham, a route by which boys from the lower middle and artisan classes could secure access to commissioned rank was also being closed. If all of the cadets were trained at one naval college, they reasoned, then only richer parents could send their sons there. Added to this was the fact that many boys from this upper social class simply did not wish to become naval officers: hence the problem of recruiting sufficient boys would not only remain under the new scheme, but would be exacerbated. Support for this point of view was generally to be found on the more radical Liberal benches of the House of Commons, and it was opposition of this sort that the Government found most difficult to deal with.

While Selborne and his allies were able to overcome the initial opposition to his scheme, the question of education for naval officers did not come to rest and debates on the future of the proposals occupied MPs on more than one occasion.[27] The Admiralty, however, stoutly defended its record on naval officer education: as the Civil Lord of the

Admiralty, E.G. Pretyman, declared in his speech on the Navy estimates in 1905, 'The training at Osborne has been, and continues to be, an unqualified success.'[28]

But the Selborne scheme had not, apparently, gone far enough for Sir John Fisher, who had returned to the Admiralty as First Naval Lord in the autumn of 1904. In that year, a committee chaired by Admiral Sir Archibald Douglas had reported that more training would be needed before any Executive officer presently in the service would be able to perform even the most basic duty of an Engineer officer afloat. Fisher argued that the committee was behind the times. Under the Selborne scheme this would not be the case, simply because now 'These two distinct branches of knowledge [seamanship and engineering] have been taught together from early youth.' But Fisher was aware of the urgent need to raise the status of Engineering Officers in the fleet, so that 'all class distinctions would be forever abolished, and all officers would serve on equal terms . . .'.[29] He therefore pressed for a truly 'common entry' for all naval officers (at this stage he also included Royal Marine officers) – all would go to one College and, while there, all would learn engineering and the other skills required of a junior naval (and Royal Marine) officer.

He also acknowledged the force of the social exclusivity argument:

Surely we are drawing our Nelsons from too narrow a class . . . combined with the cost of the subsequent training our present system excludes all but a very small fraction of the population from serving the King as naval officers. It admits the duke's son if he is fit, but it excludes the cook's son if he is fit or not. It ought to admit both, *but only if both are fit.* . . .

There seems to be only one way of solving this problem. Initial fitness must be secured, as at present, by careful selection at the outset, and if the promise is not fulfilled as time goes on – if brains, character, or manners prove wanting – ruthless exclusion, whether of duke's son or of cook's son, must be the inflexible rule. But do not exclude for poverty alone, either at the outset or afterwards. Let every fit boy have his chance. . . .[30]

All of this was to have its effect on the entry and training of naval officers. As Fisher recognised, the Selborne scheme had its limitations. Under its provisions, while all officer cadets would receive the same course of training in the same institution and separate training for Engineer Officer cadets would be done away with and the College at Keyham closed, there would still be separate 'branches' of the service that future officers would have to choose to enter. It was hoped sufficient numbers would choose to serve in the Engineer branch, so that the list of Engineer Officers would be filled and Selborne was keen to point out that once a cadet had chosen his branch, he could not thereafter change it. Once a cadet had reached the rank of Lieutenant he would specialise permanently in Engineering, the Royal Marines, or one of the Executive branches (Those who did not choose a branch became 'general service officers'). The two former would not be able to rise to command ships or fleets, and the Engineer and Executive branches would remain separate.[31]

While Selborne had suggested it might be ten years before the Admiralty reconsidered his scheme, Fisher was working on its reform as early as September 1905.[32] Before he made any definite plans, he wanted to see how the new cadets – those recruited under the new system up to two years earlier – were doing. Accordingly, he approached Rosslyn Wemyss, Captain of Osborne. His time there, Wemyss, declared, had convinced him that the Osborne cadets:

> will turn out far more capable all-round officers than the present generation of young officers serving at sea, and I see every reason to believe . . . that they will be . . . perfectly capable of taking charge of a watch in the engine-room of a battleship.

He went on:

> there is no reason why cadets entered under the New System should not (indeed there is every reason why they should) *all* be eligible to attain the very highest ranks in His Majesty's Navy. . . . If this principle be allowed, the sooner it is given out the better, for the following reasons:-
>
> (1) I have observed a tendency on the part of the parents of some of the cadets at Osborne to hope at least that their sons might never become Lieutenants (E), with no chance of commanding ships or fleets, and I have a suspicion that, for this reason, they have in some cases even discouraged their sons in engineering studies.
>
> (2) Carefully as I have striven to discourage, and even to stop, any

inclination among the cadets to talk of specialising into various branches of the service, I believe that, lately, they have taken to discussing this matter. Indeed, on one occasion, I heard a cadet say, 'Oh, I am not going to be an Engineer!'

(3) Keen as the cadets are about engineering at present, there is no doubt some danger that when, on going to sea, they mix with other Naval Officers, some of them who would, perhaps, of their own inclination, take up engineering, might be discouraged from doing so. . . .

The fact of giving out now that such disabilities are done away with would effectually put a stop to all these ideas, and would, I have no doubt, give an immense impetus to the Engineering training. . . .[33]

Similar views were expressed by Captain W.E. Goodenough, the Captain of Dartmouth College.[34] It was also the opinion of both a former and a present Engineer Officer at Osborne. The former, Engineer Commander H.W. Metcalfe, had no doubt that

the restriction originally put down in the new scheme for the entry and training of officers, whereby those officers specialising in engineering are debarred from rising to command fleets, might have the most serious and adverse influence on the Service in the future. . . .

Many of the smartest lads at Osborne have raised this point with me – 'we love engineering and would rather be Engineers than anything else, but we do want to command our own ships and our own fleets'. The parents of promising boys also must naturally be influenced by this possible 'bar sinister', and many who would otherwise have offered their sons for the Navy will not do so, on this account.[35]

The latter, Engineer Commander C.J. Taylor, had 'no hesitation in saying that the new scheme of training naval officers as carried out at Osborne is on correct lines' but steps needed to be taken to ensure engineering remained popular.[36] The headmaster at Osborne, Cyril Ashford, was equally clear in his opinions:

It is difficult for anyone not in close touch with the teaching at Osborne to realise how enormously receptive boys of this age are for all the practical sides of engineering work; their freshness and flexibility of mind makes their rate of progress unexpectedly rapid compared with that of older pupils, and the work they turn out in the shops is excellent. . . . I have no hesitation in saying that the broader education now given will immensely increase the officer's control over his men. . . . I believe that the Osborne and Dartmouth course will provide a suitable foundation for the much fuller and more specialised training that will doubtless be provided for Sub-Lieutenants. There appears to me no clear reason why a period of specialising in engineering should be more detrimental than a period spent in special work in T[orpedo], G[unnery] or N[avigation].

Ashford went on to sound a clear warning:

The announcement, at an early stage, that an Engineer Officer is at least eligible for higher executive rank would go far to remove many difficulties that are likely to become very serious in the very near future at Osborne and Dartmouth with regard to the distribution of cadets to the different branches of the Service.[37]

This was almost exactly what Sir John wanted to read. Now, he declared,

It can confidently be stated that, not only have these young officers fully and completely realised the anticipations which were formed at the inception of the scheme, but in many respects their progress has far exceeded anything that was thought possible.

It is now certain that these cadets, owing to their longer and more practical course of training, will be better equipped than their predecessors to take their positions immediately as Executive Officers of the fleet. . . .

This has been raised above the level of mere conjecture.[38]

What was equally apparent, though, was that to fill the numbers of the Engineer branch, an additional incentive was needed. This would be what Fisher had always wanted. Engineers should now be allowed to command ships and fleets. All officers, given the quality of the training they were now receiving, should be able to serve in any branch of the service, at any time in their career. In other words, 'interchangeability' between Engineer and Executive Officers would have to be introduced.

The result of Fisher's efforts was the publication in November 1905, by Earl Cawdor, the First Lord of the Admiralty, of a memorandum. The 'most important' feature of this

> was that there was no necessity for a permanent division of officers into three distinct branches and that the provision of officers for Engine Room duties and for service with the Corps of Royal Marines could be effected by an extension of the specialisation in force already in the Navy for Gunnery, Torpedo and Navigation.[39]

To the fury and horror of the conservatives, both within and outside the Navy, complete 'interchangeability' had arrived. Fisher had correctly predicted there would be considerable opposition to this development.

> There will be immense opposition: there always is! Bows and Arrows died hard in the Navy . . . the Bow and Arrow party are still with us. . . . They can't bear the 'Dreadnought'. . . . They'll hate Heaven, probably. . . . They certainly won't like all the harps playing the same tune. Fancy! Complete interchangeability! Admiral Lambton and a Lieutenant (E) exchanging harps! It will be hell! . . .

He singled out as one of his opponents in Parliament Carlyon Bellairs MP, 'a retired Lieutenant with four years' sea service'.[40] Bellairs opened an assault on the scheme in the Commons in March 1906, and over the next three years continued to lead the attack on it in the House.[41] He had some allies. There were, for example, debates about the new scheme of training in the Commons in March 1907 and a major one in 1908,[42] but the Government held firm until after Fisher's retirement. Then, in 1912, the Admiralty appointed a committee, named after its Chairman, Admiral Sir Reginald Custance. The aim of this committee, according to the newly appointed First Lord of the Admiralty, Winston Churchill, was to make the education of future naval officers 'less ambitious, more simple, more practical, more thorough and more directly centred on their fitness for specific duties as naval officers'.[43]

While much of the Custance Committee's report relating to Osborne dealt with details of the College accommodation,[44] opponents of the new entry arrangements cited its reports to show, in the words of one steadfast opponent to change, Admiral Lord Charles Beresford, that the new naval officer training scheme 'has entirely broken down'.[45]

Churchill did not go so far as this. He admitted there was a shortage of naval officers, but he proposed to get round this in several ways. As an emergency measure, he intended to recruit Sub-Lieutenants from the Royal Naval Reserve. As a more permanent step, he would introduce promotion from the lower deck and he would also introduce the selection of cadets from among boys aged between seventeen and a half and eighteen and a half. His other proposals had not actually been recommended by the Custance Committee: first, he intended to raise the age of entry for cadets to between thirteen years and four months and thirteen years and eight months. This would suit the requirements of preparatory schools, since it was the age students took their public school entrance examinations, and he hoped older boys would be less prone to childhood illnesses. Secondly, he proposed to reduce the cost of attending Osborne and Dartmouth in the hope of attracting a greater number of boys from a wider social class. The first of these steps would begin in December 1913,[46] the latter does not appear to have been taken.

One of the main ideas behind the training programme stemming from the Selborne scheme was that cadets were to receive a broad-based liberal education, as well as a specifically naval one. Any new naval college would therefore have to act not simply as a naval training college but as a 'naval public school'. It was, as one modern authority has remarked:

> a public school in that most of the work was similar to that on the modern side of a public school, it was naval, not so much because of the naval subjects taught, which occupied a comparatively small number of hours, but because its reason for existence and its atmosphere were naval.

For this reason, 'the use of naval terminology' at the Colleges was not 'mere affectation':

> Cadets were not merely picking up the slang of a public school,which would help them there but not in after life: they were beginning to acquire the vocabulary of a profession in which immediate action had often to be taken, even in peacetime, and in which the words and phrases which started that action had to be terse, unambiguous, and not blinded by loose usage.[47]

Hence the Royal Naval College, Osborne, came into existence to act both as an introduction to the Royal Navy and to educate boys in some of the basics of the humanities and other academic subjects, which they would not have acquired because they had not gone to public school.

But its primary function, as was stressed at the time by Professor J.A. Ewing, the first Director of Naval Education, was to serve as a 'source of supply' to the senior College at Dartmouth. Ewing was anxious to stress to the parents of prospective cadets both the indivisibility and broadness of the new training course:

> The two years' training at Osborne is followed by another two years in the senior college at Dartmouth. During these four years the boy receives a broad and liberal education in the subjects of a modern side at a public school, along with a much greater amount of practical science and engineering than any public school gives or could give. Each of the colleges is furnished with a large workshop, in which the engineering training is given by naval officers of the engineering branch. The time spent in the workshops, together with that spent on theoretical subjects directly connected with engineering makes up one half of the cadets' working time. The cadet's life [he admitted] is a very strenuous one, but great care is taken to guard against over-strain.

He went on to stress the main difference between the two naval colleges and contemporary public schools:

> A highly important feature of the Colleges is their naval character; not only does the curriculum include a certain amount of teaching in seamanship and navigation, but the boys are under naval discipline and are breathing a naval atmosphere throughout their course.

He pointed out that, despite the 'many difficulties in combining organization under a naval captain' with the work of a civilian headmaster and other masters, 'experience has shown . . . the difficulties are not insurmountable'.[48]

As far as cadet education is concerned, the new scheme has attracted positive comment in recent times.

To meet modern requirements, a foundation of essential knowledge was necessary, which should include the humanities as well as fundamental knowledge of mathematics and science. If this was to begin at the age of twelve or thirteen, then a progressive system coordinated with instruction in Service subjects could be arranged, interrupted as required by a training cruise. This . . . was the basis of the Naval Public School education of four years for a cadet entering at thirteen years of age. . . .[49]

'To meet modern requirements', however, meant lowering the age of entry and both educating and training the cadets for longer: hence the need for a four-year land-based course. The intention was that, from now on, 'All cadets would be taught by new teaching staff in an institution firmly dedicated to the new scheme.' Professor Ewing declared himself 'very anxious to see that Dartmouth College develops on entirely new lines without *Britannia* interference or even influence'.[50]

This ambition led to another problem: how to keep the 'new scheme' (Selborne) cadets separate from, and uninfluenced by, the 'old scheme' (*Britannia*) ones. In the event it was agreed that, when the new College at Dartmouth formally opened in September 1905 – when, that is, the first of the 'new scheme' cadets had completed the first two of their four years' training – the senior 'old scheme' cadets on the *Britannia* would be sent to sea, as usual. On this one occasion, the next two terms of cadets there would also be sent to sea, in two cruisers specially appointed for the purpose. This would leave only forty-two 'old scheme' cadets in residence at Dartmouth, to be joined by sixty-three 'new scheme' Osborne cadets – but the two terms would be kept strictly apart.[51]

But the decision to lower the recruiting age of cadets and extend the period of their shore-based training had had one more immediately apparent consequence: the buildings at Dartmouth as designed would be too small to hold the number of cadets to be recruited. The initial design was only to hold four cadet terms, whereas now there would be the equivalent of twelve terms of cadets being trained at any one time. Hence, a choice existed: either expand the College at Dartmouth, or provide some additional space elsewhere. In the event, both options were adopted. Even before the main Dartmouth building opened in September 1905 'a new block containing a single gun room was begun on the east side of the existing works' and by the end of 1907, another new block, containing five more studies and a reference library, had been opened.[52] In the meantime it had already been decided that another, junior, College was also needed. This would hold the cadets during their first six terms' – or two years' – training. But where was it to be located? And who was to take charge of it?

It might be said that, in the event, the Admiralty was fortunate: as it was looking for land on which to build its junior College, the country's greatest landowner was looking for a way of ridding himself of an unwanted property. In 1831 King Edward VII's mother, then Princess Victoria, had visited East Cowes on the Isle of Wight to lay the foundation stone of the local church. In 1845, now happily married, and having decided that it was 'impossible to imagine a prettier spot – we have a charming beach all to ourselves – we can walk anywhere without being followed or mobbed', she decided to purchase a house nearby. This was Osborne House, standing in a 1,000 acre estate.

With the assistance of Thomas Cubitt, Victoria's husband Albert redesigned the building, creating, between 1846 and 1850, a new Italianate 'Marine Residence'. Osborne became Victoria and Albert's most favoured residence (except, perhaps, for Balmoral) and they spent all the time they could spare there, taking their children with them. When Albert died at Windsor in 1861, Victoria retired to Osborne and, seeing it as sacred to his memory, she endeavoured to keep it exactly as it had been at the time of his death. She herself died there on 22 January 1901.

Whatever his mother may have thought of Osborne, the new King was not enamoured of it. As early as December 1901 he had been favourably impressed with an Office of Works plan to establish a convalescent home there. At about the same time – and apparently at the suggestion of his friend Sir John Fisher – he decided to offer part of the estate to the Board of Admiralty as a site for the new College. This offer, we are assured, 'was at the time particularly welcome, as no other place was immediately available'.[53] The King, having reached an agreement to retain a suite of rooms in the house to enable him to stay there for the annual Cowes Week regatta, on 11 August 1902 presented the whole Osborne Estate to the nation.[54]

Once the property was secured and with the decision taken to build a College there, the Admiralty rapidly set to work. In the House Committee on the Navy Estimates on 30 March 1903, Pretyman, in requesting a vote of £40,000 for the project, extolled the virtues of the new site. It was, he declared, an admirable one, with a water supply and drainage already to hand and with existing stables available for conversion to classrooms, offices, etc. He also pointed out that it was overlooking the River Medina, where an excellent site for College workshops was located. He went on to describe what needed to be built. The accommodation buildings were to be bungalows, constructed of a material called uralite. No wood was to be used in their construction and the floors were to be of concrete with paving. The bungalows would be heated by steam and would accommodate about thirty students each, up to around 200 in the first instance. A gymnasium and a recreation hall would also be provided. He noted that all should be finished quickly (by, he hoped, August 1904 at the latest) and that the nature of the building and site were such that the College could easily be added to.[55] By a rather curious arrangement (Pretyman did not advert to it in his speech) it had been agreed that the Office of Works would build the College and be responsible for its maintenance, although the Admiralty would foot the bill.[56] In the event, however, a civilian contractor was taken on to do the initial building work, as the Office of Works apparently requested too long to do it.[57] Moreover, in May 1903 the Admiralty also decided that the new buildings should be lit by electricity – only to discover that the generator was only powerful enough to supply the Kingston workshops. Accordingly, an agreement with the Isle of Wight Electric Light Company, who had already suggested that gas was not the answer to the lighting problem but whose proposals had been initially rejected by the Admiralty, was needed after all.[58]

It is, however, apparent that the actual building of the College was a somewhat hasty affair. Pretyman's estimated date of completion – August 1904 – may have been accurate, but the College had to be ready to receive its first students almost exactly one year earlier. The first cadets recruited under the Selborne scheme would be joining in September 1903. By this time the central buildings of the institution and at least some classrooms and workshops had to be completed and, although there would be time to add to cadets' accommodation later, some dormitories at least would have to be ready.

Recruiting staff for the new College also took some thought. In January 1903 Selborne had a meeting with Professor J.A. Ewing. At this time, Ewing was Professor of Mechanical Engineering at Cambridge University. He was also a friend of Lord Kelvin, the physicist, and Charles Parsons, designer of the *Turbinia* that caused such a nuisance at the 1897 naval review. This scientific background seems to have impressed Fisher and

Selborne and, at their meeting, Selborne offered Ewing a newly created post, that of Director of Naval Education.

Ewing accepted, and began the task of recruiting staff for the proposed new College. His most noteworthy appointment was that of Cyril Ashford, senior science master at Harrow School, to serve as headmaster. This is a clear indication of the importance science was to have in the new College's curriculum.[59] A third man, Captain Rosslyn Wemyss, was chosen to be overall head – Captain – of the new institution.

It was also decided that Ashford and Wemyss would move on to the senior College of Dartmouth with the first of the 'new scheme' cadets. This would help ensure the introduction of the new scheme into the established institution. When this happened, in September 1905, Wemyss remained in overall command of both Colleges. Ashford was eventually succeeded by Charles Godfrey, a mathematician: another clear indication of the 'science' outlook of the College at Osborne.

Building of the College carried on apace during 1903, and on 4 August the King himself made an 'inaugural visit to the College'. The *Illustrated London News* reported the official opening of the College in September 1903 and its status at that time:

> A formal official inspection on Sept. 12 took place of the inaugural ceremonies of the new Naval College which has been established in the grounds at Osborne. The classrooms are in the quadrangle of the old stables, and at Kingston there is provision for boat work. On Sept. 12 cadets friends crossed the Solent on the *Volcano*, and were received by the Governor, Captain Wemyss, and other members of the staff. The cadets went into residence on Sept. 15.[60]

The College's 'Governor', then Captain Rosslyn Wemyss, had a staff consisting of a Commander, who acted as Second-in-Command, four Lieutenants, two Engineer-Lieutenants, one Engineer Sub-Lieutenant, one Captain RMA, a Chaplain, a Staff Surgeon, a Surgeon, a Staff Paymaster and an Assistant Paymaster. In addition, several Warrant Officers and Petty Officers were retained for disciplinary purposes. Ashford, the headmaster, had a staff of nine masters under his command. (There were no naval instructors at first, but some of these joined later.)[61]

By Easter 1916 staffing had increased notably. By this date, the 'naval staff' comprised, besides the Captain (Hon. H.E. Holmes à Court) and the Commander (E.S.H. Boyle), one executive Lieutenant-Commander and one Lieutenant, one Engineer Commander, one Engineer-Lieutenant Commander, five Engineer-Lieutenants, a Chaplain, a Fleet Surgeon, a Fleet Paymaster, two Naval Instructors, two Surgeons, two Assistant Paymasters, a Carpenter Lieutenant-Commander and a Gunner. The 'Professorial Staff' comprised a headmaster (Charles Godfrey), five heads of department, ten senior masters and twenty-three assistant masters (with six others serving either in the Navy, at the Admiralty, or in the Army).

The number of cadets, too, increased dramatically, not least because of the pressure of war. The first term, the St Vincent term, numbered seventy-two cadets, who were followed by another seventy-two in the Drake term of January 1904 and seventy-six in the Blake term entered in May of that year. Cadet numbers remained at about this level, until over 100 entered in the Hawke term of September 1914 and 122 (the largest number ever taken) in the Grenville term of January 1915.

All of this, of course, was in the future when Wemyss and his associates reflected on the College opening. Wemyss himself had very favourable impressions of the opening and of the first cadets:

> We have all the boys in, safe and sound, and I must say I am delighted with the appearance of them all; nice, gentlemanlike boys – every one of them happy as the day is long. . . . Luckily today was beautiful and the place looked charming. The parents that came with their boys were all delighted with the place and buildings and well they may be.

He also reported to Fisher on how well things were going:

> Our first day with the cadets has been most successful. The boys landed at Trinity Pier organised, and knowing what to do, and I am very much surprised and pleased at the way in which Lieutenant Fullerton had already got them into some sort of shape in that short time.
>
> [To-day] . . . they had an hour's drill, then an hour with the Head Master, and I had them shewn round everything, playgrounds, Kingston etc., by the Officers.
>
> This afternoon they have been playing, football and hockey as if they had never been in any other place in their lives. They seem a

first-rate lot of boys, and up to now have shown a great deal of keenness. The way they turned out and dressed this morning at 6.00 a.m. and then fell in, was, I think, very wonderful. Nobody late, and everybody knowing exactly what to do.

To-morrow (Thursday) they get into the proper routine, and the instruction begins in earnest.

The Steward so far has proved himself excellent, and their meals are exactly what I wanted them to be. Excellent food, lots of it, plain, and well served – like a Mess and not like a School – good, plain, clean and not luxurious.[62]

Ashford was also pleased at developments, but a little more cautious than Wemyss:

I am more than satisfied with the way things have shaken down . . . of course it doesn't go like clockwork yet, as it will soon, but I am delighted with the keenness of the boys. . . . Naturally the Cadets can't shake off their school-boy way of doing things at first – they're too young not to forget occasionally, but if we aren't tied down to produce miracles at passing examinations I will guarantee to produce much more able and scientific Officers than any first-class examination product.[63]

When it opened, the College had not, of course, reached its greatest extent and it occupied only about 40 acres. By 1914 this had increased to 60 acres, and as an aspiring cadet (or their parent) was informed:

The approach to the main entrance from East Cowes is by a magnificent wide thoroughfare, about a mile and a half in length, called York Avenue: a steadily rising sweep of hill, carpeted with brown sand, and flanked by beautiful sylvan estates, from amidst the foliage of which peep forth elegant villas. Indeed Osborne College is set amidst truly arcadian surroundings, and the first impression of the new arrival must needs be one of a tender and delightful landscape.

Passing the lodge at Prince of Wales' Gate, a fine expanse of carriage drive leads directly up to the College block. The Osborne Naval College is laid out upon the bungalow system, which in addition to being picturesquely beautiful, nestling in its superbly

wooded grounds, is also extremely convenient. The quarters are laid
out in the form of a large quadrangle, the nucleus to them having
been furnished by the solid masonry walls of the former Royal
Stables. The bungalows are built of stout wooden frames, lined
inside and out with a brownish, compressed, felt-like material known
as uralite. The space between these two walls is packed with asbestos,
so that the buildings are altogether fireproof.

This source, a guide for possible future naval officers and their parents
and guardians, continues in an even more exuberant fashion:

The situation, upon a high plateau, is one of healthiest that could
possibly be conceived, the foundations consisting of a sub-soil of
gravel which is naturally most effectively drained. The surrounding
views are singularly striking in the luxuriance of beauty. On the one
hand, the old-fashioned town of Cowes rises in a gabled and
sparkling cluster from out of the lapping waters of the famous
yachting anchorage; on the other hand the famous Spithead
roadstead stretches across to Portsmouth – with its wonderful wealth
of naval associations a most fitting proximity to the College of the
rising generation of sea officers.[64]

The Admiralty itself, in 1914, was a little less ebullient than this, but it
admitted something that McKenna, First Lord for many of the pre-war
debates about Osborne, was at repeated pains to deny, namely that the
Osborne dormitories were of a temporary type:

The College grounds form a large and very level plateau some
60 acres in area at the top of a hill between Osborne Bay and the
River Medina, at a height of about 170 feet above the sea. . . .
[B]elow them, on the right bank of the river at a distance of about
five-eights of a mile, are the College workshops. . . . A portion of the
Osborne site was granted by King Edward for the purpose, with
buildings on it which admitted of conversion into class-rooms,
dining-room, etc. Dormitories, officers' quarters and other necessary
parts were added, for the most part in the form of temporary
structures of the bungalow type, and these were supplemented as the
requirements of the College increased, especially during the first two
years of its occupation.

When the College opened, its centrepiece, as the *Illustrated London News* had reported, was the former stableblock of Osborne House. This formed the building known as St Vincent, and comprised classrooms and the College dining-room, where all the cadets could eat at one sitting. Another permanent building, called Nelson, served several purposes. As the Admiralty itself declared, this was:

> a large hall . . . for assemblies and entertainment. On Sundays 'Nelson' is rigged for church, there being no permanent chapel. A part of the same large hall also serves as gymnasium.[65]

One other permanent building utilised was the former estate police station, which was converted into the Captain's residence. The civilian headmaster and most of the other officers were also provided with residential quarters, but the other masters had to 'live out', though they were at least provided with a common-room next to the headmaster's office.

In 1903, however, the building of the College was not fully complete. Most importantly, when it opened only three dormitories, each designed to house thirty cadets, had been built. These dormitories did, however, set the pattern for future developments. They were built parallel to each other, united by a corridor which abutted on the end of the Nelson block. These dormitories were provided with 'an annex containing baths, etc., and opposite . . . on the other side of the corridor is a small sitting-room where the cadets may read, write their letters, and so on. A cabin attached to each dormitory is occupied by one of the officers' – and a close watch kept on its occupants! Like the large buildings, the dormitories were given the names of illustrious naval heroes: Hawke, Rodney, Anson, Drake, Duncan, Howe, Cornwallis, Collingwood, Blake, Benbow, Grenville and Exmouth. Unlike the large buildings, however, they were not built of brick or stone, and problems soon arose out of this.

But there were some advantages to the Osborne site. The workshops at Kingston, for example, were quite impressive:

> The engineering department . . . includes for the most part under one roof a large fitting and machine shop, a shop for carpentering and pattern-making, a smithy, a foundry, a boiler-making shop, drawing office and engineering lecture rooms.

Given the importance of engineering in the curriculum, this level of provision is not to be wondered at. Nor is the Admiralty's pride in the fact that over two hundred cadets could be engaged in engineering work at the same time.

Finally, there was one attribute of the estate that was considered of great importance to the new College:

> the level stretches of the Osborne Estate which adjoin the main buildings of the College provide playing fields so ample that the principal cricket pitches can be rested during the winter, sufficient other ground being available for football and hockey.[66]

The new College had been built very quickly. It was, as Sir John Fisher proudly remarked:

> built in one-twelfth of the time, and at one-eighth of the cost, of the palatial stone buildings at Dartmouth, but equally effective, and to hold the same numbers. . . .
>
> Last January the designs did not even exist.
>
> Only just so many of the bungalows have been erected as required for occupation, so as to improve as we go along. Already we have discovered an additional joy; for in the next series of bungalows required in January, a separate sitting room will be provided at the end of each bungalow.
>
> The bungalows take three months to build. . . .[67]

He would have been equally pleased to discover that the cost of the College had come within the amount of £160,000 allowed in the Navy estimates. On 5 January 1906 the Office of Works sent the Admiralty a detailed (although not quite final) list of expenditure. The Office noted some expenses had exceeded estimates: this included a sum of £237 on servants' quarters, caused by the need to repair flood damage, and of £885 on three cadets' dormitories:

> This is due to the expectations in regard to intended dormitories on which the revised estimate was based not having been fully realised. More work had also to be done in the surrounding ground than was anticipated.

Changes to the St Vincent block, including new windows, bigger rooms, and 'the extension of the hot-water supply . . . required larger tanks and increased the cost considerably' to an excess sum of £510. A £341 surplus was also spent on drainage, which was due 'to contingencies that could not be foreseen', and a new cold meat store and coal store had to be built, making a surplus fee of £248.

The Office was, however, careful to point out that savings were made on other estimates (£232 on lecture rooms and £284 on Petty Officers' quarters, for example) and 'sixteen of the estimates were not based on quantities and that the work had to be done very hurriedly on more or less incomplete information'.

So far, £153,284 had been spent – a total saving of £6,716 on the estimate. There was, though, one main reason for this. In the original estimates, £6,500 had been set aside for the construction of a church: and £150 had been spent on it. The letter continues:

> The Board trust that it will not be thought that they are offering advice on a matter of policy which does not fall within their province if they suggest that the need for a Church might be altogether obviated by a continuance of the present arrangement for holding Divine Service, which, it is understood, would be considered quite satisfactory by the Officers of the Naval College if certain additional fittings were provided.
>
> The present practice . . . is to hold the Church Services in a portion of the large hall in the Nelson block, the other portion of which is used as a gymnasium. The fittings in question could be supplied at a small cost, while the new Gymnasium might be built on a suitable spot in the vicinity, thus rendering it unnecessary to use the Hall for secular purposes and providing a Gymnasium which would be in many respects an improvement on the existing one.[68]

At least part of this suggestion was agreed to by the Admiralty: Nelson continued in use as a Church – but also as a gym – during the whole life of Osborne Naval College.

Responsibility for the upkeep of the buildings was still, however, an unsettled affair. Matters relating to this came to a head in 1908/9. At the beginning of 1908 it was agreed between the Admiralty and Board of Works that inspection and servicing of the main steam boiler would be undertaken by Portsmouth Dockyard and the (naval) engineering staff on site at Osborne. The Board of Works still wished to be consulted if large repairs involving structural alterations were carried out – and agreed to the Admiralty's suggestion that it should remain responsible for large repairs.

When the Admiralty suggested in March 1909 that this system was 'cumbersome' and it would be better if it took full responsibility for all works at Osborne, the Board of Works rejected the proposal. The Board noted the King wished it to remain responsible for *all* works at the Osborne estate. It appears, however, that in August 1910 the Board of Works suddenly handed all College maintenance over to the Admiralty, but it was the Admiralty, this time, which was reluctant, claiming it had no maintenance staff available. In the end, although not for another year, the transfer was agreed. From 26 August 1911 the maintenance of the College became the responsibility of the Board of Admiralty, although it was accepted that the 'consent' of the Board of Works was needed to any future alterations to the College.[69]

There was certainly plenty of work for the Admiralty to do on College buildings. Most significantly, the number of dormitories was increased, so that by 1913 it stood at twelve. Each of the newer dormitories were designed to house thirty-six cadets, though numbers in some of them were eventually increased to forty. A considerable increase in the hospital accommodation was also apparent.

In July 1909, the Civil Lord of the Admiralty reported to Parliament that

we have completed . . . an isolation hospital. It seems that boys of 13 years of age – the age at which they enter Osborne – are peculiarly susceptible to all kinds of diseases – chicken pox, measles, etc., and there had been no proper accommodation, but the isolation hospital has now been completed.[70]

This building alone was not, however, sufficient. As a direct result of an influenza epidemic that swept the College in 1910 and resulted in 260 cases, it was decided additional hospital accommodation was required. This resulted in a large new 'infectious hospital' being built, some distance away from the main block.

Provision for sick cadets was described thus in 1914:

There is . . . a liberal provision of sick-quarters, comprising a 'sick-bay' in the main College buildings and a large hospital a short way off, with separate wards, which allow infectious disorders to be effectively isolated . . . the hospital contains four wards with 80 beds for the treatment of infectious cases, and there is also a separate establishment consisting of a converted dwelling-house outside the College, which contains 18 beds, as well as 16 beds in the College sick-bay.[71]

On a lighter note, in 1907 a new recreation room had been constructed. This was

a brick building, rough cast outside, with red brick facings and buttresses, and tiled roof. It consists of a large recreation room, 81ft 9in long by 40ft wide . . . entrance hall, instructors' and cloak rooms. Over these last mentioned rooms . . . situated at the east end of the building is a gallery, 40ft by 13ft 6in. . . . The floor is of maple, the walls are lined with matchboard to a height of 8ft. Ample light and ventilation are obtained from windows all round the building, also from dormer windows above. The room is heated by means of two radiating stoves, and is lighted by electroliers.

This building [we are told] fills a long-felt want, especially in wet weather, relieving any congestion in 'Nelson' which might be occasioned at such times. It has been set aside generally for first-year cadets. . . .[72]

But cadets did not always get everything they might have wanted. One of the longest-running questions about Osborne was that relating to a swimming pool. Initially, since the College was near the Solent, it was deemed acceptable that, if they wished to learn to swim, they could do so in the sea, as J. Newman M.P. was informed by the First Lord of Admiralty in June 1910.[73] But such a brief written reply did not satisfy Newman. He renewed the attack in July, pointing out that cadets could not swim in the sea in the winter, while the Solent was a dangerous place all year round. McKenna admitted that he was aware of this, and the Admiralty was considering building a pool at Osborne – but he added that there was a perfectly good swimming pool at Dartmouth, so cadets could learn to swim when they got there.[74]

A year later Newman further enquired after progress. This time McKenna informed him a sum had been taken in the estimates but no work had yet been done.[75] But Newman was not alone in his campaign. In 1912 Douglas Hall wrote to the new First Lord, Churchill, about the swimming pool only to be informed that the Admiralty was aware of the question and was considering building one.[76] A year later Hall again asked about it. He was told money had been taken in the estimates, but work on it would be carried out in conjunction with other works at the College. When Sir Henry Craik asked why the delay had occurred, when the need for a pool had been evident for some time, the Parliamentary and Financial Secretary of the Admiralty, T.J. Macnamara, told him it was probably delayed pending the report of the 1912 Custance Committee.[77] All of this was rather unfortunate for the cadets – since the Admiralty had already banned bathing in the Solent.[78] Like so much else, however, the Osborne swimming pool was to become a casualty of the First World War.

But work of a rather different kind was undertaken at the College: indeed, it soon became apparent that urgent building work was needed at the College to maintain and repair, rather than to extend, the establishment. This became particularly true of the cadets' 'bungalows'. The speed of building of the cadets' dormitories was not matched by their durability. As early as March 1907, one MP had suggested that the uralite structures at Osborne were a source of infection. He added that in his opinion 'it would be better to rebuild the whole College in brick, rather than complete the new "Infectious Hospital"', as the Admiralty proposed.[79] The Admiralty was anxious to dispel this notion and stated that the uralite had been checked by a medical expert and was 'free from irritant properties'.[80] Following the serious 'flu epidemic of 1910, Admiral Lord Charles Beresford raised the issue of health: he suggested that the Admiralty had gone against the advice of civil engineers, and that it should have spent the money on 'more suitable structures'. McKenna refuted this, and stated bluntly that the illnesses at Osborne had nothing to do with the buildings, which, he pointed out, were designed for a long life span: they were not, in that sense, 'temporary'.[81]

The idea that the buildings were a source of infection because they were 'temporary' persisted amongst MPs, however, and the question was discussed again in March 1911. McKenna pointed out once again that the uralite in the buildings was not a source of infection, and he reiterated that they were not 'temporary' – they were, he said, simply not expected to last for one hundred years.[82] But during 1911 the Admiralty came under increasing pressure. During August, Herbert Richmond noted in his diary that he had spoken to Admiral Sir Arthur Moore, the Commander-in-Chief, Portsmouth, and had learned from him that 'the

College at Osborne is coming to pieces and the question of rebuilding it must come up'.[83]

In November 1911 Douglas Hall, MP, enquired whether, given the evident unhealthiness of the site, the College was to be rebuilt, while Admiral Beresford wondered whether it was going to be altered to make it more healthy. George Lambert, the Civil Lord, informed them that the Admiralty was looking into the matter of rebuilding, but several MPs were not unduly impressed. Hall gave it as his opinion that an inspection of the College had already been made, and the buildings had been found to be in a terrible state, with damp and even holes in the walls. George Lambert explained that, in these instances, repairs had been carried out.[84] Admiral Beresford returned to the offensive in March 1912. He again asked the Admiralty whether the real cause of illness at the College was not simply that the buildings were unsuitable for habitation, as they were prone to damp (none of the buildings having a damp course). In particular, he wanted to know if the recent painting undertaken at the College was solely to prevent rising damp. Lambert responded that the buildings did have damp courses, that the painting was done to preserve the structure and for the sake of appearances and finally, that all of the buildings 'have been put into a satisfactory condition'.[85] Matters in fact reached such a point that the new First Lord, Winston Churchill, had to tell the Commons, in November 1912, in response to a written question, that there was no intention of moving the College from the Isle of Wight: this suggestion, he added, had never seriously been put forward.[86]

Even while he said this, however, a searching enquiry into the situation and conditions at Osborne was already under way. The Fourth Report of the Custance Committee, dated 20 September 1912, despite Churchill's assertion, had explicitly considered the question of whether Osborne should simply be rebuilt, or whether it should be moved to a new site.

The College did not come out well in the evidence gathered by the committee. H.A. Hood, the Captain, informed them that, in his opinion, the College dormitories, in particular, were of poor quality. He explained that the walls were so thin it was practically possible to kick a hole in them, while the areas around the windows tended to leak when it rained. He also stated that the College was too full: it would be possible to squeeze more boys in, but only by blocking some of the dormitory windows. Hood favoured the rebuilding of the College: the dormitories, he stated, should be constructed of more permanent material, and should be built further apart. The site itself, he felt, was not unhealthy.

When questioned again, though he argued that rebuilding of the College on a site nearer the workshops was his preferred option, he did not think the cadets should be forced to live on a building site while the rebuilding work was going on. Fleet Surgeon Murray Jones, who had only been at the College for five weeks, not surprisingly backed Hood up. While he believed the site itself was not unhealthy, he felt many of the buildings were damp and all were too far removed from the workshops. Jones' superior, however, Sir James Porter, the Director General of the Navy Medical Department, was not at all impressed with Osborne. The site itself was unhealthy, he declared, the lighting in many of the buildings was bad and the supply of milk and fresh water inadequate. The best thing to do, in Porter's opinion, would be to rebuild the College elsewhere.

The Custance Committee Report reflected many of these comments. They concurred with Hood in stating that the College was currently too full, the site was damp, and it was too far from the workshops. They reviewed the College accommodation and, while the committee noted with favour some of the changes that had been made since the 1910 epidemics – in particular improvements to the heating and the provision of closed-in verandahs on the hospital – they were far less impressed with the dormitory accommodation. They felt that uralite was not a suitable material for permanent buildings, and added that the removal of asbestos from some of the dormitories in 1911, had resulted in walls that were too thin and buildings that were difficult to heat.

The committee recommended rebuilding the College, but near to the existing site. First, they stated that all the new buildings should be built in brick, and provided with wooden floors. Extra stoves should be provided, rather than inefficient central heating. Two temporary dormitories should be provided while this was going on: they estimated it would take two and a half years to complete the work. The cost was estimated at £31,405. To this, the committee added £4,400 for a swimming pool. Given the current proposal to increase the intake of cadets from seventy to eighty-seven a term, two additional dormitories were needed as well as extensions to the workshops (including servants' quarters) and four more classrooms – and possibly further extensions to the dining-room and hospital.[87]

MPs were very anxious to learn the findings of the committee, asking a series of questions about them in late 1912 and early 1913, while the Admiralty was equally anxious to keep them at bay while its recommendations were considered by the Board. [88] The Committee Report was at last made public on 24 March 1913.[89]

In the event the Custance Committee report had relatively little impact on the buildings at Osborne. Money for the recommended changes – including the new swimming pool – was included in the estimates for 1913–14, but nothing of any great significance was undertaken before the First World War broke out in August 1914. Perhaps the last word should come from Lord H. Cavendish-Bentinck. As late as March 1916 he enquired about progress on the Osborne swimming pool only to be informed that work on it had been postponed pending a decision on whether or not a new College was going to be built. In any event, as he was reminded, boys could learn to swim at Dartmouth.[90]

By 1917, with the war at its height, the Royal Naval College at Osborne had reached its greatest extent. The Admiralty had formulated a clear idea of the kind of cadet it wanted, and had recruited increasing numbers of them during the first years of the war. The buildings at the College had been extended to take account of this increase in student numbers.

It is evident that the introduction of the new schemes for officer recruitment had run into considerable opposition before 1914. Attempts to block common entry for all officer cadets had failed (except for Royal Marine officers, who had eventually been left out of the standard entry). Despite strong opposition from conservative and radical sources both within and outside of the Navy, Fisher had pushed through his proposals by 1906. At the same time, new Colleges had been built for the cadets at Osborne and Dartmouth and had opened their doors in September 1903 and September 1905. The Admiralty and Board of Works had continued to squabble over responsibility for the construction and maintenance of the buildings at Osborne, but by 1910 this had fallen firmly within the Admiralty's sphere of operations. The result was a large College of several permanent buildings, including classrooms and workshops and a collection of uralite bungalows, which were used as dormitories for cadets. All, by 1917, were full, and some were in a less than perfect condition.

Before looking at cadets' life at the College, however, it seems necessary to investigate in a little more detail Admiralty recruiting strategy and the type of boy that was recruited. It may then be possible to determine the success (or otherwise) of the policy developed, against such tenacious opposition, in the years leading up to the First World War.

CHAPTER TWO

Recruitment and Recruits

The first term of seventy-four cadets to enter the Royal Naval College, Osborne, began their studies there in September 1903. To gain entry, these seventy-four boys had undergone both an oral and a written test, and a medical examination. Each one came from a different family background, and each one, it may be assumed, had his own reasons for going there. The Admiralty, in its turn, had its own reasons for accepting them.

The Admiralty, as may be imagined, was very anxious to recruit boys of the 'right sort' into the Navy. Perhaps the best summation of what it was looking for can be taken from the semi-official publication issued in 1914, *The Entry and Training of Naval Cadets*. This brief pamphlet tells us, as it told the parents and guardians of twelve-year-old boys just before the outbreak of the First World War, that 'there is scope and need in the Navy for many types of men and varieties of talent', but it went on to be a little more specific:

> that boy has the best chance who is resolute, resourceful, quick to decide, and ready to act on his decision. He must be no slacker, but keen in work and play. He should be sound alike in wind and limb and in the big and little principles of conduct . . . cheerful, unselfish, considerate. . . . He should give promise of being responsive and observant, closely in touch with his surroundings, but master of himself. . . .

It was made clear that boys who were not cast in this mould – 'the boy of sensitive, poetic spirit, the ruminating young philosopher, the scholar whose whole heart is in his books' – would not find a place in the Navy.[1]

As was noted in Chapter One, the Admiralty also laid down more specific regulations regarding prospective cadets. In the last days of the old *Britannia* system, the age at which cadets were taken on was between fourteen and a half years and fifteen and a half years. This had been reduced to twelve and a half years when Osborne Naval College opened its doors, but was raised in 1906 to twelve years and nine or ten months, and again, to bring it in line with age of entry to public schools, to between thirteen years and four to eight months in 1913. It was made clear then that applications were not to be made on behalf of boys until they had reached twelve and a half years of age. It was explained in 1914 that:

soon after the boy is 12½, but not before that, his parent should write to the Assistant Private Secretary of the First Lord of the Admiralty, who will send a form of application and other necessary papers. 'Influence' is quite unnecessary and is not likely to be useful. Anyone may apply, and every application is considered on its merits. . . .

The regulation as to age is that a candidate must be more than 13 years and 4 months old, and not older than 13 years and 8 months, on the 1st December, 1st April or 1st August preceding the date of admission. Consequently, a boy who reaches the age of 13 in April, May, June or July is eligible for admission in the following January. If the birthday falls in August, September, October or November he is eligible for admission in May; if it falls in December, January, February or March he is eligible for admission in September.

Applications for admission in January must be received at the Admiralty by the end of the preceding September, those for admission in May must be received by the end of the preceding December, and for admission in September by the end of the preceding April.

Thus, for example, a boy who was born on 31st July 1901 is eligible for admission in January 1915, and application must be made on his behalf to the Assistant Private Secretary before the end of September 1914. It may be made any time between the end of January 1914 (when the boy is 12½) and that date. A boy born on 1st August 1901 is eligible for admission in May 1915, and in his case application must be made before the end of December 1914.[2]

It was consistently pointed out that 'candidates must be of pure European descent, and the sons of either natural-born or naturalized British subjects' – the 'burden of proof' in doubtful cases rested with the parent or guardian. Candidates would also have to pass written examinations and a medical before admission.[3]

Parents and guardians had to undertake to pay the cadet's fees. These amounted to £75 a year, although it was possible for those who were sons of Royal Navy, Army or Royal Marine officers or Admiralty civil servants to apply for one of a 'limited number' of reduced fee places – in this case, if successful, the fee was reduced to £40. However, 'in this selection their Lordships will have regard solely to the pecuniary circumstances of the cadet'. In addition to this, parents and guardians were expected to find about £8 per term for the expenses of the cadet – washing, repairing boots and clothes, pocket money (1/- per week) instruments, school books, sports etc.[4] – and between £35 and £50 for outfitting him.[5] The fees were to be paid termly.

The only amendment of significance to these regulations came in 1916, during the war, when King's Cadetships were introduced. These were granted to:

> the sons of officers of the Royal Navy, Royal Marines or Army who have been killed in action or who have died of wounds received in action, whether afloat or ashore, or have died through the destruction of their ship, or have been drowned or have suffered other violent death due directly and wholly to war service, or who have died of disease attributable to active service.[6]

The terms of these cadetships were quite generous. They amounted to a remission of all fees while at College, and an allowance of up to £40 for outfitting a new cadet. Any serving cadet who suffered the loss of his father could receive a King's Cadetship and would receive full remission of all future fees. The Treasury, not surprisingly, was somewhat opposed to this measure on the grounds of cost, but the Admiralty, to its credit, stuck to its guns. It was agreed in August 1916 that sons of RNR officers and Warrant Officers would also be eligible but the number of cadetships at any one time was not to exceed one hundred.[7]

Cadets' parents and guardians also had to sign a form stating that they agreed to withdraw their boy 'immediately' should the Admiralty request it 'for any reason'. Plenty of reasons for withdrawal were offered:

> Cadets who fail to reach a certain standard, or who . . . are considered unsuitable for the Naval Service may be required to withdraw. . . . This rule will apply to those who do not show an aptitude for Naval life, as well as those who make insufficient progress, or whose constitution is weak, although no disease may have developed.

The Admiralty would receive reports on cadets' progress every year. Cadets would receive 'merit marks' in all subjects, to be determined 'partly by examination and partly by the marks gained for current work during the year'.[8]

A cadet's parent or guardian would generally be issued with a warning about his lack of progress 'a term in advance', though this was not considered essential and was not always adhered to. Although this sounds harsh, it was noted in 1907 that, of 588 cadets so far entered under the new scheme, only 43 – or less than 7 per cent – had been withdrawn.[9] The Admiralty was also at pains to point out that, in cases of doubt, the cadet would be kept on and given another chance, even if he was 'put down' a term.[10] If a cadet was withdrawn, which could be at either the parents' wishes or the Admiralty's request, the former would have to pay £25 for every term passed in the College.[11]

From the start, the Admiralty stressed that candidates would be admitted to Osborne without selecting which of the three naval branches (Executive, Engineer or Marine) they were going to serve in. (By 1914 it had been decided that most Royal Marine officers would enter the Corps directly, and 'very few' Osborne boys would join them.) The Admiralty was careful to state that not even candidates who scored the highest marks in the entrance examination would have the choice,[12] but all could volunteer for a specialist branch when they reached commissioned rank.

The Admiralty also had to deny constantly allegations that the whole admissions procedure was settled in advance. In the pre-Osborne days all candidates for cadetships were 'nominated': some directly by newly appointed Admirals and Captains, but most by nominations for which application had been made to the Admiralty. Under the new scheme, all cadetships – except a few from the Colonies – were open to free competition. The Admiralty strongly denied that candidates were nominated by members of the Cabinet – though it had to admit in 1910 that some 'recommendations' of colonial boys were made through the Secretary of State for the Colonies. As late as 1919 Walter Long, the First Lord of the Admiralty, found it necessary to inform the House of Commons that the only information the Admiralty required in order to select candidates were medical particulars and a confidential report from the boy's headmaster.[13]

Age was only one consideration to be borne in mind when searching for Osborne recruits. Where the boys were to come from, whose character fitted the other, rather restrictive, categories, was not so certain. As surviving records of College Interview Boards held in 1903, 1905 and 1915 show, the fathers of prospective candidates held (or had held) a wide variety of appointments.[14] In November 1903 the Board, which met between 4 and 12 November, had before it the names of 193 candidates for admission to the College. Of these, the largest occupational group of fathers was that of soldier, with thirty-four being listed as currently serving with the Colours, or having retired, in both the British and Indian Armies. Next in number were those simply described as 'Gentleman', some of whom had, no doubt, retired from other occupations. Only nineteen of the fathers served with the Royal Navy (and one in the Royal Marines), and two listed their occupation as having a connection with the Merchant Navy. The remaining fathers came from a wide variety of middle-class backgrounds. There were twenty-nine businessmen, often described as 'merchants', from both the commercial and the industrial worlds, and nineteen clergymen, as well as civil servants and stockbrokers (six of each), dentists (two) and doctors (eleven), lawyers (ten), and engineers of various types (six). Perhaps not surprisingly, the academic world did not figure largely; there was one university lecturer, one inspector of schools, and one museum curator. There was also a journalist, an architect and two artists, among others.

Two years later, in the interviews held at the end of October and beginning of November 1905, the number of applicants had dropped to 167. There had been very few changes in the occupation or position of fathers, compared with 1903; 'Gentlemen' again figured highly (twenty-five), as did soldiers, past and present (twenty-one). There were fifteen fathers with a Royal Naval background and, once again, only one Royal Marine, together with one 'shipping master' and two 'shipping owners', twenty-two 'merchants' of various sorts, fourteen clergymen, twelve civil servants, eleven lawyers and engineers, ten doctors (but no dentists) and three stockbrokers. Only one father had any connection with the world of education (holding a College Fellowship), but on this occasion there was also an artist, an actor and a policeman from Burma.

Ten years later 110 boys were interviewed for admission. Once again, their fathers were drawn from a wide range of middle- or upper-class occupations, and there appears to have been little overall change in the background of boys going to Osborne. In 1915, however, the largest single group, broadly defined, was that of 'merchant' with twenty-one names, followed by regular Army officers (fourteen, with the addition of another ten men who were 'temporarily' in the Army – not necessarily as officers) and Gentlemen (twelve). In this group, only two fathers were noted as serving in the Royal Navy, and none at all in the Royal Marines, and only one shipping owner. There were, as before, a relatively large number of men drawn from the legal and medical professions (ten each) and the clergy (six). Nine listed their profession as engineer, but, as before, there were only a few involved in education (two, one as a headmaster, and the other as an inspector of schools). While there were no actors listed on this occasion, there were, among others, a journalist, an architect and an artist.

Taken as a whole, these figures tell us much about the background of prospective naval officers. The most obvious surprise is that so few of the boys appear, at first sight at least, to have had a naval background. This revelation, however, must be treated with caution. The interview lists for 1903, in particular, have a good deal to say about some boys, and are careful to point out if a boy had any naval connection. It was noted on the application of one, for example, whose father was described simply as 'M.A. (Oxon) Artist', that his two great-uncles had been Admirals in the Royal Navy, as was one of his cousins, two others of whom were Army officers. A similar tale is told of another candidate: his father was a surgeon in civil life, but his great-uncle was Admiral Sir William Shadwell. In all, eighteen boys in 1903 may be said to have come from a 'naval family', in addition to those whose fathers actually were in the service, to which might be added a further thirteen who had relatives in both services and eight who had relatives in the Army. Even so, the apparent lack of naval background of so many of the cadets is somewhat unexpected. Less so is the fact that many of the liberal arts professions are under-represented, so that in this respect, at least, the Admiralty seemed to be getting the kind of applicants it was looking for.

The Admiralty carefully reviewed its lists of candidates in its preparations for the admission interview. While under the 1902 regulations for admission 'nomination' was no longer strictly required for a naval cadet, the interview list for 1903 leaves no doubt that it helped to have 'friends in high places'. It was noted next to the name of one prospective cadet that, besides having a father who was a Vice Admiral, 'Lord W. Kerr will nominate' (perhaps not surprisingly the word 'passed' has been added in another hand). One candidate, whose father directed a museum in South India, nevertheless had powerful allies, including

'Earl Roberts, who is interested' and 'Lord W. Kerr, interested (but not personally)', while another was 'supported' by an MP. Both of these boys passed. But other boys were not so fortunate. One, although supported by the presence of one Admiral, two Lieutenants RN and one Midshipman in his family, did not secure entry.

It is clear that the boys themselves had a variety of motives for wishing to join the Navy. Some, indeed, evidently had no choice in the matter. Several former cadets put the matter bluntly:

My father wanted me to go into the Navy.[15]

At that tender age I had no great ideas other than being a train driver or a soldier, but my father was very anxious for my brother and myself to go in the Royal Navy and that was it.[16]

I was never asked if I wanted to go into the Navy. My father was Commander-in-Chief of the Home Fleet at the time I went to Osborne. . . .[17]

As for my own wishes in the matter, I had not been consulted. . . .[18]

One declared that he had joined: 'Because my parents conned me into going . . . they said . . . I was not prone to seasickness and therefore I'd make a lovely sailor.'[19] On the other hand, there were those who had much more positive reasons for going. For some it was a simple: 'I always wanted to go into the Navy.'[20] 'I always wanted to go into the Navy and I hadn't any other particular reason.'[21] Although one admitted, 'I've no idea why. . . . I'd no naval background and I always wanted to go into the Navy.'[22]

Others were influenced by some happy memories of their own. One

lived at Portland and I used to see the ships' masts. I knew the name of every ship in the Navy, I think when I was nine or . . . ten. . . . And my father was a doctor, actually, but instinctively a sailor, and loved the sea. Heredity, I think, came into it a little.[23]

Another thought, 'the reason was because I'd done a lot of sailing on the Norfolk Broads and I rather thought the Navy would be like the Norfolk Broads.'[24] A third had seen the Royal Navy in close-up:

When I was six . . . some of the British fleet came and anchored in the Port of London . . . my father. . . . I don't think he did it advisedly to get me to volunteer to join the Navy, he may have, he never said so but he said, 'Let's go and have a look.' So we went on board a destroyer. I became instantly and absolutely fascinated. She was a nice clean little ship and I remember being lifted up by a sailor . . . he cocked one of the guns up. . . . I was fascinated by this and by a lot of other things. When an old lady said to me 'Are you going to be an engine driver, my little man?'. I said 'No, I'm going to be a naval officer.' My father . . . was absolutely delighted, of course, that he didn't have to pay my public school fees.[25]

Outside influences could also be brought to bear:

I loved the element of the sea, but that was largely based on happy associations of summer holidays but I'm not sure the main reason wasn't, it was very much the thing to do from our prep. school. Our headmaster was right in with the naval world. This was the greatest honour any boy could have, to get into the Navy, the thing to do.[26]

At least one father used directly personal persuasion to interest his son in naval service:

I was put in a sailor suit when I was about five and my father was in the Navy. I was always rather amused at something he said which probably had no bearing on it but he said 'My boy, I don't want to influence you in any way but the Navy's the finest profession in the world. You can do that or lick stamps in an office from nine o'clock in the morning until ten o'clock at night, nothing much else to do.' I don't think I believed him. Still. There's no doubt that the Navy was regarded as a top profession in those days.[27]

Some boys had more intimate reasons for wishing to join the service:

When I was four I vividly remember . . . I received a postcard from an uncle of mine. In fact he was my only uncle. . . . I think he was a captain in the Royal Navy and he was quite a well-known figure and rather in a way a family god to us. We were very proud of him. . . . He sent me a postcard with a picture on it of sailors scrubbing decks.

They had bare feet, water was washing about all over the place and I said to myself, 'My golly, that's the way to live, that's the way I can get my feet wet without being ticked off by nanny when I walk through all the puddles,' which was my chief sport at the time, and I never varied at all since that. This story sounds a little bit jaunty but it's really seriously true and it had a great effect on my career because I began to realise that the Navy was in some sort of way a vocation. I didn't join it just for a job like so many people do, I wanted it to be my life.[28]

One other former cadet remembered that

A favourite first cousin of mine some years previously had said he wanted to go into the Navy and so I followed him and said I wanted to go into the Navy. He didn't go into the Navy. I found it more convenient to say that I was going into the Navy when people ask you what you're going to do when you grow up and that's why I went.[29]

while another was

sorry to say I cannot give you any really good reason. . . . My family had no tradition in the Royal Navy whatsoever nor can I honestly say I was very interested in a nautical life. I really think the reason I joined the Navy – you must remember I was only twelve and a half when I had to make this momentous decision – was that I thought I should be a smash hit in my naval uniform at children's parties.[30]

It is, therefore, very difficult from the oral records to categorise boys' reasons for wishing to go to the Royal Naval College, Osborne. It is fairly clear that the majority of them wished to go, mostly without any real degree of family pressure being exerted on them. The factors that gave rise to these wishes in the first place were clearly many and various, but a positive desire to enter the Navy certainly predominates. There was a significant minority, however, who displayed no great enthusiasm to join the Navy and who did so simply because their father or family wished it, or because they felt they had no other real choice.

Once a boy had made known his wishes (or had been informed by his parents what his wishes were), the boy's parent or guardian now had to apply for their son's admission. It was, of course, essential that the boy conformed to the regulations as regards age and nationality, but the

Admiralty desired to know a great more than this. It was necessary for the parent or guardian of each candidate to complete 'Cadets – Form A' on his behalf. This form asked for details about the boy's educational background, and the name, address and occupation of his parent or guardian. It also required the signatory to declare that, if successful, the boy would 'adopt the Navy as his profession in life' and that his parent or guardian would pay the Admiralty all fees and costs, while the cadet was at Osborne and Dartmouth, as well as an allowance while he was Midshipman and Acting Sub-Lieutenant.

In addition to Form A, the boy's parent or guardian was required to complete a 'Statement of Medical Particulars', the information on which had to be confirmed by the family doctor. The Admiralty, by 1914, at least, had made it quite clear to the public that the state of health of potential cadets was a serious concern. *The Education of a Naval Officer* commented that:

> Every candidate must be in good health, and free from any physical defect of body, impediment or speech, defect of sight or hearing, and also from any predisposition to constitutional or hereditary disease or weakness of any kind, and be in all respects well developed and active in proportion to his age. . . .

Not surprisingly, therefore, the health of every candidate was enquired into in some detail on the application form, with questions covering matters ranging from the quality of his eyesight to whether or not he was incontinent. The candidate's parent or guardian was also asked whether the boy or any of his 'near relations' had ever 'been afflicted with consumption, scrofula, gout, asthma, epilepsy, or insanity', and whether he had had smallpox, scarlet fever or measles – while some of these would not preclude admission to Osborne, others might well disqualify the candidate. Besides this information, the Admiralty enquired about the state of health of both parents and any siblings and whether, and if so why, either parent or any siblings were deceased.[31]

In addition to this personal and medical information, the admissions panel requested a report from the boy's teachers. This posed twelve 'strictly private and confidential' questions, as well as requesting general comments on 'the boy's capacity, and the promise he shows, judging by the progress he has made, and his conduct both in and out of school, since he has been under your care'.

The specific questions themselves reveal a lot about what the Admiralty was looking for. It wanted to know, for example, whether the candidate was suited for the Navy and was 'advanced' intellectually, whether he was particularly good at languages or 'practical mechanics', and whether he was 'keen' at work and play. But other questions indicate that the Admiralty wished to know far more about each boy's character:

6. Does he tend to lead other boys? If so, is his influence on them good?

7. Is he physically strong and active, or are you aware of any weakness?

8. Is he frank, truthful and obedient?

9. Have you detected in him any offence against morals?

The last question wanted to know whether he had any 'private or special tuition' to prepare him for the qualifying examination, which all candidates, once they had passed the interview and medical, had to undertake.

The Admiralty was clearly content with this questionnaire and proposed only a minor modification of it to the Custance Committee of 1912, namely adding that the boys should be compared not only with their fellow applicants, but also with candidates for naval cadetships on other occasions.[32] These three forms between them certainly give a clear impression of the kind of boy the Admiralty was seeking and, if fully completed, would have enabled the Applications Committee to decide with some confidence whether or not he should be invited for interview.

From all of the details required from parents and guardians, doctors and teachers, it is apparent the Admiralty paid careful attention to the kind of boy it was admitting to the service. The sums of money required and, more particularly, the commitment required from the parents and guardians were also significant. The medical questionnaire showed that any doubts about a boy's health, not to mention reservations about his character expressed by his teachers, could very well terminate a candidate's naval career even before it started.

Numerous boys were nevertheless invited to take their candidacies a stage further. This would involve them in a journey, usually up to

London, where they would have to undergo an interview, followed by a medical and a formal written examination. The actual location of these events varied widely. The Interview Committee that met in March 1913, for example, was 'in Spring Gardens' just by Admiralty Arch.[33] That held in the summer of 1917 met 'at a club in Trafalgar Square', while that for October/November 1917 met at the Russell Hotel.[34] After the war the venue appears to have changed again – and not for the better: the Board for autumn 1921 met in 'a whole lot of huts in St James' Park . . . there was a sort of hutted encampment'.[35]

The Admiralty made no secret of the fact that the Interview Committee was the most important element in selecting candidates for admission. It was a special committee, appointed by the First Lord of the Admiralty for each occasion it met (three times a year), and comprised

an Admiral as Chairman, the Headmaster of a public school, or some equally high authority in education with experience of boys, a Naval Captain, and one of the First Lord's Secretaries.[36]

The committee could be made up of some eminent figures. The Recruiting Committee sitting in June and July 1908, for example, had Admiral Sir Michael Culme Seymour as its chairman, together with Revd Dr H.B. Gray, Warden of Bradfield School, Captain L. Halsey (Flag Captain, Devonport), Mr Edward Packe and Mr Roland Nelson as its members.[37] In 1921 the Recruiting Committee was chaired by Admiral Sir Doveton Sturdee, victor of the Battle of the Falkland Islands, and the Headmaster of Rugby School also sat on it.[38] Not that the fame or importance of the committee members necessarily had much of an impact on the young men they were interviewing; one recalled that 'the oral examination was done in London by about three retired Admirals, I think they were retired, from the age I was then they certainly looked it'.[39]

Another former cadet remembered 'a lot of rather alarming gentlemen sitting round a table: they fired questions at me'.[40]

Before being admitted to the presence of these 'rather alarming gentlemen' all candidates had to write a short piece for the committee to read. The subject of this varied greatly. One candidate was told that he had three minutes 'to write an essay on what are good manners'; another to write something on a rather more exciting subject – 'a fight between an airship and an aeroplane'.[41] One young man's effort caused his interviewers considerable amusement:

before the interview, while we were waiting, we were told to sit down and write ten lines on one of three subjects which were set on a piece of paper. The subject I chose was, 'What do you imagine the interview board will be like?' I said something to the effect that 'I imagine five old men sitting round a table asking me questions about various things.' That was handed in. When I arrived at the door, the door was open and I ushered in before the . . . board. They were simply bursting their sides with laughter.[42]

Another candidate, who had to write an essay on the difference between the Navy of Nelson's day and the present, was helped in its preparation by a Petty Officer.[43] One other cadet faced a challenging essay subject:

. . . while waiting for the interview we were given a slip of paper and we were given ten minutes to write an answer to the question. The question that I selected was 'Do you think war is necesary?' or . . . something like that. I thought for about eight and a half minutes and then I wrote, 'Yes, war is necessary because if there was no war there would be no need to have a Navy and I want to join the Navy so war is necessary'. . . . And that was that.[44]

The committee would then interview the boy for some fifteen to twenty minutes, during which time, so the Admiralty informed parents and guardians, 'questions are asked as to his school-work, his interests, his tastes: he is made to talk. Only very rarely is he hampered by shyness.'[45]

Surviving candidates had very vivid recollections of their interview day:

I remember one of the interviewers saying to the other, 'nicely dressed'. That was thanks to my headmaster who procured me a new suit for the occasion. I was a slovenly boy. I wasn't usually dressed like that. I thought the going was good.

This particular candidate, like many others, remembered some of the questions he was then asked:

I was taken by the schoolmaster to a map which was hanging on the blackboard and there was a port in Russia which I must have known.

I couldn't get it. He tried to help me by saying, 'It rhymes with "the back of a tiger".' But of course the answer was Riga.[46]

Another recalled how he

> went into a room where there were four chaps round a table. I think one was Lord Selborne, he was a big man; I don't know who the others were. The first chap who I thought was Lord Selborne said so you are Hamilton, aren't you? I said yes sir (I said sir to every question to them all). Your father's Capt. Hamilton on the *Bulwark*. Yes. Is your mother still in Malta? Yes. Have you ever been to Malta? Yes about 5 or 6 years ago. Do you remember anything about it? No nothing. Have you been to France or anywhere except Malta? No. Do you remember any old naval battles? Yes, the battle of the Nile. Who was the Admiral? Nelson. Who did he fight against? The French. What do you call the ruler of France? (I forgot at first then said) the Emperor, the Republic, I mean, no, the President. Of Germany? Kaiser. Russia? The Tsar. Of America? The President. What is his name? (I had forgotten). I don't know. Do you know any river in America? The Mississippi. In France? The Seine. Who is the old Admiral? Sir Henry Keppel. (Then one of the others). How big is this room do you think? 40 by 55 feet. They grinned. Who was John Bryte? [sic]. I don't know. Who was Pitt? A great statesman. What were his cheif [sic] reforms? I don't know. What does consol mean? (they spelt it to me). (I said) Like a British consul in a foreign land? (they laughed). They asked me a lot more general questions like this. . . .[47]

Another remembered that he was

> rather frightened by it because one went into a large room and at a big table there were a whole lot of austere looking gentlemen, some naval, some civilian, sitting round it. They soon put you at your ease, I think. They asked you all sorts of questions, geographical questions, history, even Latin, I don't know why because Latin was never part of one's training after one went to Osborne.[48]

A third commented that the Board 'asked me various questions, nothing to do with the Navy. They asked me if I went abroad to a strange country and wanted to farm there, what would I look for? Things like that.'[49]
Geography intruded itself on several occasions:

. . . they asked me what my hobbies were, I think I said 'painting and stamp-collecting'. Then the Admiral said, 'Have you got any stamps from North Borneo?' I hurriedly thought 'I don't know where that is.' I said no. He said, 'Have you got any stamps from the Leeward Islands?' I did know where they were. So he said, 'There's a map behind you. Show me where the Leeward Islands are.' I was able to do that.[50]

. . . I remember rather vividly the last question they asked me. They pointed to a map on the wall which was of China. . . . One of the interviewers said, 'Point out the Huang Ho.' I was able to do that because I'd seen it before.[51]

Candidates' sports and pastimes also came under scrutiny:

I was asked what I did or what games I played when I wasn't in organised games such as football or cricket. I told them that as my father played golf, I played golf and so did my brother and 'What else?' I was asked and I said, 'Similarly, my father plays billiards and of course I enjoy that game very much.' The first question was asked me by, I think, an Admiral, 'What's the stymie rule of golf?', which of course everybody knew. But the headmaster of Radley was rather different and he asked me how many times I was allowed to pot the red off the top spot which I also knew. . . .[52]

The main purpose of the interview was not, however, to test the candidate's knowledge, as the Admiralty freely admitted, but to assess his 'suitability'. Looking back, many of the candidates reached this conclusion for themselves:

There were none of them really testing questions, I think they were really after . . . your attitude of mind on the whole. Looking up my answers to some of the geography questions afterwards I knew I'd got most of them wrong.[53]

On second thoughts he

may have made the grade by insisting that my title of Dnieper for what was really the River Volga was the right one and I wouldn't budge from that and they may have said, 'This chap's going to stick to his guns and you can't do much about him, let him through.'[54]

The Admiralty wanted to make the interview appear quite straightforward, but it is difficult to gauge how the candidates themselves viewed it at the time. Some were expecting worse, and were 'greatly relieved' by the experience itself:

I remember being utterly terrified in the waiting room because rumour went round that we ought to remember the number of the taxi we came in and the number of windows in the interview room and that sort of thing. However, that didn't happen. But . . . my twin brother went in before me and came out looking almost human, which relieved me greatly, and when I went in they started laughing because I was so like him and this infuriated this little boy. I was told to sit down and one of them said 'Are you called Tweedledum and Tweedledee at school?' I was very upset about this and I said 'No, sir, certainly not.' We were called Gowlland Major and Gowlland Minor, sort of putting them in their place. They all laughed a lot. Then I told them I'd beaten my brother at geography the last term and they let me off the rest, it was rather a good interview on the whole.[55]

For some the interview, however important, was not a bad affair: 'I suppose the whole thing depended a good deal on the president, kind of chap he was. I found the whole thing very friendly and quite easy . . . no great obstacle at all.'[56] Others were not quite so fortunate:

they asked you questions about anything just to see how you responded and they asked me a question . . . about the Persian Gulf. There was some row going on at that time round about where the Euphrates comes out and I hesitated. I got a little confused and the examiner . . . I think they were schoolmasters . . . pounced on me and bullied me a little. . . .[57]

At least one came away with still more negative views: one candidate simply remembered being 'terrified of the whole procedure'.[58]

On the whole, however, it may be said that the Admiralty Interview Committee did its job well – at least from the point of view of the candidates. The interviews themselves appear to have contained a judicious mixture of factual questions along with more probing ones regarding boys' personalities and interests. Most boys certainly seem to have been able to stand up to their questioning – but this, of course, is based on the recollections of the ones who passed.

Once the interview was over, the committee members voted on the grade the boy should be awarded. A range of seven grades was used and, on the basis of this, the First Lord would select those candidates who could go forward – providing they were physically fit – to the written examination. From comments written on the surviving interview lists, it is clear that the committee members placed character at least as highly as academic attainment in awarding their grades. One candidate, interviewed in November 1903, was described as 'bright and intelligent' and awarded a B+, while another was also awarded this grade but he had been 'pulled down from alpha by sickly appearance' – neither of these boys were finally passed by the Board. Of two other boys, who were both successful, one received alpha + and was described as 'good all round' while the other, with the same grade, was felt to be 'very promising'. One candidate was evidently a 'grave, serious boy', but this did not help his case, and at least one other was 'spoilt by public school' and awarded an omega grade. Still others were described bluntly as 'very poor at all subjects' and 'not good at anything' – not surprisingly, both of these candidates received an omega grade and neither of them passed. In contrast to this, one boy, whose Latin was 'poor' and algebra 'weak', was nevertheless able to go forward.[59]

The health and physical fitness of candidates was ascertained at the same time as their interview. The boys were expected to be both fit and strong. They had to carry out physical exercises for the benefit of the doctors:

> Of course, one had a medical examination too, the same time. I remember one had to climb up a rope quite naked using only one's hands, which was rather trying but I'd been training for that 'cos I was told that was something you had to do so I got over that one alright.[60]

Another successful candidate remembered that he passed the medical examination even though he had been unable to climb the rope.[61] The candidates also had their eyes tested. While this seems to have been conducted rigorously, at least in the first instance, it would appear that parental pressure, judiciously applied, could nevertheless make a difference at a later date. One cadet remembered:

> they failed me for eye-sight 'cos I did a bit of painting and I knew the difference between peacock blue and green and when they showed

me a bead which was peacock blue I called it blue. They said I was colourblind. However, my father knew I wasn't, had me examined again and I got through.[62]

In another case, it was – apparently – the boy's mother who made the difference:

they wrote and told my mother that I had failed for eyesight . . . I had a second shot but they still wrote to my mother and said again I had failed for eyesight. My mother being a woman of great enterprise wrote back and said that if they looked at their records of the previous year they would see how much my eyes had improved during the past twelve months. . . . Whether that influenced the Admiralty or not I don't know but they did revise their decision.[63]

The problems of at least one candidate, however, escaped detection altogether: 'I wore specs for reading, for astigmatism, and I was very careful not to show that I wore specs, because eyesight was a very particular problem. You had to be 100% on eyesight.'[64]

But there were some things the boys could not hide. It was noted on the record of one 1903 candidate for admission that he had 'appeared before C[ee] & would have been awarded B+ or alpha – except for stammering. Sir H. Neale called and said stammering was now understood to be cured'. Unfortunately, another hand has added 'not cured' – and another hopeful candidate's attempt to join the Navy was brought to an abrupt halt.[65]

Those who had passed the interview and medical fitness test now faced their last obstacle: the written examination. The Admiralty pamphlet *On the Entry and Training of Naval Cadets* was careful to point out that the reason for the change in the age of entry to Osborne made in 1913 was to bring it up to the age at which boys left Preparatory Schools and went to Public Schools. Hence, boys would have a choice about whether to take up an Osborne cadetship or go on to Public School. The Admiralty also pointed out, however, that their test was a small hurdle to clear: 'All but a few of the selected candidates are successful in passing this test. . . . All . . . who pass the test enter Osborne; the examination is strictly a qualifying one, not a competition.'

No secret was made of the fact that it was the interview which had decided whether or not a boy had a future at Osborne. It was felt the interview could ascertain far better than a written test whether or not the boy had the necessary 'qualities' to make a good officer.[66] Moreover, it was believed a 'competitive examination' could lead to 'cramming, a specially mischievous thing at an early age'. The Admiralty experts were especially keen to avoid this: 'Any special preparation for Osborne is to be deprecated, especially anything that savours of cramming.' For this reason, parents were advised that they should send their sons to any one of the many 'excellent' Preparatory Schools available:

> There is no need to look for an establishment which devotes itself to the training of naval candidates, and no advantage in choosing such an establishment. It is preferable that the early education of the Osborne candidate should not in any way be distinguished from that of other boys.[67]

Some parents seem to have followed this advice, and sent their sons to 'ordinary' Preparatory Schools: '. . . the school was a very classically-minded school. They liked classically-minded boys and they were getting a tremendous amount of Winchester scholarships just at that time.'[68] Others, however, clearly did not do so. One boy, for example, explained that 'I went to an extremely efficient prep school which specialised in sending boys up for the Navy. . . .'[69] Another was 'crammed by a prep school. It was an institution called a naval academy which set out to get boys passed into Osborne and made a speciality out of it. . . .'[70]

The amount and nature of preparation for the examination itself also seems to have varied. Some former cadets recollected nothing out of the ordinary in their school work during this time:

> I think we did the usual sort of sweating that one did for exams at school. . . . I don't remember doing any special thing at all.[71]

> I didn't cram any more than one normally does at a prep school where one is given past Navy exam papers which were much the same but no more difficult than the common entrance.[72]

Others received some more special treatment. For one, it was '. . . my headmaster of my preparatory school [who] took a great deal of trouble to try and coach me to take this exam'.[73] Another was fortunate: '. . .

I was lucky in Uncle Gusford who was actually the cramming master for those who wanted to go into the Navy.'[74]

All of these candidates had applied for cadetships after the age of entry had been raised in 1913. Before that time there is little doubt the majority of Osborne boys had attended special 'cramming' establishments. The Admiralty's changes appear to have made some difference, but it is clear that the 'cramming' element was not totally done away with after 1913, although less reliance was placed on crammers after this time.

The examinations themselves were held over two days in December, March and July every year, and comprised papers in six subjects: English, history and geography, arithmetic and algebra, geometry, French or German, and Latin.[75] The English paper involved writing from dictation and noting 'the gist of a short passage read aloud to the candidates'. The history and geography papers had 'special reference to the British Empire'. The arithmetic and algebra paper was primarily devoted to the former, and included such matters as the multiplication of fractions, 'simple proportion, ratio and percentage' and so on. The algebra section included the meaning of algebraic symbols, problems leading to the solution of equations and similar questions. It was stressed that the geometry paper included both practical and theoretical geometry, comprising, among other things, simple deductions from specific theorems and theorems based on those included in the Common Entrance to Public Schools examinations, as laid down in the Cambridge University Ordinances. The French or German examinations included 'an oral examination to which importance will be attached'. Finally, the Latin paper included 'easy pages' for translation (both to and from Latin) and 'simple grammatical questions'.

As noted in the Regulations, these examination papers seem quite daunting. Indeed, in 1908 J. McVeagh gave the House of Commons his opinion that some, at least, of the papers were unsuitable for boys under thirteen years of age. Reginald McKenna, the First Lord of the Admiralty, denied this, stating that the papers were set by the Oxford and Cambridge Universities Examinations Board.[76] However, few of the candidates had any recollection of the examinations, and this in itself would suggest the papers were not too difficult. Only one former cadet recollected 'quite a stiff written examination'.[77] Another pointed out that the examination was 'quite potsy', and that 'the entrance examination itself was . . . extremely easy for anyone who had any kind of education at a reasonable

Preparatory School'.[78] While a third thought 'It was very simple. . . . I'd been doing common entrance exams for some time and the Osborne one was like falling off a log, it really was.'[79] The intentions of the Admiralty appear to have been achieved in this respect: the standard of the examination was, approximately, equivalent to that of the Public Schools' Common Entrance Examination and most candidates passed:

> We all sat at individual desks and we were given these papers which was very like the ordinary common entrance for a public school. All the same subjects and I don't think there were any great difficulties there. I very much doubt if anyone failed that.[80]

All the boys who reached the necessary standard were now to go to Osborne: it was up to their parents and guardians to equip them for this. The Admiralty laid down strict regulations as to what each boy was to bring with him. Besides a uniform, summer and winter 'working suits' and other clothes (including shirts, underwear, braces and socks, waterproof or 'Pegamoid' coat, football and gymnasium wear), cadets were to be supplied with sheets and pillowcases, clothes- and hair-brushes, a portmanteau and a 'travelling bag'. The Admiralty could, and did, supply some of this, but the cadets' families would have to pay for it. The one concession was that, for the first year at Osborne, cadets could continue to wear suitable black boots that they already had.[81]

Fully equipped, the cadets set off to Portsmouth ready to be shipped over to the College by steamer. This was a day that was vividly recalled by many:

> We went by train to Portsmouth. We were then fitted out with our new uniforms by Messrs. Gieves who gave us all lunch at the Keppel's Head which Gieves could well afford to do seeing they had the contract for all our uniforms. It was a very cold day and then we were all lined up on the jetty in our pegamoids, those black stiff oilskins, the thirty of us, the new term. We looked rather like a row of penguins with sailor caps on and we went on board HM tug *Pert* which took us across the Solent to Sandquay [sic] and there in the gathering dusk we were marched up along a very steep hill clutching our little Gladstone bags and beginning to get a bit weary and apprehensive. Finally, we arrived at the Royal Naval College, Osborne, where we were fell upon by a horde of hairy petty officers who took charge of us and from then on the naval scramble started.[82]

Messrs Gieves, a tailoring firm specialising in naval outfitting, provided the vast majority of cadets with their uniform:

> The forty of us assembled in Portsmouth at Messrs. Gieves, 22 The Hard and we were then outfitted with our uniforms for which we'd previously been measured and fitted in London and we were all dressed in this totally strange uniform. Gieves then stood us a lunch. . . .[83]

On at least one occasion an important member of the firm appeared to inspect the cadets: 'We were inspected by Mr Gieve from whom we'd all bought our uniform. He came to see if we'd got our ties on straight and all that sort of thing, which was rather amusing.'[84]

The cadets were sometimes inspected by other important figures. In September 1913 and January 1921 the Commander-in-Chief, Portsmouth, performed this duty, while in September 1918 it was carried out by the Duke of Connaught.[85] At least one cadet thought they would not have been impressed with what they saw:

> Because it was pouring with rain we had to wear our pegamoid mackintoshes which were provided as part of the uniform by Gieves and when people complained Gieves said, 'Well, they're all going to grow so everything looks a bit long.' We were all dressed in uniforms which were about five sizes too big for us. The pegamoids in particular were very large and anyone who could have looked at this row of cadets, they appeared to have no feet and no hands because the sleeves of the pegamoids were much too long and jutted out over our hands and they were also practically down to our feet and were resting on the ground and we had no feet at all. It must have been a very extraordinary sight.[86]

Once on board the ferry, the cadets were ordered to 'fall in' and for one party this meant trouble:

> We were addressed as the tug cleared the harbour, one of the cadet captains said 'Fall in'. So we shuffled about the place and our term officer got on to the hatch cover of the tug and said, 'Now, you remember this, when I say "fall in" I mean "fall in" and I expect you to move.' So we were shuffled in a place in two ranks and he gave us a few words on what was going to happen.[87]

This austere introduction to naval discipline was somewhat exceptional, but all cadets had lessons to learn, even on the ferry. For one group, this was how to salute:

> . . . one cadet . . . lifted up his hand very sharply, caught it under the peak of his cap which fell off and went over the side. Of course, everybody hooted with laughter; the poor little chap . . . he burst into tears. He arrived at the College on his first day . . . hatless. Of course, he was in trouble from the very first day he got there. . . . We were very young of course and we were all rather frightened, I think.[88]

On arrival at Cowes cadets were faced with a march to the College, a distance of some 1½ miles, a long way for the heavily laden young boys:

> When we got to Cowes the dusk was falling and it was wet, one of those muggy January days. . . . The Admiralty seemed to think we should have many clothes on and working from the outside downwards you had your new uniform cap which was, of course, very uncomfortable, winter serge quality suit . . . very thick monkey jacket under which was an equally thick waistcoat with brass buttons, trousers same material, a thick flannel shirt, rather unfamiliar stiff collar and black tie and a thick long-sleeved vest and thick long-legged pants and black boots on top of which we put on our British warms, the ordinary British warm overcoat in naval cloth and because it was raining we also put on our oilskins . . . called pegamoids. [We were] armed with this and carrying quite a heavy leather overnight bag which contained our toothbrushes and things. . . .

It is not surprising to learn that these particular cadets arrived at the College 'in a rather wet and perspiring condition'. Even then, though, their long and tiring day was not over. Once in the College, they had to go to the store to collect various items of equipment, and then, finally, they made their way to the dormitories:

> We got into the College and . . . the rest of the terms were not coming back till the next day so the thing was largely unlighted and I can remember a sense of certain desolation. . . We went into a place called the Cadet Store which had a counter painted in a good old green paint which was largely reserved for hospitals, very dreary, where a Chief

Petty Officer issued us with certain other items of clothes and equipment which didn't come from Gieves like, for instance, the lanyard. . . . You put it round your neck, which had your key ring, which had a name plate on it, and also the key of your private till which was a locked drawer in your sea chest in which you were supposed to keep any valuables. . . . Having been issued with all those things, I think we had a bit of supper and then went down to our dormitory.[89]

To round off the day, the cadets were stood by their beds and were

given an outline of the rules for dormitory work, dressing, undressing, gongs for doing this, gongs for doing that, gongs for saying our prayers, one and a half minutes for that, the way to fold our clothes on our sea chest and so on.

At least,

It was all very kindly done, but there was no nonsense – nobody was ever going to get bored at that place, I came to the conclusion, because there was always somebody after you in some way for something or other. But you didn't go about with a guilty conscience unless you really had one.[90]

So ended the first day of cadets' experience of life in the Royal Navy. For some, it had clearly been a rather difficult day: others appear to have coped with it well, especially considering their relative youth. For most, it was probably not so very different from what would have happened to them had they gone to public school; for the remainder, the introduction to the rigours of naval discipline was abrupt, but all would have to face up to it in the very near future. There can be little doubt that the majority of cadets must have been exhausted by their experiences and they surely appreciated the beds in the dormitories in which they had been placed.

The cadets now securely bedded down were those boys who had survived a rigorous selection procedure to secure places at the Royal Naval College, Osborne. The Admiralty had received applications from boys who wished or had been told they should wish to join the Royal Navy from a variety of backgrounds. It had a very clear idea of the type of boy it was looking for, both in terms of character and physical fitness, and of the commitment required of parents or guardians. The entrance procedure was designed to test all of these factors. As preliminaries, parents had to show they were willing to contribute to the costs of training their sons and that the boys were fit. The boys' teachers were also called upon to submit a report on them. If these passed muster, the next stage in the procedure, the interview, was undoubtedly the most important element in it. This was clearly recalled by survivors of the College, but it is difficult to draw many general conclusions about it. The questions asked were many and various, but the responses of the boys all appear to have shared characteristics of spontaneity and vigour and all, of course, overcame this hurdle. The 'character' of the boy, as assessed at the interview, did most to determine whether or not he would go to the College: only if he was deemed physically unfit or not intelligent enough would he be prevented from attending. The medical examination and the final stage in the admissions procedure, the Qualifying Examination, seem to have presented no real obstacles.

Had the recruiting system worked? One former cadet has left a considered and probably fair answer to this question:

> What was the Board looking for? Poise? What they saw might have been sedulously laid over a shaky interior. Brains? Certainly not. Many of the boys they passed were astonishingly stupid. Manners, breeding or smartness? Perhaps these were sought but how difficult to detect smartness in a boy when he is palpitating with anxiety and has just endured hours of waiting in a billiard room. . . . Yet there is no doubt the system had its merits. Guided . . . by confidential reports from headmasters . . . influenced by their knowledge of gunroom officers, the Board . . . aimed to pick out not so much the ready-made article as those of malleable qualities. . . . From my year has come a VC, triple and double DSOs, submarine commanders whose name will go down in history, airmen, destroyer captains of renown, musicians and scholars. . . .[91]

The successful candidates had now begun a two-year stay at Osborne and it is necessary to see how they fared while there, and at the same time assess how far they lived up to the plans of the authorities who devised them. Only then can an answer be attempted to the key question of whether or not the College was a 'success'.

CHAPTER THREE

Classroom, Workshop, Sports Hall and Playing Field

The Admiralty and its expert advisors devoted a lot of attention to the question of what their officer cadets should learn. In 1914 the Admiralty informed parents and guardians that:

> The aim of the course as a whole [at Osborne and Dartmouth] is to provide as far as may be possible a liberal education, together with the groundwork in mathematics and science, engineering, and navigation, which the professional requirements of the officers make it necessary or desirable that they should possess before they go to sea. The claims of the technical subjects are so strong that the curriculum inevitably leans towards the side of mathematics and science, and their applications, and it is through the medium of mathematics and science as instruments of education that a great part of the mental development of the cadets proceeds. But the claims of the more humane studies are not forgotten: English, history and modern languages take an important place.[1]

When, to this, are added the demands imposed by the need to learn the rudiments of naval discipline, as well as the time devoted to sports and games, it is apparent that the cadets at Osborne had a great deal to do. This impression is not diminished when a more detailed examination of the syllabus provided in 1912 is made. In that year the Board of Admiralty asked the Department of Education to send in Inspectors to review the provision of education at Osborne. For their benefit, the College provided an explanation of the objectives of teaching of English and history at Osborne. These were

(1) to give the necessary practice in writing and speaking English;
(2) to give the power of reading and using books; (3) by the study of

suitable works in literature and history to give that general acquaintance with the ideas and thoughts of mankind which is necessary to enable naval officers to take their place among the educated and cultured members of other professions.[2]

It was noted that 'special stress' was laid on naval history, particularly the 'lives and exploits of the most famous seamen and the most striking episodes in naval wars'. This was to help provide the basis for the understanding of naval traditions and set up models of conduct. Two years later, in 1914, the Admiralty provided the public with a more detailed breakdown of the full Osborne syllabus. They were informed that cadets were expected to learn the history of England from the Renaissance to the present, and 'a parallel study (necessarily sketchy) of the principal movements in the history of Europe'.

In English, cadets were to have training in both language and literature, 'reading poetry and prose from the point of view of literary interest and learning a few selected passages by heart'. In addition, all cadets were to learn either French or German (half were detailed for each language) and it was noted that 'a utilitarian rather than a literary treatment is pursued, for time does not permit the study of any literature, and conversational methods are adopted in teaching'. Geography, including a 'brief discussion of the influences of climate' and a 'very elementary sketch of astronomical geography', to help the later study of navigation, was taught.[3]

Mathematics was included in the Osborne syllabus, although 'it is borne in mind that the subject is meant to serve these boys as a tool'. Science, too, was taught with this in mind: it included 'easy mensuration, hydrostatics, mechanics, heat, and the most elementary outlines of magnetism and current electricity' but this was supplemented by what was taught in the engineering classes.[4]

Engineering was deemed to be of particular importance, mostly in its practical form. Cadets at Osborne began to learn the rudiments of using tools in pattern-making, fitting and turning and forging. They also began 'to learn something of seamanship and to acquire the art of signalling by means of semaphore, Morse and Flags'.[5]

Finally, all cadets received elements of religious education and not only on Sundays. This included standard study of Bible stories and the Prayer Book, as well as 'lectures . . . on the sources from which the Books of the Bible have been derived': special provision was made for Roman Catholic cadets.[6]

Outside of the classroom, all cadets were expected to spend from one and a half to two hours a week on 'gymnastics and physical training' and, in addition to all of this, 'Games receive much attention' since, the Admiralty informed its readers, 'The all-round knowledge of games which the cadets acquire is likely to prove a useful asset to them later in their care of men.'[7] The matches and teams were arranged in the Ward Room, and posted after the cadets' morning work, 'Except when excused on medical grounds, cadets are required to be out of doors and actively employed during certain hours: in this sense games (of some sort) are compulsory.'[8]

It is, therefore, not unreasonable to assume that cadets had a very busy time of it, but curiously this was not the unanimous recollection of former cadets. One remarked: 'You were kept pretty hard at it. There was the usual class hours which took place. Of course, in the summer the afternoon work was done in the evening after daylight so that you could play games.'[9] But another had a different impression about working hard:

No, I'm afraid I didn't. I'd worked very hard at my prep school because, of course, it was determined to get me through and so I had to work very hard. But when I got to Osborne there were so many other interesting things to do, more sports, there was rowing, there was rugger, cross-country runs, gymnastics. It opened up a whole area of education which I'd never met before and I thoroughly enjoyed it.[10]

The most general response was that 'like all small boys you did what you had to and managed to keep up',[11] though at least one 'worked fairly hard. I was frustrated because I wasn't very good at work but I enjoyed the outdoor life at Osborne and the games. I was very interested in the gym which I generally got top place at.'[12]

Overall, it is very difficult to generalise what cadets thought of the academic rigour of the regime: opinions range from those who did not work hard, through to the ex-cadet who felt he worked 'too hard. I was low down in my term and I did have to work jolly hard. Never worked harder since. That's true.'[13] On balance, though, the full nature of the curriculum would seem to suggest that any cadet wishing to do well at Osborne would need to put in some effort to do so.

In addition to work carried out in the classroom with term mates, all cadets on entry to the College were organised into 'what they called "tutor sets" . . . all of us not from the same term, though we did most things together'.[14] The Admiralty's description in 1914 made both the composition and purpose of the tutor sets clear to prospective cadets' parents and guardians:

> The cadets are also grouped in 'tutor sets', each of which is associated with a particular master who serves as their adviser in matters of study. This ensures that out of study every cadet comes into fairly close relation with one of the masters as a personal friend, and remains in that relation throughout his stay at the College. At Osborne, 22 of the masters act in this way as tutors. . . . The tutor watches the general progress of his cadets and reports on it to the Headmaster. In the tutor sets boys of various seniorities are mixed.[15]

Very few of the cadets interviewed had any recollection of this system, and those who did remained uncertain of its purpose. One remembered that:

> on the educational side you had tutor sets, which consisted of a section from each of the six terms . . . your tutor was one of the senior masters who was . . . I suppose in charge of your education. . . . I don't think we played games as tutor sets because I think we just had a unity as a tutor set because we met there in the evenings and your tutor was a sort of link with your specialist teachers.[16]

Another former cadet recounted how

> We all went at one period a week, I think it was, to a particular master who was our tutor. I don't know whether it was his job to see how we were getting on in normal subjects but I seem to remember in the period we had some voluntary subject we studied. I remember one of mine was astronomy. But I've no doubt he also was concerned with our general education.[17]

Two other cadets had particular reasons for remembering their 'tutor', one, at least, for pleasant ones:

> When you went [to Osborne] each was allocated to what they called a tutor. I suppose the idea was rather on the lines of universities. It

was someone you could go and discuss your studies with, perhaps. In fact, it didn't amount to anything at Osborne at all. I had a remarkable character, yes, I'd forgotten him, Hughes-Games. . . . You went to your tutor as a matter of course. Everybody in the tutor set, which would be about twenty I suppose, adjourned to one of the classrooms on a Sunday, to meet your tutor and hear what he had to say. And if you hadn't been doing awfully well in your work he'd give you a roasting. Well conversely, I was astonished and rather embarrassed when after we'd been there a month I was hauled out in the tutor set and presented with a shilling by Mr. Hughes-Games because I'd come out top of the term in the order. They had these monthly orders. The whole marking there was intensively competitive. There was practically nothing that wasn't marked. And you were flat out the whole time. At the end of the time they gathered up all the marks in the various departments I suppose and they added them up and put the monthly order up on the board. And I was given a shilling for being top of the term. And this was repeated on two occasions after that.[18]

Unfortunately, another cadet remembered his tutor at Osborne for less satisfactory reasons:

Though our Term Officers were our principal mentors we were each allocated to a Master as 'Tutor'. I suppose he was intended to look after our moral and spiritual welfare, but in my own case he did nothing of the kind. I can remember just one invitation to tea in my Tutor's house, when he entertained us by playing a gramophone. But it was an incident on the playing fields which really aroused my hatred for him. He and his wife were watching a game of football, and the woman remarked, 'Roskill plays quite well.' 'Yes', he replied within the hearing of cadets on the touchline, 'But I don't like him. He is a Jew boy' (which was less than a half truth). This remark was of course repeated with glee in the dormitory that evening. I never lived it down, nor did I forgive A.P. Boissier for making it. Later he became headmaster of Harrow, and I learnt with some relish that he had been anything but a success in that capacity.[19]

Hence it is clear that at least one of the tutors at Osborne was not the 'friend' of the cadet the Admiralty had hoped he would be.

To investigate in more detail the education provided at Osborne, two important sources can be used. The first of these is contemporary with the College and comprises some of the Annual Reports drawn up by the Royal Navy's own Directorate of Education, together with the more detailed findings of the Department of Education Report of 1912, referred to earlier. The second is the memories of those who experienced the education at first hand and whose memories of the College have survived very well over the years. From these sources, it may be possible to draw some more definite conclusions about the nature and quality of the education provided at Osborne.

The Director of Naval Education's Annual Reports are general reviews of the previous year's developments in the College and include information on student numbers and staffing, as well as some comments on teaching and the curriculum. In the Report for 1905, for example, the Director noted that the engineering syllabus had been amended to allow greater concentration on steam turbines and that, with the enlarged workshops completed, moulding, casting and copper-smelting was now taught, as well as carpentry, pattern-making and fitting and turning. In addition, classes in mechanical drawing had been made more systematic.[20] In 1906 changes were made in the history, English, geography, mathematics and physics syllabi and 'streaming' of boys had been introduced in languages, mathematics and science. The Report covering that year also gave a breakdown of how much time was devoted to various subjects. In the first year the most time allowed for any one subject was the fifteen periods assigned to the teaching of engineering, although only half a period was given over to 'preparation' in this subject. In the other subjects, the figures were: for mathematics, nine and a half periods; for science, five and a half periods; for French, six and a half periods; for history, three and a half periods; for English, three and a half periods; for geography, two and a half periods; for divinity, two periods of teaching only; with three periods of teaching only given over to 'gymnastics and drill', and two for seamanship.

In the second year, following changes made (there was to be one less period of English, and one more of physics, together with one more period of 'revision' in history, French and physics), the figures for classes in each subject were as follows: mathematics, eight periods of teaching, one of revision and one of preparation; physics, three periods of teaching, two in the laboratory and one preparation; in French, six periods of teaching and one of preparation; in History, three periods of teaching of 'English, Foreign and Naval History', and one of preparation; in English two periods of teaching, with one of preparation in alternate weeks together with one period (devoted to English Literature) on Sunday; religious instruction was to consist of two one-hour periods every Sunday; geography of two teaching periods and one period of preparation in alternate weeks; and seamanship of one period only, devoted to signalling.[21] No comparable changes were reported in 1907, but in 1908 the study of German for half of the cadets was introduced.[22]

There matters rested until May 1912, when the Department of Education Committee paid a visit to the College.[23] In their report, the ten inspectors (who also visited Dartmouth) made some general observations as well as some more specific comments on the education offered at Osborne. Generally speaking, the committee was quite understanding. It noted that while some of the students at the College were 'really able', the 'ability of a considerable number is not high, and in a small proportion of cases is distinctly low'. While it saw the reasons for the importance of science and technical subjects to these particular boys, it was unhappy at the limited time devoted to the humanities. The inspectors were also convinced that some of the less bright boys were being pushed a bit too hard and no boy had overmuch time for private study. They were pleased to see that classes were small (usually of some sixteen to eighteen boys) and that each cadet was streamed separately for the different subjects he took.

Looking more specifically at the subjects offered, the committee felt that the time devoted to the teaching of both English and history was too short: but at least the classes were small and the teaching staff at Osborne and Dartmouth cooperated with each other. The inspectors had a few specific suggestions for the English classes, but praised the course on the whole, as they did the history courses, though they felt these would benefit from a shortening of the period covered and help in note-taking being offered to the cadets. The naval history course of Geoffrey Callender, however, received their full approval. In the cases of both English and history, the committee felt that some revision in the course examinations would be beneficial.

Geography was also praised by the committee, with the recommendation that more time should be devoted to the astronomical side. Modern languages did not come off quite so well. The inspectors felt that the students were good at the oral element, but less so in the written language and that in this instance the co-ordination of courses between Osborne and Dartmouth was not particularly good. The committee also felt that the mathematics course might be somewhat too specialised and the weaker boys might have to try and learn too much. On the whole, though, they felt that the average ability was high in this subject.

More space was devoted in the committee's report to the science courses. In these cases, it noted the high standard of the cadets but also felt that some things could be done to improve the syllabus further. The inspectors proposed that, in addition to the physics currently being taught, some chemistry should be added to the curriculum – but to make room for this some elements relating to electricity or mechanics could be dropped (as optics already had been). They also suggested that more revision work was needed, together with more practical work in the laboratory: text books should be used and less time devoted to lectures.

The committee felt that the engineering lectures were good and that the system of training in the workshops was almost perfect. It did not, however, make any comments about the physical training and games the cadets had to undertake.

While the committee felt that the cadets perhaps had too little time for individual effort, its overall conclusion was favourable. In the few years of the College's existence, the inspectors felt, the 'experiment' had a 'very high degree of success and will get better in future'. It is not surprising that the Director of Naval Education's Report for 1912 noted the existence of this Report and that most of the committee's recommendations had been implemented.[24]

The result of the committee's visit was that from 1912 the time devoted to various subjects in the Osborne curriculum changed somewhat. From then on, cadets would receive only one hour of engineering lectures, together with eight hours in the engineering workshops and only a quarter of an hour 'preparation' per week. In mathematics, the figures were seven and a half hours of teaching and one and a quarter hours preparation. In science (by which was meant solely physics and not chemistry), two and a quarter hours of lectures, one and a half hours laboratory work and one hours preparation per week. In French or German, these figures were three and three-quarters of an hour for teaching and half an hour for preparation. In history, one and a half hours was given over to both. In English and geography, the figures were one and a half hours and a quarter of an hour respectively for teaching and preparation in each case and in religious instruction, there would be one and a half hours teaching per week only. Two and a quarter hours per week were spent in gymnastics and three-quarters of an hour per week each in seamanship and in signalling.

These figures indicate that, although some changes to the curriculum had been made, the overall structure of the College course had not been greatly altered.[25] This amended syllabus lasted effectively throughout the existence of the College and this certainly suggests the Admiralty and other appropriate authorities were happy with it. The question remains about whether those on the receiving end were equally satisfied by it.

Most former cadets appear to have had a favourable recollection of their studies at Osborne. The majority believed that they did

The ordinary standard work which one would have done at Public School, with no Latin, no Greek, possibly more mathematics and I think we started physics which I hadn't been taught, science, very limited science at my prep. school, but at Osborne I think we . . . started with physics, optics, hydraulics and so on. French we had. . . .[26]

As another remarked

. . . it was a very general education. Maths, French we had, no more Latin of course, that was dropped out. We started on physics which we hadn't done anything of and of course, engineering, seamanship, extras, extra sort of naval training. A certain amount of naval history . . . was a bit of an extra. But basically the training there was very much the same as you would have got at a public school with the exception of a few naval subjects.[27]

The abandonment of Latin was noted by another cadet, who remembered being taught 'All the standard subjects but we dropped Latin. . . . All the others were the standard, Maths, History, English – the usual subjects taught at any public school in those days.'[28] But one former cadet, echoing the findings of the 1912 Committee, believed, 'the humanities were hardly recognised'.[29] Another remembered that 'None of the arts – music or literature – was taught', simply because 'there was no time'.[30] Only some of those interviewed had any special recollections of the 'purely academic' subjects they were taught and these were not invariably very favourable. One remembered learning to speak German to a certain extent, as war with Germany was looming and they thought it would be just as well if they had naval officers who could understand German broadcasts and that sort of thing. So I learnt German up to a point; I wasn't particularly good.[31]

Considering that languages were supposed to be taught practically, it comes as a surprise to learn:

I was taught to forget all the French I knew really and truly. . . . When I was a child, I'd had French mademoiselles for three years running and I was pretty good at French. Then they started teaching us French grammar and things at Osborne and knocked it all out of my head pretty well. I thought at the time anyhow. And there was something in it, too. . . . I got very bored just learning grammar and nothing else when really I could talk pretty fluently.[32]

Even when recollections of the language teaching were more positive, it is apparent that they were not always taught in the manner their Lordships advertised: 'Good teaching in French. . . . A book we did was Victor Hugo's *Les Misérables*. . . . That was good . . . but that was rather skimped, that side.'[33] One student, however, had a different experience of the teaching of French, and this would indicate that, in at least one case, the staff taught French in a way that their Lordships would have approved:

Mr Poole . . . would allow no word in his class from beginning to end, if it wasn't in French, and he had a unique way of teaching it, and I think it was absolutely the tops. I have been able to get along in French all the rest of my life on that.[34]

Whatever the standard of foreign language tuition, it did not serve one eminent student particularly well: 'we had the heir to the Belgian throne [in our term]. . . . The only thing I can remember . . . was the Belgian Crown Prince failed in the French exam, which we thought was rather fun. . . .'[35] Another, though, was able to profit from it. This was 'the late Duke of Kent, Prince George'. He was, apparently, a

charming, very self-effacing, very shy but delightful chap and sometimes we used to tease him a little bit and he used to be so confused. . . . He, of course . . . was extremely good at history and extremely good at French, but otherwise I regret to say he wasn't very high up in the term.[36]

One cadet commenting on the teaching of English at the College, thought

 . . . we weren't taught what I've always understood to be the teaching of English, like parsing and analysing the parts of speech and that sort of thing. As far as I can remember if you could get round the English master he would read you John Masefield's *Right Royal* or something like that. I never quite knew what I was supposed to do in English.[37]

But another remarked on how the authorities 'were especially keen on the English language. They took great care to cultivate our elocution and writing'.[38] In history, what was taught was, at least, fairly clear: 'basically naval history as laid down by [Geoffrey] Callender . . . naval history – only naval history. . . .' [39] This meant that the cadets

 . . . were confined practically to naval history you see. There wasn't time to do the rest of it so we got a slightly compartmented view of history, no relation to what was going on in, say, the continent, or anything like that. . . .[40]

From this it would appear that the hopes of the Admiralty in framing the wider history curriculum were not fully realised.

As far as geography was concerned, one former cadet thought he was taught 'very basic geography. I can't remember learning about the geography of the land or anything of that kind, it was just places I think. . .'.[41]

There were some more positive recollections of the mathematics taught. Even though it was recalled by one former cadet that 'in mathematics we did not go on to astral navigation or anything like that', another felt that the mathematics course 'was a very good grounding and I don't think it was very difficult . . . we did very little navigational mathematics'.[42]

The physics course also appears to have made a positive impression on the students:

. . . physics, that's the element of science of what I was introduced to as mensuration, measurement, and I began just to discover what accuracy was in measurement both in weight and in drawing and in all sorts of things through this and we had very sensitive scales, balances we called them. They were a complete novelty to use.[43]

Another former cadet commented that 'Physics consisted of what is now about eighty disciplines of different sorts. Physics covered geometry and everything like that.'[44] This provides at least a hint that the Admiralty's wishes were met as far as the physics course was concerned, but it is apparent that the purely academic subjects generally did not have much impact on the cadets. It is not difficult to see the reason why: namely, that considerably more of their time was spent on other, albeit allied, activities. These were recalled by many of those interviewed:

We did seamanship, navigation and a great deal of engineering in the workshops at Kingston. Soon after or almost before the end of our time I think it was realised that engineering was perhaps rather too much and it was curtailed down at the workshops. But we did a lot of seamanship, navigation, practical seamanship and of course in the summer term there was a lot of sailing, pulling boats and other practical things like that. I don't think there was anything else very special that we did but the engineering at that time, we did a great deal of it.[45]

A second remembered that

. . . a considerable amount of time was spent on purely nautical subjects and also even more time was spent on engineering in the workshops down at . . . Kingston. . . . But we did spend I think it's true to say the best part of – at least a quarter of – our time on engineering work which at that time was being very much pushed.[46]

This was good news for some:

I was very interested in it [science] indeed, and I think that quite a preponderance of my attention went down to a place called Kingston down on the river where we had our workshops, the College workshops. Accuracy again in joinery . . . there was a little foundry they had down there and so . . . we could actually melt brass and things like that. The classroom work on heat and steam was quite interesting.[47]

The 'engineering' course was, as one ex-cadet, who later specialised in it, commented, 'really nothing much more than workshop practice and machine drawing, no theory about it at all . . . the theoretical side was left almost entirely to Dartmouth'.[48] The experience of this course, however, certainly lived on. Actually getting to the Kingston workshops was itself something to be remembered, as well as what happened there:

The third part [of the curriculum] was extensive practical work in the manual subjects basic to engineering as was taught in the workshops at Kingston on the bank of the river, to which we were marched, in fours, by the term PO and the Engineer Lieutenant of our term. 'Tiny' Dalton was a massive man, well over 6 ft tall, and any talking in the ranks would be greeted by the threat of a huge stick waving over one's head. The curriculum at Kingston included pattern-making, turning with a lathe, use of all tools – metal and woodwork – and each cadet made something of his own choice – calipers or the like. . . . We also, of course, had lectures on simple engineering – boilers, turbines and reciprocating engines, and the relatively new Benz-petrol engines.[49]

Another cadet had detailed memories of the work undertaken at Kingston:

The first thing we had to do, we were given a lot of mild steel and a hammer, a chisel, and we had to remove about an eighth of an inch, chip it off and then file it absolutely dead smooth. I've never discovered why. When we'd done that we were given a block of . . . cast iron I think it was, and a different chisel but the same hammer, and had to do the same thing all over again. I know that took me weeks, it was a very slow job. Then after that we got on to brass . . . and had to do some turning on a lathe. We had to do a nut and bolt and do a screw thread on a lathe which is extremely difficult because if you went too far the whole thing seized up and the belt came off and the instructor came along, he was extremely angry. . . . We went through a blacksmith's course I remember and I made a small pair of pliers which I took home to my parents who were very impressed. Carpentry we did too, a certain amount of that . . . there was a copper smithy too . . . as well as a blacksmiths. Sort of general basic training it was.[50]

One thought that he and his colleagues had

. . . learnt a good deal of the basics of foundry work and blacksmith's work and carpentry . . . and most of us enjoyed it very much because it was a change from the academic work up in the College.[51]

But it could have its drawbacks:

we did a pretty tough engineering course starting with what was always chipping and filing in which you always came away with your fingers all mangled . . . they went on later to more technical procedures like milling and grinding and making small objects. . . .[52]

Despite the apparent dangers, however, the general view of the Osborne engineering course seems to have been very positive – even if it was risky:

. . . we had quite a lot of time there . . . literally knocking one's fingers about and that sort of thing with all the things one does do. That was very useful to me all my life in the service because it really did give a very good background of what goes on in a steamship.[53]

One former cadet stated his opinion very decisively:

I would like to say one thing about that and that is the practical engineering side at Osborne was out-of-this-world good. To any boy who was interested it was literally priceless. Every term we did many periods in, shall we say, one term the foundry, another term on lathes, and another term on boilers and blacksmith, absolutely everything . . . if you were that way inclined you could turn out an expert on any of those subjects.[54]

Another summed up the overall view of the engineering course well:

. . . few held it to be a waste of time. . . . It was borne upon us that everyone had to know at least something of the other man's job and the upper deck officer needed to know the problems of the engineer and the conditions under which the stokers worked. . . . We accepted engineering as part of the scene and either exulted in it or hated it according to taste.[55]

While the cadets spent a good deal of time learning some rudimentary practical engineering tasks, they were also being introduced to 'seamanship'. These classes were not so well recollected. What they involved, according to one witness, was simply 'tying knots, bending hitches and occasionally down in the boatyard we went out being taught to row'.[56] But the general view appeared to be that 'not so much' work was done on the River Medina: as was noted, 'Osborne is a mile or so from the Medina.'[57] One cadet could not 'remember . . . any boat training at Osborne. I don't think we had any boats.'[58] While another supposed 'we did a bit of cutter work, of sailing and cutter work at Osborne but I can't remember very much. . . .'[59]

Others, however, had different and more detailed recollections:

There was boatwork. I suppose it was a sport to be taken down to the river to be put into a double-banked cutter, thirty foot cutter, that is six oars each side, twelve oars, and taught to row or pull an oar as we called it, we never called it rowing. It was pulling an oar and sitting on a fixed seat in a ship's boat. One thing I remember we got that boat outside the river and it was lovely going down in good weather . . . past Cowes, past John Samuel White's shipyard where they were building destroyers. . . . [There was] a fair amount [of boat work], no sailing. It was all this rowing and the steam launches we had for teaching us how a reciprocating steam engine worked. . . .[60]

. . . Sailing, yes, we did, we had blue boats down on the Medina which we used to go out in and we also all went out in service cutters, Montague cutters and that type of thing. We did quite a bit of sailing. . . .[61]

White's shipyard was clearly on the receiving end of more than one visit from the Osborne cadets: 'Upon the sluggish waters of the Medina we sailed in cutters or, taking the helm of steam pinnaces, steered exultantly past Samuel White's yard and into Cowes Roads.'[62] Other cadets recalled special cruises made on steam ships out of Osborne – even if they did not do much else in the way of boat work:

Very little from Osborne. There weren't the facilities. The Medina was a fiddling little river and there was not much to be done about that . . . there was a pulling regatta. It was always inter-term things. Apart from that, part of the engineering course was to go out in the little steamboat . . . I think it was Queen Victoria's own . . . into the middle of the Solent, and be instructed in the actual workings. We had a triple expansion ordinary engine with a coal boiler and everything. You got taken down into the engine-room which was absolutely gleaming, perfect. The stoker had obviously been kept there for that purpose and all the copper and bright work, pipes and everything were gleaming. The slightly oily and hot smells down there, I can remember rolling about and feeling increasingly seasick in the middle of the Solent, while the engineer officer lectured to us on what we'd learnt about academically ashore.[63]

We were taken out on this little steamboat . . . that was on the Medina and took a hand at the helm aboard her, and also went down to the engine room. But we didn't do an awful lot of actual work afloat, not at Osborne.[64]

These trips could on occasion be quite exciting:

We embarked on Sunday evening and on Monday morning steamed down to the Needles and anchored at the entrance to the Hamble River. On Tuesday we went ashore to have tea with Lady Fullerton and a game of footer [sic]. On Wednesday we returned to the buoy in the Cowes Roads and went up to the College for the Trafalgar Night sing-song. We got back at 11.00 p.m. Thursday at noon we arrived at Portsmouth and after going round the Dockyard and visiting the sail and rigging lofts and HMS *Caesar*, we went to tea with Sir John and Lady Fisher and had the honour of being the only class who cleared the tea-table to the last crumb. Next day, Friday, the *Neptune*, an old battleship, sold out of the Navy to a German firm, was to have left in tow of a powerful tug. The tide caught her . . . and she bore down on the *Racer* – when within 20 yards the towing hawser parted, and she drifted up the harbour with the tide, and in a few minutes struck the *Victory* at the port gangway. Next day we returned to Cowes.[65]

One interesting fact, however, is that the cadets at Osborne did not have to go afloat to begin to learn the rudiments of that vital element of seamanship, how to row. As one cadet remarked: 'There was a service cutter on a sort of revolving platform and that is about all we had from the seamanship point of view, I think.'[66] It is, of course, impossible to learn how to row on dry land, but learning how to handle oars and co-operate with others in the boat was of use.

Perhaps the best summing up of the 'seamanship' experience at Osborne was that offered by another former cadet and it did not simply involve boats:

I don't think we had much river work, it's strange, I can't remember much river work or on boats from Osborne. Some of our people may remember but I can't. There was a tremendous lot at Dartmouth so I get a bit mixed up with the boats that we always went out . . . in Dartmouth harbour because the river was broader and there was less going on but Cowes was pretty crowded always and I don't think we did much river work. But I remember being taught how to row a cutter, a 32-foot heavy boat. We used to do that on land. We used to climb into this thing and get out – toss the oars. They were very heavy ash oars and we had to learn to toss the oars and then we'd put them out and row and we rowed on dry land with these huge heavy ash oars. If I was lucky and I was small I was put in the bow so that I had a lighter oar but that's the kind of seamanship we did there. The other seamanship was connected with the mast. That was a very fine feature of Osborne. There was a mast . . . we all used to climb up this thing and I enjoyed it very much. . . . I didn't mind heights in those days and climbing to the top into the lubbers hole or if you were more adventurous you'd go round the outside of the top and climb into it that way. . . . Then you could go up to another top if you also were adventurous and didn't mind falling down. In my time I think only one cadet ever fell and there was a great net underneath so that he probably came to no real harm. There was this net about eight feet off the ground, so you could run about underneath it, but it would save lives alright . . . we enjoyed the mast.[67]

But not everyone did 'enjoy' the mast:

> We had this great mast with, thank God, a net underneath it. . . . We
> were told we'd jolly well got to climb it at least once in our career. I
> tried this and I was absolutely paralysed with fear half way up the
> shrouds, the ratlines and managed somehow to crawl up to the top
> and [after] about . . . a minute or two of terror up there . . . I
> crawled down the other side without falling off. . . . I crawled down
> the other side.[68]

The net apparently served its purpose well on at least one occasion. It
is reported that one cadet fell from the mast head-first and trapped his
head in the net, to the horror of onlookers who assumed he must have
broken his neck. Fortunately, he managed to extract himself
unharmed.[69]

On another occasion, however, there was a problem. One former
cadet, who was not 'frightened' of the mast but 'didn't like it much'
thought

> You may be surprised to hear that the Navy did produce a net
> underneath in case anyone fell off, which they did from time to time,
> but no-one ever hurt themselves falling off the mast by mistake. I
> know one of my friends hurt himself very considerably jumping off it
> for a bet. . . . I think somebody bet him six bull's eyes or something
> he wouldn't jump off the top of the mast but unfortunately, as he
> didn't fall loose . . . he hurt himself quite badly.[70]

Memories as to whether or not it was a requirement to climb the mast
are conflicting. One cadet did 'remember climbing it. I can't say I was
ever particularly enthusiastic but we did have to climb the mast.'[71]
Others, however, were less certain about the *necessity* of climbing it,
though they had no doubt about the fact that they had ascended it, for
one reason or another:

> I certainly did go up at various times. There was a net of course all
> round the bottom so that if you did happen to fall off you would
> probably just land in the net and you would [not] hurt yourself. I
> think probably we did have to. As I say I certainly did do it several
> times.[72]

I can't remember whether we had to; we certainly did. It was an accepted thing that you did, I don't remember being driven up it or anything like that. . . . We certainly were allowed to climb it and we were expected to climb it.[73]

One ex-cadet, who attended the College during the First World War, remarked that 'people used to get sent up there now and then but I can't think why',[74] suggesting that the College used 'mastheading' as a disciplinary measure – a rather unlikely suggestion. Another, who went there in the last days of the College, commented that 'The mast was still there but we never climbed it'[75] which would imply that by this time the authorities felt the mast was unsafe, even though a new one had been erected in 1917.

It would appear from the recollections of former cadets that – at least until after the First World War – cadets were required to ascend the mast, but only once, and only to the platform, and it was perfectly acceptable for them to use the lubber's hole to get on to the platform. Those who enjoyed the experience could go higher if they so wished and on more than one occasion. Whatever their outlook, many ex-cadets recollected the mast and the pleasure – or otherwise – of ascending it. One was happy enough: 'I had a good head for heights, so I was prepared without any trepidation to go as high as I possibly could up the mast.'[76]

Others were not quite so confident:

We all climbed the rigging, the most intrepid going over the futtock shrouds which I personally saw no point in attempting, rather like a fly on a wall upside down. Most of us got on to the platform through the lubber's hole.[77]

For some, it was simply something that had to be done:

I did but I've got no head for heights. But everybody had to. . . . Some, of course, loved it and one or two fell off, I remember, and were caught in the net below. I went up the regulation height but no further, once. Thankfully got down again. It was quite a height when you're up there but some cadets, they loved it. They were like steeplejacks, went right up to the top and practically stood on the truck at the top. But not me.[78]

Ascending the mast could, however, serve more than one purpose. It was not only one element in the seamanship course, but it was also

one of the things that you told your Cadet Captain at night . . . because the College was very keen that you should take exercise of some sort so a log was kept of what you'd done and all the way up the dormitory in the evening the Cadet Captain'd say, 'Now, what did you do, Thomas?', I'd say, 'Went for a run' or played hockey or played rugger or something and everybody had to say what they'd done to take exercise. One of the things you were allowed to do was to go over the mast so that was an easy one really for some of us.[79]

It is, perhaps, not surprising that cadets' recollections were not dominated by memories of their academic work and that the engineering and 'seamanship' elements of their course – particularly if the ascent of the mast is included – should stand out. To an extent, one of the aims of the authorities, the promotion of engineering, seems to have been achieved, at least as far as the time devoted to it is concerned. Time spent in the workshops and smithy appears to have had far more of an impact than time spent in the classroom. Of all the 'purely' academic subjects only history – specifically naval history – stands out in cadets' memories. This is no doubt due in most cases to the flamboyance of the teacher, although it might be assumed that young men seeking the Royal Navy as a career might already have an interest in the achievements and personalities in the history of their chosen service.

Another reason why cadets did not recall their academic classes was, of course, because they spent a considerable amount of time outside of the classroom. They were expected, as the Admiralty was anxious to point out, to spend their afternoons on various sporting activities. Although the 1912 inspectors did not include this side of the College's work in their investigations, it is very apparent that this side of things was very important to the cadets at the College.

As one former cadet noted 'all forms of sport were very strongly encouraged and it was considered to be very important'.[80] Another remarked, 'I think we had more or less compulsory games, we certainly had compulsory boxing . . . we were encouraged to play. The playing fields at Osborne were very fine.'[81] Various types of sport were played – quite what cadets did depending very much on what they enjoyed or what they were good at:

I played soccer and cricket. The first time I'd ever come across them in my life were squash courts at Osborne, which I didn't play. I played a bit of tennis, but normally tennis was left to the afternoons where cricket or other organized games were not played. . . . I did some boxing. . . . There was also some quite intensive training in plain gymnastics, box-horse work, cartwheels and all that sort of thing, horizontal bar, in fact all the normal gymnastic stuff.[82]

Another cadet declared that 'I always enjoyed cricket very much. . . . I used to love cricket but I was never very adept at it.'[83]

Some ex-cadets were really thrilled at the importance of sport in the College curriculum. 'We had an immense number of playing fields at Osborne; it was really quite wonderful. We played a game every day. You were expected to, in fact.'[84] Others were not so happy, but nevertheless found themselves at work on the playing fields, or elsewhere:

I was one of those people who thoroughly disliked all organized sports. Therefore, I did everything in my power to avoid them. When I say organized sports I mean things like rugger and soccer and cricket. I was a fairly good cross-country runner, not very good but reasonably good so I was quite keen on the cross-country runs. . . . I tended to [do that] if I had to do anything, and we had to because we had everything logged [which] we had to do in the way of exercises, and so on, I used to go in for things like squash rackets or roller-skating or something like that. . . . Naturally . . . we were compelled to play things like rugger, rugger was a very very popular thing for the College and therefore we were all put through rugger. We were all made to box which I absolutely hated . . . I was just boxing-shy, but I was put into the ring. Out of sheer self-preservation I tried to hit back rather vaguely but . . . I just wasn't good at that sort of thing.[85]

Some cadets achieved more in their boxing:

We had boxing competitions. Everybody had to box somebody of their own weight. . . . I earned three points for my term and a bloody nose laying out another cadet who incidentally became a cadet captain.[86]

Of all the team games, rugby appears to be the one cadets remembered most clearly. One teacher, W.L. Bunting, had 'captained an English rugger team way back . . . so he encouraged us to play rugger. . . . I was very keen on athletics and rugger. . . .'[87] Another cadet noted simply that he had been 'a rather keen rugger player',[88] while a third recalled 'No particular emphasis on any sport, but possibly rugger a little bit more than most games.'[89] At least one ex-cadet had a particular reason for remembering it: 'The only time I went sick I think I was knocked out playing rugger once and they sent me off to hospital for one night. . . .'[90]

Others recalled playing hockey:

I just looked on classes as rather a bore and waited for getting out for a game of hockey . . . I loved hockey. . . .[91]

I don't remember playing rugger at Osborne, but certainly we played hockey and soccer.[92]

Some, however, were less certain that this game was actually played at Osborne:

We played hockey, I think a bit, which I rather enjoyed.[93]

I can't remember if we played hockey or not. I'm not sure at Osborne. We certainly did at Dartmouth.[94]

There were, however, some more detailed recollections of some of the individualist sports that cadets undertook. Foremost among these – no doubt because it formed a part of the curriculum separate from 'games' – was work in the gymnasium.

You played a game of some sort every day; we went to the gym or something or you did a certain amount of physical jerks with a hard-faced PT naval instructor making you jump up and down and climb ropes. . . . You didn't have much time to be idle.[95]

Sometimes 'games' could be added on to the other tasks facing the cadets:

At the end of studies in the afternoon there was what was called VG, voluntary gym. The PT instructors all turned up in Nelson and stood behind the box-horse and we all had to vault over these horses.[96]

One point that had been noted at the time was also recalled by a former cadet, who did 'Much more swimming at Dartmouth because there was no swimming pool or anything' at Osborne.[97] Those cadets who attended the College after swimming lessons in the Solent had been stopped apparently received no swimming lessons, and none of those interviewed recollected any. It was not that they were not kept busy in other ways, though:

> There were games every day and one more or less had to do [them]. . . . We had to report every day that we'd done something. We were looked after all of the time, there was no room for hole-in-the-corner, holing up with a bottle of beer or anything illegal if you could get it.[98]

As another former cadet remembered:

> In the evening, we had what was known as the inquest and you had to report on what you had done during the day. Of course, if you hadn't played a game such as cricket or something you had to say you [had] taken physical training or boxing or something or other and if you didn't there was a lot of trouble.[99]

But you could also get into trouble for the opposite reason:

> We were always encouraged to do lots of exercise and games. . . . In fact, it was there we had a system of daily routine records where . . . a cadet captain used to come in with a notebook and say 'Gowlland, L., what did you do to-day?' and I used to say: hockey, gym, swimming or whatever. . . . There was one chap in my term called Martyn who made a real good thing of this and he used to string off about eight things he'd done in the afternoon . . . run, football, boxing, hockey, cycling, boat work and all the rest of it, which was great fun of course and it had to be stopped.[100]

There is no doubt that being good at games had its compensations:

> . . . it was a great asset: if you were good at games you got a lot of privileges . . . if you were much brainier and weren't good at games it didn't really stand you in such good stead, at that time anyway. Perhaps it did later on but not at Osborne and Dartmouth. If you were good at games it really did help you along a lot.

When asked quite how it helped, however, this witness replied:

> That's rather hard to say, I think perhaps your standing amongst the other cadets really. 'Oh, he's got his colours. He's quite a chap, you know.' You had a special badge on your blazer and everybody knew that you were in the 1st XI or whatever.[101]

But being a less good sportsman was not regarded as too disadvantageous, at least by one cadet:

> It was entirely sport-orientated, as were most prep and public schools. Being not good at games myself that relegated you in the pecking order a bit but I don't think in that respect it was different to any other boys' educational establishment of that period.[102]

It would seem from this statement, as well as a study of the syllabus, that sports and other practical subjects, such as seamanship, overshadowed the classroom to a great extent. One witness remarked that:

> . . . the academic side was very limited. It was one of the tensions between the academic staff and the rest. The academic staff felt that we weren't – there wasn't enough room, scope within the total syllabus of life there to provide a really proper academic education and indeed there wasn't, in my opinion. . . . Sport . . . and technical stuff like seamanship, knots and splices, navigation, etcetera, stuff which could easily have been done later on, much easier, but there it was.[103]

But another pointed out

> I loved Osborne; it is a very happy memory. It provided a lot of things which preparatory school couldn't provide. It opened up [what] was really a new sort of life. Not perhaps from the academic point of view but it was a pseudo-naval education.[104]

On the other hand, one former cadet recalled that between academic and non-academic subjects there was 'what I'd call a balance. I never felt it overdone one way or the other. I liked the practical side. . . .'[105]

Much, it seems, depends on definition. Bearing in mind what Osborne Naval College was designed to do – that is, to educate young boys who would in due course become naval officers, and nothing else – then the curriculum appears to have been carefully thought out and can be justified. To encourage more of the boys to specialise in engineering later on, their early introduction to some basic principles of the subject is clearly a good idea. Similarly some introduction to elements of seamanship and training for command seems worthwhile. Also, given the views of the time, it is very certain that physical fitness in its widest sense could not be neglected. All of this, added to a full academic timetable, would clearly be too heavy a burden for the boys. Somewhere there had to be a compromise, and that was made in the classroom subjects. It was no doubt hoped that any lacunae in the boys' education at this stage could be filled up later on, when they found the time to do some reading on their own. This, as the Education Inspectors' Report noted, was clearly something they did not have much time to do at Osborne.

It is not surprising that the recollections of the College survivors should be clearer when looking at the practical side of life at the College. Not only was more time devoted to it, but the excitement of such activities as ascending the College mast or trying to navigate a cutter down the River Medina would obviously live on. It is only occasionally that the classroom teachers and their activities are recalled so vividly.

Staff with teaching responsibilities at the College fall into several categories: civilian masters, brought in to teach the boys in the classroom and oversee their general academic development; naval officers, who acted as Term Lieutenants, and their Engineer Officer second-in-commands, who taught the boys seamanship and oversaw their engineering education; and naval Petty Officers, who acted as tutors in two areas, as cadet mentors and as physical training instructors. It was with the first two of these groups that the 1912 Education Inspectors' report was concerned. They felt that the thirty-four civilian masters were, on the whole, 'extremely competent', that the average teaching skills were 'high' – several were 'brilliant', in fact – but there were a 'few poor ones'. They specifically praised the teaching of English and history, and noted that the modern languages staff were enthusiastic and hard-working. They felt that the ability of the staff who taught mathematics was high, that they cooperated well with staff who taught physics, and that the teaching of science displayed 'vitality' and was 'as far as possible from being stereotypical or conventional'.[106] They were somewhat less satisfied with the skills of the naval officers, who were moved too frequently (every two years). They felt the Engineer Officers in particular gave well-prepared lectures but had insufficient training as teachers. It is very interesting to compare this generally favourable report with the recollections of the cadets who received this tuition, and to see which teachers, civilian or naval, stood out in their memories.

In general terms – and perhaps not surprisingly – most of those cadets who were interviewed had very positive recollections of the general quality of teaching at the College. One considered that 'our masters were of the finest possible character',[107] while others thought 'that generally speaking, they were good, outstanding, masters . . .'[108] and 'they were all different and we, I think, were lucky in the masters we had . . .'.[109] Even the majority of those who admitted the difficulties of forming a judgement on such matters were of the same opinion:

> . . . they were very good. I thought the academic staff was . . . insofar as I was able to judge those things . . . very good.[110]

> It's very difficult to tell but the standard of those who taught us was in my view very high and they were extremely observant. . . .[111]

Notwithstanding the difficulties of recruiting teachers during the First World War

> there's no doubt we had very good masters or [they] seemed to us very good masters. Most of us had come from preparatory schools and there they'd been rather scraping the barrel for masters because so many had to go to the war, so many had been killed and they were either young boys almost who taught [us] or aged men who didn't care a raspberry. But at Osborne they were very hand-picked and excellent, I would say.[112]

Another veteran of the College admitted

> I had no opportunity of comparing it with anything except my prep. school. I haven't been to a public school so I don't know but I would have said the quality of the teaching was very good indeed. The masters were all popular and we were never hostile to any of them.[113]

One former cadet recalled how his father's actions seemed to support the notion that teaching standards were high, at least in one case:

> I think it was higher than we realised at the time, because my father, who at that time was headmaster of Harrow, made an excuse for coming down to see his son at Osborne and really I knew perfectly well what he wanted was to snatch one of the excellent Osborne masters to come to Harrow, poaching . . . one of them was Mr Boissier, who was tutor to Lord Louis [Mountbatten], who became headmaster of Harrow in turn. . . .[114]

Other memories were not so positive. One cadet, who felt the teachers generally were 'very good', could not 'really remember anything special about them'.[115] Another, similarly, could remember:

> very very little about the Osborne teachers. Of course I was there during the war and all young men had been sent off to the war. I don't really think they were a very first-class lot of teachers looking back. I can't really say, I don't remember them well enough to say. I expect they were very adequate in their way but no sort of outstanding ones that I can really remember at all.[116]

One outstanding cadet could recall:

> Morning and afternoon instruction followed a fixed plan. The teaching was, I think, competent though generally uninspired, and no master . . . made any lasting impression on me.[117]

It may be that the war had a negative effect on teaching standards, but not everyone who was there during this time felt the same. Another former cadet commented:

> To my way of thinking the masters were themselves very hand picked and very well chosen.
>
> As the war started we did lose some of the younger masters . . . and we got those who'd been sent to us from public schools, in some cases from public schools that had had to be closed because of the war. So we made up the numbers pretty quickly. And I don't think the standard was reduced at all. I think it was generally very good

indeed. I certainly think as far as I was concerned the masters did a very good job indeed without exception, I think.[118]

This was indeed the dominant recollection of the teaching at Osborne, whenever the particular cadet was there. Even those whose careers did not prosper in the Navy were prepared to state their high opinion of the academic staff. The standard of teaching was, as one who made his career in the Army concluded, 'very high indeed. . . . One couldn't find the slightest fault'.[119]

While most former cadets had some more or less positive memories of their civilian teachers, far fewer had anything to say about the naval personnel, at least not in their capacity as teachers. This, of course, has a lot to do with the fact that many of those interviewed went to the College during or immediately after the First World War, at which time many of the duties of the naval staff were taken over by the civilian masters. But those cadets who did pass comments on the naval personnel were not always very positive. One, who generally recounted the history of the College in the most glowing terms, had this to say:

> The seamanship instruction and the pilotage [were] handled to quite a considerable extent by the naval officers and when the original staff were sent off to sea when the war broke out first of all we got the more senior, more elderly ones coming back and I think in a way they were not quite so good at it. There was no real lowering of standards but it's just they were a little bit slower on the uptake I think. In some instances they were quite elderly. I remember the commander who was sent to us was really beyond it. . . .[120]

Another, who was not unduly impressed with his civilian masters, was even harsher about his naval teachers:

> I don't say they were unfit for sea but I don't think they were a very extra-special lot really. Of course later on I think they were chosen for the job of training of cadets, specially selected for that. I should doubt if they were at Osborne. They probably said, 'Here's a chap who can't go to sea, not fit for sea, we'll send him to Osborne to look after the cadets.' That may be a little bit unfair but looking back I think that could have been so.[121]

However, there were some different opinions: 'We were taught joinery by very very good teachers, the old pensioners who taught us'[122], while the Petty Officers attached to the term 'were very carefully selected and they were mostly gymnastic experts. . .'.[123] Engineering was also 'very well taught' by naval personnel.[124] Even the usually harsh Captain Roskill agreed, though, as he made clear, this was for special reasons:

> The instruction periods I enjoyed most were those devoted to boatwork on the river Medina and to practical work in the shops at Sandquay [sic] on the river banks. It was only in the workshops and on the river that we came into contact with the 'lower deck', from which carefully selected pensioners acted as our instructors. These men were for the most part splendid examples of the British long-service rating, with all the uncomplaining patience, fortitude and humour of their class. They were quite uneducated and often did not really understand the theoretical basis of the subject they were required to teach, learning it parrot-wise from the appropriate manual. Yet their practical experience and deep wisdom made theoretical knowledge almost redundant. And they could distinguish instinctively the good officer, who really did know his job and looked after his men, from the inefficient, negligent or tyrannical type. . . .[125]

In general, therefore, the recollections of former cadets give more than a little support to the findings of the 1912 Education Department Inspectors. Most were quite certain that the standard of tuition they received, at least from the academic staff, was good or very good. But there were numerous teachers at Osborne, some of whom stayed there for quite lengthy periods, and it is interesting to see which of them were particularly recalled – for good or ill – by the ex-cadets.

Without a doubt the one teacher best remembered was the 'most remarkable man named Geoffrey Callender. . . . It so happened I was in a class which was taught by him. I must say he was quite inspiring.'[126] Some former cadets, whose memories of Osborne were otherwise somewhat limited, when asked if they could remember any of their teachers, responded:

> I don't really: I remember of course Geoffrey Callender, a very good historical teacher. I can't remember any precise detail. I learnt French, I know.[127]

> I had a tutor whose name was Mr Gibbons. The teacher who impressed me most, I think, was Geoffrey Callender who taught us naval history and English. No, I don't think I have any other particular impressions.[128]

> Do I remember much about the teaching at Osborne? Well, we much enjoyed the naval history teaching which was given by Mr Callender who was a very popular master there.[129]

Others, 'of course' remembered Callender, and also why they did:

> I remember, of course, Professor Callender who taught naval history, his principal book, he handed it out to us, is called *Sea Kings of Britain* and I think he produced a further volume later on. He was very good at teaching. He had a keen sense of humour and a very attractive voice which made history extremely interesting to us.[130]

> The person I remember very well was Professor Callender who taught me history. He made history very interesting, and he particularly emphasised the business of the British Navy, that then was, intercepting the Spanish treasure train as it crossed the Panama peninsula, taking all the wonderful golden things and other things they got from the Inca civilization in Peru.[131]

The quality of Callender's teaching, another former cadet remarked, was

> First class, absolutely. Old Geoffrey Callender's classes were a gift in themselves. He had a marvellous way of putting it across . . . he really was an absolute genius. He would throw his academic gown over his shoulder and become Queen Elizabeth knighting Francis Drake, that sort of thing. It's the sort of thing that brings it home to you.[132]

On at least one occasion, Callender had to address his class on matters other than naval history, as was memorably recalled by Stephen King-Hall. He explains in his memoirs that two boys were 'discovered experimenting with what are called the facts of life'. As a consequence, the Chaplain was ordered to address the cadets on the question of sex and all class teachers were instructed to find out what the boys knew about it. In King-Hall's case, this task fell to Callender:

Cadets and parents at Portsmouth Dockyard, 1910 (Courtesy Mr J. Milner)

Inspection of cadets by Admiral Sir H. Meux at Royal Naval Dockyard, Portsmouth, before embarkation for Osborne, 15 January 1913 (Royal Naval Museum; 1982/82)

Cadets en route for Osborne (Courtesy Mr J. Milner)

The Drake Term, 1910/11 (Royal Naval Museum; 1981/125 (1 2))*

The mast, with cadets on the platform (Royal Naval Museum; 1986/60 (9*17))

An early view of the dormitories, with Officers' quarters in the foreground. The mast is a prominent feature (Royal Naval Museum;1981/1061 (10))

Officers' quarters; the gardens have yet to be laid (Royal Naval Museum; 1981/1061 (12))

A general view of the dormitories and Officers' quarters, 1917 (Royal Naval Museum; 1980/47)

The St Vincent block (Royal Naval Museum; 1986/60 (9*22))

Dining-room, St Vincent, laid out for main meal. Cadets occupied benches along the sides of the tables (Royal Naval Museum; 1986/60 (9*21))

Cadets outside their canteen (Royal Naval Museum; 1986/60 (9*30))

The reading rooms, attached to each college dormitory, with an unoccupied mast (Royal Naval Museum; 1986/60 (9*35))

A dormitory. Large standard sea chests are at the end of all cadets' beds, which are carefully not placed directly below the windows (Royal Naval Museum; 1986/60 (9*20))

The reading room and wash-houses at the end of each dormitory (Royal Naval Museum; 1981/1061 (14))

Exterior of the dormitory bungalows with covered walkway and marine sentry visible (Royal Naval Museum 1981/1061 (9))

Cadets 'doubling' between classes (not, as the original picture is labelled, 'at morning exercise') (Royal Naval Museum; 1981/1061 (15))

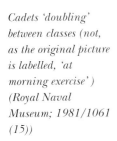

The Kingston machine shops (Royal Naval Museum; 1981/1061 (8))

*Cadets assembled outside the Kingston machine shops (Royal Naval Museum; 1986/60 (9*28))*

*A cadet at a 'turning machine' (Royal Naval Museum; 1986/60 (9*23))*

Cadets engaged in engineering tasks: some are filing, others operating lathes (Royal Naval Museum; 1986/60 (9*25))

Cadets at lathes in No. 16 Machine Shop, Kingston (Royal Naval Museum; 1981/1061 (11))

'An engineering instruction' (Royal Naval Museum; 1981/1061 (6))

Cadets engaged in metal filing, as recalled by many veterans (Royal Naval Museum; 1986/60 (9*16))

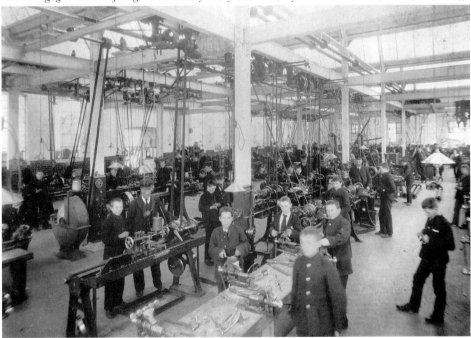

Cadets at metal-working class (Royal Naval Museum; 1986/60 (9*26))

'In the laboratory, Kingston': two civilian masters are present (Royal Naval Museum; 1981/1061 (4))

In the forge at Kingston (Royal Naval Museum; 1986/60 (9*29))

Cadets at a technical drawing class (Royal Naval Museum; 1986/60 (9*24))

*Cadets in the carpenters shops: Petty Officers, as always, are to hand (Royal Naval Museum; 1981/1061 (5) top and 1986/60 (9*14) bottom)*

Cadets in drill dress (Royal Naval Museum; 1981/1061 (13)

Rope splicing drill (Royal Naval Museum; 1986/60 (9*37) middle and 1981/1061 (3) bottom)

*The gym, in Nelson,
ready for action
(Royal Naval
Museum;
1981/1061 (1))*

*Cadets undergoing
circuit training in
Nelson (Royal Naval
Museum; 1986/60
(9*18))*

*A physical training
class in Nelson
(Royal Naval
Museum(1986/60
9*19))*

Cadets in an outdoor physical training class (Courtesy Mr J. Milner)

The boxing match (Courtesy Mr J. Milner)

The rugby team (Courtesy Mr J. Milner)

Cadets pulling cutters (Courtesy Mr J. Milner)

A scholar, a bachelor, and to all appearances devoid of passion, he at last forced himself to address a leading question to the class. Unfortunately, he used such long scientific words that no one could make out what he was talking about.

Poor Mr Callender tried again.

'Has any boy in this class ever slid down the bannister?'

All hands rose in the affirmative.

The questioner warmed to his task.

'Let any boy who whilst sliding down the bannisters felt a guilty but pleasurable sensation hold up his hand.'

Nobody moved.

Mr Callender smiled his satisfaction and remarked: 'You will be well advised not to slide down bannisters. The class is dismissed.'[133]

Some of the other teachers were fondly remembered besides Callender, and several seem to have made a lasting impression on their cadets: 'There was a very excellent French master called Lassimonne. He was a Frenchman but he taught it in a very pleasant lighthearted manner and I think one learnt a lot of French from him. . . .'[134] Although another ex-cadet remarked: 'I always remember the French master who was called Mr Lassimonne. We all rather laughed about him. . . .'[135] He was remembered as a 'caricature of a Frenchman. . . . His top hat tapered outwards to start the ample elipse of his figure which came in at his ankles and small feet.'[136]

Some cadets, besides Roskill, also recollected A.P. Boissier: 'a very good history teacher . . . always known as Boss-eye . . . who I think afterwards went to Harrow either as headmaster or deputy headmaster'.[137]

Another teacher who was recalled by quite a number of former cadets was the French master W.M. Poole, who wrote the French grammar; '"le vieux Poole" we always called him' and he was 'quite unlike Geoffrey Callender, very severe, very serious', but whose classes in French have already been commented on.[138] Other memories of Poole were perhaps less flattering: 'We had Monsieur Poole who taught us something . . . French I think. He went off as the headmaster of a girls' school and came a cropper so I heard in later years.'[139] It was the classes of 'an old man called Poole' that caused one cadet to lose all his knowledge of French.[140]

Another language teacher, E.J.C. Green, lived on in the memory of one cadet for a very particular reason:

. . . the chap who taught us French was an Englishman called Green who had a French wife and an appalling French accent. . . . My last job in the Navy was naval attaché in Paris and I never lived down that accent . . . it got me into very great difficulty really because the one thing I learnt or remembered from my French instruction . . . was an idiom which I used on two occasions.

The first time was when the cadet in question was a midshipman in HMS *Malaya*, attending a dance in honour of the then Crown Prince of Spain. Unfortunately, he was seized by the Admiral in command and 'thrown into the arms of an absolutely typical Spanish Grand Duchess who stood seven feet high with a mantilla and comb'. They began to dance, but tripped over one of the deck towing clenches:

. . . she was flat on her back on the quarter deck, and I was on top of her. I picked her up and dusted her down and pointed [to] some chairs on the quarter deck and the inevitable occurred. She said, 'Do you speak Spanish?' and I said, 'Non parler espagnol', countered with 'Do you speak English?', and she said, 'Non parler inglese' and countered with 'Do you speak French?'. I thought, 'Hale, your chance has come, your idiom that you learnt . . .' and I said, 'Moi, je parle français comme une vache espagnol.' She got up and walked away. Thirty years later I was naval attaché in Paris at one of the first dinner parties we gave. After I'd taken on the job we had all the top Admirals of the Ministry of Marine for dinner and Madame Rebufelle . . . asked me if I spoke French at dinner. There was one of those dreadful pauses where everybody stopped speaking at that particular moment and I said, 'Moi, je parle français comme une vache espagnol.' Again there was the most deadly hush and it was then explained to me that it wasn't 'une vache espagnol' it was 'un basque espagnol'.[141]

It is not altogether just that this rather unfortunate tale should stand as a summary of the language tuition at Osborne and Dartmouth. It does, nevertheless, suggest pretty conclusively that the standard of language tuition was not all that it might have been and at least one cadet suffered for this in later life.

Two other masters, W.L. Bunting and R.W. Bates, were remembered, though only one ex-cadet explained why:

We had a Mr Bunting and a Mr Bates and they looked after us for our first term which due to the 'flu epidemic only lasted six weeks . . . we saw . . . quite a lot of them even if the term did only last six weeks.[142]

Another recollected master was H.G.W. Hughes-Games, who 'used to teach us or train us in rugger'.[143] 'His great claim to fame was that he played rugger for Wales and had torn the ears off two members of the English team'[144] – or so it was said! He was 'a remarkable character . . . a tiny little man with a beard and a funny way of talking'.[145] This was also remarked on by another ex-cadet, who thought Hughes-Games (Hugo) was a 'great character', and who was his tutee at Osborne: 'He had a peculiar impediment in his speech, and his favourite expression when censuring a cadet was "You are fat, thlack and howwible".'[146]

A further master, James Watt, was also among those recalled by former cadets: 'James Watt was tutor to the Royal Family. All the then Princes had been under him at Buckingham Palace. And he was assistant headmaster and I was in his tutor set. . . .'[147] One cadet in particular had striking memories of this individual:

. . . the mathematics taught by James Watt was a very good grounding. . . . Our masters, James Watt and co., used to conduct us to the musters that we had in Nelson. . . . He used to take us there and he would march past the Commander and . . . give an order for eyes right and lift his mortar board. I can see him now lifting his mortar board as he went past. He was rather ancient but he stood up and took his hat off, marvellous man . . . very strict.[148]

This was during the First World War, and Watt and his civilian colleagues were undertaking a duty normally reserved for the term officers.

Some former cadets recollected several masters, without going into much detail about them:

Who else now? Gibbons, Bunting, geography. A chap called Saunders in the physics lab. Culme Seymour, that's an old naval name. He, I think, was maths. . . . Grenfell was one. Nicholls, nice chap, he went in for bird photography as well as his duties. . . .[149]

. . . one or two of our teachers, Wolfe – always known as 'Daddy Wolfe'. He taught us mathematics. . . . Callender taught us history.

I remember one who taught us science, which was a completely new subject, and all taught very well, very interestingly. . . .[150]

There was an old bird called Ranson who taught us maths. He was very good and there was . . . Hughes-Games, I think he taught us history. My term officer, there were two of them. There was a chap called Bunting . . . and the other was Bates. They took the place of term lieutenants of course because the war was on. This was 1915.[151]

Others remembered only a few of their masters: 'Physics, of course, came into the science and these two people Boissier and Uphide who went on to Harrow and Eton later used to teach us. . . .'[152] and one recalled Charles Godfrey:

The headmaster was a man called Godfrey who'd written a number of books on education and he was also a great mathematician and had written mathematical tables and that sort of thing. He constantly came round into the classrooms to see how things were going, and occasionally broke in and asked questions himself.[153]

From these memoirs it is possible to see how some teachers managed to cope with the limitations imposed upon them by the syllabus. Exceptional masters seem to have been Callender – universally recalled with respect and affection, although not solely for his teaching activities – Boissier, Poole – though here the record is mixed – Watt and Hughes-Games. Others, such as Lassimonne, appear to have coped well and inspired some affection, although a few, such as Green, were apparently not so well liked. It appears that former cadets respected their teachers, and felt that the experience in the classroom, workshops, and on the playing fields at Osborne was a positive one. There are, of course, exceptions to this, even among those who were interviewed, where a favourable impression was only to be expected.

But, while plenty of time was taken up by the activities described in this chapter, they formed only a part of the overall experience of the life at Osborne Naval College. Before the teaching day even started, cadets had to prepare themselves for a varied day at work. Once teaching and games had finished, and during the limited free time available on Saturdays and, especially, Sundays, cadets had plenty of things to occupy themselves with. It is to these activities that we must now turn.

CHAPTER FOUR

Daily Life at the College

The subject of living arrangements at Osborne includes a variety of matters, most obvious of which is cadets' sleeping and study accommodation. The dormitories were recollected by several former cadets, one of whom was particularly struck by their flimsy nature:

> All the dormitories . . . were made of stuff called uralite which was a sort of elaborate kind of hardboard. In fact it wasn't very hard and if you were fooling about it was very easy to put your foot through the uralite.[1]

It was rumoured that on one tour of inspection the officer commanding Osborne, Captain H. Hood, did exactly that.

Cadets' recollections of the quality of their living accommodation differed widely. At least one felt the standard of accommodation was 'very good', and another, who went to the College in 1913, thought it was 'first class, we had a very good dormitory'.[2] Another commented that 'They were beds, not bunks or anything of that sort. . . . Yes, I think it was very comfortable really.'[3] Some, however, were not quite so positive: 'they were quite comfortable. . . . I wouldn't say they were luxurious but they were adequate for boys of our age, far better really than a prep school.'[4]

'They were' remarked another witness, 'about right for 1917 in a place of that sort,'[5] while a third added 'They were pretty good really. I'd come from a prep. school, of course. You have very comfortable beds.'[6]

Others agreed that conditions were 'adequate', but, 'very, very different from what we had been accustomed to'.[7] This appears to have been the general impression and even those who accepted that the dormitories were comfortable did not usually enthuse about them. One recalled that he had

> a pretty ropey bed, the usual sort of school bed. . . . We had what was called a gun-room which was really a sort of reading room cum large

place opposite where each dormitory had its own . . . hard benches and one or two ropey chairs. . . . It was alright for a little one, not too bad.[8]

Some former cadets did not recollect their accommodation as favourably as this. One, who entered the College in 1910, recalled that living conditions were 'poor' while another remarked that Osborne was 'not at all' a comfortable place to live: 'It was a botch up.'[9]

The general view was that the buildings also tended to be cold:

three or four of our dormitories were . . . like a chicken brooder shed holding some thirty boys each and they were heated, or so-called heated, by coke stoves. It was really rather painful to wake up on a really cold winter morning at about six o'clock or so when the old pensioner would come along and start lighting up these coke stoves because the smoke went everywhere except out through the Charlie Noble [chimney] through the roof. . . .[10]

Although some felt that, even in the winter, the dormitories were 'reasonably warm',[11] it would seem that, on balance, their heating was not particularly good.

One cadet thought 'generally . . . the facilities were fairly good. Apart of course from the fact that they were temporary buildings and not permanent ones',[12] which gives a good impression of the quality of the uralite dormitories. Uralite had been chosen primarily because it afforded a rapid and cheap method of construction: under the initial plans, however, the dormitories were also intended to be as permanent as the brick buildings of the College. But the fragile nature and the evidently declining quality of the buildings did not escape the notice of the authorities. Hence, the Fourth Report of the Custance Committee of 20 September 1912 had pointed out that, in its opinion, uralite was not a suitable material for permanent buildings,[13] while the 1917 Committee had reported that, in its opinion, the dormitories were cold and damp, and the conditions were made worse by the dust and dirt spread about by the archaic steam heating system in use, which also 'dried out' the air in the rooms. It did not help matters, the committee reported, that windows in dormitories were left open all night. The conclusions reached were that, at the very least, the steam heating should be shut off longer at night, that the temperatures in the dormitories should be taken at varied intervals and more often, and that each dormitory should have a minimum and maximum thermometer and a wet and dry thermometer to measure humidity.[14]

Contemporary evidence, coupled with the cautious comments of former students, would suggest that the standard of living accommodation for cadets at Osborne was not especially high. The comparison between other preparatory or public schools would also seem to indicate that cadets at Osborne were not particularly well accommodated. Fragile, apparently temporary, dormitories – no doubt with holes in the walls after years of use and the attention of young teenage boys, not to mention natural wear and tear – would not appear to have been especially comfortable, while the difficulties of heating the buildings would not have added to their amenity.

But the physical quality of the dormitories was only one element in the quality of life for students at Osborne. What contributed at least as much to this was the daily routine with which all students were faced during their time there. The Admiralty guide on *The Entry and Training of Naval Cadets* sums up the daily routine as it operated in 1913:

At Osborne the cadet turns out at 6.30 in summer and 6.45 in winter. He has a cup of cocoa when he has bathed and dressed, and in half an hour is ready for a short period of early morning school, which lasts till 7.45. Then breakfast is served, which is followed by 'Divisions', when the cadets fall in in their several terms in the principal hall of the College: a hymn is sung and prayers are read. At 9.00 a.m. study is resumed and is continued till 1 o'clock with an interval of a quarter of an hour for a glass of milk and a bun at 11.15. At 1.10 dinner is served, and at 2.15 (in summer) study begins again and goes on till 4.30, when the cadets have milk and buns in the mess room and change into flannels for their recreation in the field. In winter the afternoon routine is different: the hours immediately after dinner are given up to recreation, for the sake of the daylight, and study is taken from 4.10 to 6.30. Tea is served at 7, and is followed by a period of evening study or preparation which generally lasts for only half an hour. Shortly before 9 o'clock prayers are read and the cadets turn in. Lights are out when the Commander makes his rounds at 9.15. On Wednesdays and Saturdays there is no afternoon school, and on Saturdays no evening preparation. On Sundays the cadets turn out half an hour later than on weekdays.

They have a scripture lesson after breakfast. Morning service is held at 11, and after dinner they are allowed to go out of the College till about 6 o'clock, when they return for tea before a short evening service, which is followed by a period spent in the studies, during which a standard author is read or a lecture given on some matter of interest outside the ordinary lines of their work. . . . The number of hours allowed for sleep at Osborne from 'lights out' to the morning bugle call is 10 hours in the four winter months, 9¾ in the spring and autumn and 9¼ in the summer.[15]

Cadets, therefore, winter or summer, had an early start followed by a long day, of both study and 'recreation'. Former cadets' recollections of their early start bring it to life rather more than the dry, semi-official prose of the guide:

The rules were very stringent. You had to get up as soon as reveille blew . . . then you stripped off your pyjamas, rushed down the dormitory stark naked into the cold plunge at the end where you were watched over by your cadet captain who jolly well made sure that you totally immersed yourself and you rushed back, dripping wet to your sea-chest, dried yourself as quickly as you could, threw on your clothes and reported ready for the day's work. One of the most difficult things was putting on one's gaiters. We had these leather gaiters which were extremely tricky to a novice till you got the hang of it. I remember struggling with mine and some wretched cadets could never manage them . . . we had a rather curious outfit . . . this monkey jacket and . . . white flannel trousers and black gaiters and black boots and a white scarf . . . and a white lanyard on which was the key of your sea-chest. That was about it. You were given very little time to dress. Then off you went to have breakfast.[16]

Several other former cadets also recalled, in greater or lesser detail, the early morning routine. Two things, in particular, come through from their memoirs: these were, first, the coldness of the cold plunge bath and, secondly, the speed with which everything had to be accomplished:

We started, we did everything by bell. Everything was done in the most fearful rush to time. In the morning you started off by rushing into the plunge room where you . . . washed, cleaned your teeth and then at a signal you plunged into about six foot of absolutely ice cold water, in the winter covered with ice. . . .[17]

At least one cadet found the cold bath fairly easy to cope with: 'I was prepared for a reasonably cold plunge so I didn't find that offensive.'[18]

Another witness offered an unofficial explanation for the speed at which things were done: 'there was probably a race with the next dormitory to see which dormitory could dress quickest',[19] but, the speed was no doubt due rather to the demands of the authorities. One cadet's memoirs tell us that, once the plunge was over, cadets

fell in, with a towel around their waist, and awaited the arrival of the Surgeon Lieutenant who visited each dormitory in turn, looked at each cadet, and if he thought any were 'below par' they awaited further examination and anyway were given a dose of 'white mixture' (a 'depth charge' which lay at the bottom of many ills).[20]

Rather surprisingly, this seems to have escaped the memories of other former cadets, whose recollections of the early morning were dominated by the race to dress. One cadet recalled that

We leapt out of bed and as hard as we could go, got out of our pyjamas and fled down the dormitory as hard as you could go . . . into the plunge . . . and then rushed back and got dressed and we were allowed about a minute and a half to get dressed and this was all very much done to time. Then suddenly the order came, 'say your prayers'. One fell to one's knees and rattled off a prayer or two . . . the whole thing was a great rush, very exciting.[21]

Another former cadet recollected that these events in the morning (and evening) were a help in his wider education:

. . . in the dormitories was a large shallow plunge bath of about ten feet square into which every cadet was expected, made, to leap in the morning and splash himself about and get out and dry himself. It wasn't much of a hardship really because we had to conduct the whole process of dressing and undressing at such speed that we never had a moment to think. . . . A cadet captain of each dormitory . . . would have a gong screwed to the wall, worked by a string which he pulled . . . once, kneel down and say your prayers. . . . And there one began to learn the elements of seamanship by observing the boy next to one who was a little bit flier and while he was kneeling down there he was fiddling with his tie all the time and loosening the knot . . . so that the moment the gong went for finish of prayers after ninety seconds off it came over his head and it got laid down on top of his shirt, which he managed to fold in about five seconds . . . and that was all ready for the next morning. We were taught to look ahead to that extent and thereby we learnt one of the very absolute basic principles of seamanship all the time, quite naturally it came to us. Lacing up your boots and things like that, all those little actions, doing up all the buttons or getting them ready, . . . you never had to suffer from lack of anticipation.[22]

Very occasionally, however, this anticipation could have unfortunate results:

We got up to the sound of a gong at the end of the dormitory which was rung by the chap in the first bed. This chap Pedder was first in my dormitory, Boscawen, and on the first morning he'd been told when he heard reveille to ring this bell so we all got up and roared off to the plunge bath. He'd been staying awake for this, frightened about it the whole night, I'm sure, and he heard the reveille which was sounded for the seamen and the stewards to get up about, I should think . . . three quarters of an hour before we need. And he heard the reveille sounded off and he knew the reveille, he'd probably been a boy scout. So, he leapt out of bed and rang our gong and the cadet captain was very angry because he said 'Here, it's much too early, go on, get back into bed.' But that was Arthur Pedder's first morning rousing us much too early with his gong.[23]

It is clear from these recollections that the cadets' quality of life was reduced by the early start and, particularly by, the nature of the routine they had to undergo every morning, especially the speed with which they had to perform their ablutions. The authorities recognised this in 1917. The committee appointed that year made two recommendations relating to the early start. One was that the cadets should enter the plunge bath before they washed: the other, more significant, was that the getting up time should be later.[24] These proposals were accepted by the Admiralty, and the lot of the boys was therefore somewhat ameliorated. Although bed time was early, the overall daily routine appears with hindsight to have been rather severe, certainly before these changes were made.

Cadets, when out of the dormitory were not able to relax: 'You were kept on your toes all the time. You weren't allowed to walk between dormitories or anything like that.'[25] Another cadet recollected that:

Everything was done at the double. One thing was . . . you were not allowed to walk past any other term senior to you to the reading room or dormitory. So as it was arranged that the senior terms had the nearest dormitories to Nelson . . . when you first got there you had a long, long, row of corridors, and at the run. Whenever you went up or down that corridor during the day you had to run, because you were junior to all the other people you passed. And heaven help you if you were caught not doing it.[26]

At least one veteran was vehement about this facet of Osborne life: 'You may be surprised to hear that we never did anything out of a double. We doubled everywhere. We fell in for every bloody thing. . . .'[27] Sometimes, of course, this 'doubling' had to take place after dark, and this led to some excitement:

In wartime all the lights were low and we had blue lights along the corridors there, and at the end of prep . . . we were told to go to bed. We rushed along these corridors, we always did everything at a run at Osborne, and that's a picture in my mind's eye now, I can see it, 200–300 of us tearing along this corridor and breaking off to our various dormitories on the way, in this gloomy blue light. It's quite a picture. . . .[28]

Once roused, the cadets were fed with a mug of cocoa and biscuit before they attended some early morning classes, until breakfast was served, the first main meal of the day. This seems to have been quite a substantial meal, comprising tea or coffee, porridge, a hot dish (sausages or bacon and eggs, or similar), or ham, rolls, butter and marmalade. This was followed by 'Divisions', and then some more classes. Dinner was served at 1.10 p.m. – the cadets having had some 'elevenses' (milk and a bun) – and consisted of roast meat or pie or beefsteak pudding, potatoes, another vegetable and pudding (or soup and cheese). Further work in the classroom or on the playing fields followed (depending on whether it was summer or winter). Milk and buns were served to the cadets at 4.30 and tea – another quite substantial meal consisting of cold meat or buttered eggs, bread and butter and cake and jam – was the final meal of the day. On Sundays, 'high tea' was served before supper.

The Admiralty kept a close eye on the diet at its naval colleges, partly for reasons of health and partly for reasons of economy. A Committee Reporting on Osborne and Dartmouth in 1905 pointed out severely that costs were too high. One way they could be reduced was by changing the drinks supplied at meal times. The Committee argued that it would also be much healthier if the boys drank only water at meal times, as opposed to the existing arrangement whereby ginger beer, lemonade or lime juice was supplied. On 'special occasions', the committee conceded, lemonade might be supplied.[29] This proposal, while adopted, did not pass unchallenged, as a marginal note on the draft report testifies.

It proved difficult to verify exactly what the quality of the food supplied at the College was like. As one former cadet put it: 'I don't remember much about it. We were so hungry all the time that it wolfed itself down. I don't really remember it, no, I can't tell you, but it couldn't have been very bad.'[30] And this view was not unique:

. . . Looking back I remember I was always hungry. Not that I didn't get enough to eat because there was always plenty to eat but I always seemed to be hungry . . . in general I think the food was quite good there, looking back.[31]

For those who did remember, the quality of the food was at least satisfactory. 'I suppose it was adequate. We grumbled about it, most boys do,'[32] as one cadet commented, while another remarked 'No small boy particularly likes his food but it was no worse than anywhere else and I would say quite adequate really.'[33] Others were a bit more positive: 'The food was simple and good'[34] – although this comment was referring to the years before the outbreak of the First World War. Even during the war it was noted that 'this was the time, 1918, when things were pretty pinched . . . and my mother asked me questions appreciating that we needed feeding properly. "Do you have real milk? Do you have butter or margarine?" We had everything of the best.'[35] This view was confirmed by another witness.

The food I thought was extremely good considering the appalling shortages that were going on. You've got to remember it was the worst period of the U-boat blockade and there must have been terrible shortages. There were I know in my own home. . . . The food in the College on the other hand was ample, there was plenty of what I, in common with most of the others, simply adored, golden syrup, sugar and fresh rolls, that sort of thing. We had very large appetites of course because we were given plenty of exercise and working hard. So I don't think we suffered in the least from shortage of food.[36]

After the war the food remained eminently satisfactory, at least in the opinion of one former cadet, who went to the College in January 1920:

The food I always thought was excellent. We did have that funny fish at Osborne, which we used to call Medina Mudfish. But the things I remember best and enjoyed most were marrowbones and the kedgeree. . . . They were bloody good, they really were. The food was excellent.[37]

One or two other cadets had detailed memories of the food. One recollected:

We used to have boiled eggs from time to time. I personally never had a bad one but some people always found bad eggs when they had boiled eggs. I always remember the wretched steward . . . he was called Oily Albert, called Oily because his hair was all smarmed down. He was always being called up by cadets who said 'this egg is filthy'. If you smell an egg it doesn't smell awfully nice and I think nine times out of ten the eggs were perfectly all right. I never had a bad one at all personally. No, I thought the food was very good. I had no complaints about it at the time and I'm sure I never complained to my parents about it either. It wasn't particularly exciting. It was varied, sustaining and good I thought.[38]

Another remarked on:

Lunch – nothing much to say about that. . . . Tea – well, there was a break in the forenoon when you were given a bun, and then you rushed off. You had one bun, and God help you if you took another one, and a mug of water. And then in the afternoon you again went to the messroom and I think there was some bread or margarine or something. It was just after the First World War and things were pretty tough foodwise. . . .

. . . . Finally, you had a very miserable supper, what we called dogs. They were like great big dog biscuits, Admiralty pattern biscuits I suppose, and a mug of water.[39]

Overall, the quality of food provided by the College authorities seems to have been at least satisfactory. As far as can be judged, the First World War had little impact on the cadets' diet. The Admiralty clearly made considerable efforts to ensure that Osborne College was supplied with food, even while the war was on. Most cadets also seem to have had enough to eat, whether or not they considered the diet varied. Perhaps the last words on College meals can be left to a cadet describing how at least one of his fellow students found the food very edible indeed: 'One boy in my term who didn't stay in the Navy very long, but he became a High Court judge, ate twenty-four fish balls in one sitting. And we passed all ours along to him.'[40] This is probably the all-time record: another former cadet recollected that the record for his term was only about half a dozen.[41]

If, as often seems to have been the case, the cadets wanted additional refreshment, beyond that provided in Nelson, Osborne also contained a canteen, run by Petty Officer William Primmer. 'Mister Primmer' was remembered with affection by many of the former cadets, and with some sympathy:

The canteen was, needless to say with small boys, very popular and we used to have an awful thing called penny reds. We used to all rush in there and yell at poor old Mr Primmer who was in charge and I must confess his life must have been made pretty well unbearable I think by a lot of small cadets yelling for penny reds or penny yellows or penny something or other or bits of doughnut or that sort of thing but needless to say it was very popular, the canteen. . . . Mr Primmer was a real character . . . a very conscientious man, he did his best, but by Jove, with all these small boys yelling at him it must have been a pretty unbearable life, I think.[42]

There was quite a good canteen . . . run by a gentleman called Mr Primmer. If you wanted to buy something in the rush hour you just

yelled at him and held your money out and hoped to get something.
I remember the largest big Fry's chocolate bar cost tuppence.[43]

Primmer evidently kept a close eye on what was passing in his canteen.

The canteen was quite a feature because you could get extra things
to eat there but it was very sparse. But there was a man called Mr
Primmer who ran the canteen there. You could go and order things
like raspberryade. You could have a penny red off him and
occasionally there was one chocolate bar and there weren't many
chocolate bars in the end of the war. Woe betide anyone who was
recognised as having come in before and got his bar and tried to
come in again and get a second chocolate bar. Mr Primmer would
shout out, 'Stop serving, stop serving, he's cheating.' And stop
everything. But occasionally one got a chocolate bar and that was a
wonderful day. I think one could get an oatmeal bun any time and
certainly some raspberryade, penny red, but nothing much else.[44]

Some cadets, however, were more fortunate. Earlier in the First World
War, chocolate was evidently available in larger quantities and use could
be made of it:

I myself used to go to the canteen of a Saturday and buy there –
there were little blocks of chocolate about two inches square you
could get. I got some of those and I used to find that I could sell
them to my colleagues on Sundays for double the price. So I did that
a certain amount. . . . [45]

Cadets remembered clearly the difficulty of getting served:

The great cry was 'Penny red, Mr Primmer'. He seemed to have an
unlimited supply. There was a rather nice little rhyme I remember in
the *Osborne Magazine* taken from 'The Charge of the Light Brigade'.
Something like this:

Half an inch, half an inch, half an inch forward
Near the counter move the three hundred
Their's not to reason why
Their's but to do and die

And Saturday's grub to buy
Patient three hundred
Typical small boys.[46]

It was, of course, necessary to have money to pay Petty Officer Primmer and his assistants, once you managed to reach the counter. One former cadet recalled how this necessity was obtained, and then how he spent it, in detail:

His Majesty paid you a shilling a week for being a cadet, and this you received with gratitude on a Saturday. And your parents sent you back a small sum of pocket money, and from this you could draw without demand one shilling every Wednesday. So your basic income was two shillings a week. If you could get any more out of your private fund, get your mother to send you a postal order, of course you were better off. The private fund was a ludicrous business. You could only draw out of that – you couldn't say 'because I want to buy some chocolate at the canteen'. You had to put it down for certain things you could get at the cadet's office, and the favourite ones I remember were collar studs, which one was apt to lose because they were that sort of shirt and collar. And the writing paper, and things of that sort. But nobody had the slightest intention of buying any of those things, but that was well understood, but you put it down and you could get out about as much as two more shillings . . . then there was the canteen, and after games you really were hungry and those that had it rushed in. It was a little place rather like a little cricket pavilion with a veranda in front, and inside a long counter presided over by a retired – I presume – catering Petty Officer called Mr Primmer. And he had one or two female assistants. . . . [The] horde of cadets, as soon as the match was over, they'd rush in clamouring for . . . some awful red cordial, 'Penny red, please Mr Primmer' was the cry . . . you could get a penny bar of chocolate or two pennyworth of caramels which were a good bet because they lasted a bit. And more exotic things like whipped cream walnuts which cost tuppence ha'penny . . . that was to be saved up for a treat. But it was a very vital part of one's life. The rich ones had quite a lot and I can remember standing outside the canteen and gaping through the window, praying that somebody would come along and say 'Come and have a penny red'. . . . My father was a Rugby and Cambridge man and he didn't reckon we ought to have too much money. But some of my friends, their mothers perhaps were more lavish with their pocket money, and so they could get in and even treat one to a bar of chocolate, if you were lucky. And if your parents ever came down, which was pretty rare, they also could go into the canteen and then there used to be a circle of hangers-on hoping for the handouts.[47]

Only one cadet recalled that he did not spend much time in the canteen:

. . . there was no lack with us. There was a canteen but only the richer people and . . . the people who were gourmands used to go and spend time on the strawberries and cream and things. But as a member of a family of five sons, I didn't have as much pocket money as some of the others.[48]

For the remainder, however, the canteen seems to have served a very useful purpose, as both a means of enlivening the diet and also providing treats for the boys, even at the height of the First World War. The regime in the canteen was also recollected favourably, several ex-cadets remarking on Primmer affectionately. He seems to have made the best of his situation, and generally handled the scrum in his canteen effectively. Overall, it was one thing about Osborne Naval College that most former cadets still remembered vividly and it was clearly an asset to the institution.

The tuck-shop was not, however, the only entertainment provided for boys at the College, however important it may have been. While a good deal of their free time was taken up with [non] optional activities, the cadets still had Saturday evening and Sunday afternoon and evening free, as well as some time before bed time during the week. The authorities made efforts to fill this, too. As one of Osborne's most famous cadets remarked of his time there:

the grounds which really formed the park of Queen Victoria's favourite country home . . . were quite lovely. Though we were not allowed to approach the house, on half holidays and Sunday afternoons the paths through the woods and down to the sea were open to us, and in the infrequent intervals between organised games

I used to love to wander there. But our lives were so strictly circumscribed and controlled that these opportunities were rare.[49]

Another cadet reinforced the point that Osborne House itself was off limits to the boys: 'Funnily enough, while I was at Osborne I never saw Osborne House. I never caught sight of it at all and we were quite close by, just through a few trees and shrubs and things.'[50]

From the evidence preserved in several issues of the College *Osborne Magazine*, however, it is clear that the College possessed an active Natural History Society, although it would suggest that most of its time was spent in lecture halls rather than in the College grounds. In Easter term, 1916, for example, the Society heard three lectures. The first, on 5 February, was presented by Surgeon G.C. Chance, RN, who discussed malaria. The second, three weeks later, was presented by a member of the College staff, Assistant Master A.J. Bostock Hill, who talked of 'some of Nature's marvels', which included fish and insects. The last lecture, on 19 March, was by another College staff member, Assistant Master J.H. Murray, on 'Adventures while Birds' nesting'. This was illustrated with slides, taken by Murray, which were being issued in book form at that very time.[51] In the summer term only two lectures were held. One, by Assistant Master E.A. Hughes, on 10 June, discussed bird photographers and those who stole birds' eggs, while the second, 'one of the most interesting ever given to members of the Society', was given by Senior Master B.S. Wolfe on 15 July, and concerned the collecting of skeletons as a hobby! It was in this term that the Natural History Society awarded prizes: two (out of no less than seventy entries) in the Nature Photographic Competition, and one in the 'Essay Competition'.[52]

Lectures were undoubtedly the favoured way found to fill in the cadets' spare time. They were given on a variety of subjects in addition to natural history. On 24 February 1917, for example, Assistant Master Lieutenant J.D. Upcott, of the Devon Regiment, 'gave a most interesting lecture dealing with last Summer's operations on the Somme, illustrated by slides lent by the Munitions Department': it would appear he pulled few punches.[53] Sometimes these talks were on more peaceful subjects, but they were still appreciated:

On Friday night I heard the best lecture I have, or, probably, ever will hear, in my life. It lasted from 8 until 10 p.m. All the officers, masters, bluejackets, marines, instructors, stewards, some bluejackets

from Portsmouth, the families of all these people and many more of
the staff were listening to it, so there must have been eight hundred
to a thousand in the room. It was given by Commander Evans of the
Scott Expedition. There were hundreds of lantern slides, and a
whole cinematograph film. The clapping, yelling, stamping, cheering
was such that I've still got a sore throat from it. . . . He then gave us
his theodolite. The way he gave his lecture and spoke about the two
seamen who saved his life was marvellous.[54]

As far as many former cadets were concerned, however, it was not the
lectures that stayed in their minds. Memories revolved around two other
forms of entertainment in particular: musical or other theatrical
performances (usually of Gilbert and Sullivan operettas) and, on
Saturday nights, dances. As one cadet remembered:

. . . we had some very good theatricals by the staff and concerts [by]
the staff and cadets. Lectures . . . the staff and cadets put on a very
good . . . Gilbert and Sullivan, the *Mikado*, which was a very good
production.[55]

Operettas appear to have been particularly recalled:

Occasionally the officers and the masters on the staff would put on
a sort of concert which was an uproarious success . . . but apart
from that the only real theatrical entertainment took place in our
very first term, and it's absolutely engraved on my memory.
Geoffrey Callender elected to produce *The Pirates of Penzance* to be
played at the end of term. And so everybody was selected according
to their qualifications. For my sins, I'd been in the choir at my
prep. school and my voice hadn't broken yet. One or two of the
term's had, and so the cast was assembled. I remember the young
lady . . . in the *Pirates*, taken by a rather nice looking young cadet a
term above me, who I think was a descendant of Charles Dickens.
His name was [G.H.C.] Dickens, a very nice chap. His lover was a
gaunt fellow one term senior whose voice had broken, called
[G.C.] de Jersey. And the rest of the chorus, of policemen, [were]
those whose voices had broken, and . . . girls, including myself
[were those whose voices] had not. And every Saturday afternoon
in that term, which was the only free time you ever really had in the

whole week, was taken up with rehearsals for *The Pirates of Penzance*. Oh dear, we were ordered, and I think we gave three performances at the end of term, and we were rewarded by a very excellent supper at the end of it, but it didn't make up for all those Saturday afternoons.[56]

Other cadets suffered a similar fate:

> . . . it was in our second term . . . that it was decided that there would be a production of a Gilbert and Sullivan opera which was to be *The Mikado*. It so happened that I had a really nice voice though . . . [a] very good boy soprano voice. In the process of selection I was chosen to take the part of Yum Yum in *The Mikado*. So this is what we did. I'm told I made an absolutely knock-down Yum Yum but I wasn't allowed to forget it afterwards.[57]

> During our second term we did a performance of *The Pirates of Penzance* . . . in which I was one of the beautiful daughters because I could sing.[58]

The College also possessed a choir, for use in Chapel (in the summer of 1917 this numbered forty-eight staff and students in all (32 trebles, all cadets, 6 altos, 5 of whom were cadets, 4 tenors and 6 basses, all staff)),[59] but concert performers were clearly not always drawn from this select group.

> . . . occasionally we would organise a sort of college entertainment, a concert party . . . and dress ourselves up into a chorus and sing little songs and so on. It was rather outside my province because I never could sing, I could never act or anything like that so I was just one of the audience. I did get into the chorus for a little show called *Sussex by the Sea*. I was probably thrown out before the thing came to the actual production. I hope I was anyway. But it was all very amusing, all very light-hearted, perfectly happy and time went by just like nobody's business.[60]

Quite why cadets were involved in College theatrical productions was a matter of some debate. Some recollected that taking part in various entertainments was 'optional':

If you felt like it you could join a concert party. They used to put up a notice board; anyone who cared to take part in a concert or do some sort of turn, just put their name down. Then you rehearsed and if you were good enough you became part of the concert party. Some of them put on theatrical shows if they wanted to. You always could. . . . They were given the opportunity . . . some were quite good. Some were put on by the cadets and some were by the combined cadets and staff of the College.[61]

Others felt that participation was not so voluntary:

. . . at the Christmas term I was there, several cadets were hauled in to take part in amateur theatricals. I can't remember the name of the play, it was a quite well-known one going on in London at the time where the hero pretended to be a silly ass and was given a white feather by all of the girls and eventually turned out to be a master spy-catcher.[62]

Whether participation was voluntary or not, many cadets found themselves in jobs connected with these 'theatrical' productions. 'I had the job of making up one of my friends with rouge and lipstick to look like [a] girl . . . a chap called Bliss who had a very good voice, term above me. . . .'[63]

The end result of all this hard work was mixed, but is perhaps best summed up by the thoughts of one cadet who was at the College at the height of the First World War:

One used to have I think at the end of most terms some sort of an entertainment, usually a musical of some sort, performed almost entirely by the cadets, some of them were very good indeed obviously, and some were mediocre. . . . [64]

The other main form of entertainment, College dances, were vividly recalled by one cadet:

The retired band . . . Royal Marine Bandsmen . . . always came and played in the gallery of Nelson. . . . And they used to play for dancing. Well of course no female was ever allowed inside the College practically. The Captain's wife . . . was known to come in, and I believe the Captain's daughter on one occasion. But the cadets simply danced with each other, or occasionally with members of staff. It was the cadet who asked.

But Geoffrey Callender . . . was a prominent dancer. He loved it. He used to come in, in his gown and his bald head shining, and wait to be asked to dance because he always insisted on [being the] girl. And I can see him now in the arms of some small cadet revolving around, with his head thrown back, and an expression of ecstasy on his face. Nowadays, they'd probably think badly of it. There was absolutely nothing of that sort at all.[65]

One former cadet recalled dances every night – sometimes, indeed, more than one a night. While this is most improbable, some of his memories do ring true:

. . . we used to dance with each other and a certain number of the masters joined in too. I remember especially Callender, the author of *The Sea Kings of Britain*, he was very popular and danced every night.[66]

It would appear that Callender, who was also the force behind at least one Gilbert and Sullivan production, might have been responsible for the introduction of dances on Saturday nights. One cadet, who spent his time at the College before the First World War, was certain no such events had taken place during his time there.[67]

Besides these more or less formal group entertainments, term officers or tutors could lay something on for boys under their command, although any kind of 'treat' usually had to be worked for:

The term officers, I don't think, took part in [dances]; nor should they of course, because that wouldn't have been good for discipline. But . . . occasionally one was asked out to tea. There were two forms of invitation. Some of the officers played on a little nine-hole golf course which was in the grounds of Osborne House. And they would sometimes ask one of the cadets of their term to come and caddy for them. And that was a good bet because although it meant flogging round the golf course one always hoped they'd stop at nine holes though they sometimes went on to eighteen. You were then taken back to the officer's mess and given a tea which was quite beyond the ordinary tea. And occasionally one's tutor would ask one out and if he lived outside, as they mostly did, you were allowed to go to his house. I remember I had tea with Jimmy Watt . . . a very formidable old man. But it was interesting.[68]

On the whole, therefore, former cadets' recollections of the entertainments laid on for them are very positive. The commitment of many of the boys and of some, at least, of the teaching staff is evident, and displays well the concern teachers had for the pastoral welfare of their students. The excitement with which these entertainments were greeted also indicates how important the boys felt them to be during their time at the College. The whole subject throws a bright light onto what is sometimes the rather gloomy history of life at the College.

Unfortunately, other aspects of non-academic life at the College cannot be described in such glowing terms. Although cadets were relatively well fed, looked after and even entertained in their spare time at Osborne, the story of their health while at the College is not such a positive one.

Both while it was open and since its closure, Osborne Naval College has been heavily criticised for the apparent unhealthiness of its site and the consequent effects of this on its cadets. Indeed, the father of one was driven to remark that his son 'Robin, a naval cadet, was poisoned at Osborne College; this affected his heart and he succumbed to an attack of pneumonia when eighteen years of age.'[69]

No less a person than Admiral Earl Beatty felt the College was on a 'cursed spot', while Sir John Fisher's biographer tells us 'this College was never thoroughly healthy'.[70] While some of this may seem exaggerated, there is plenty of contemporary evidence to suggest that the College was not a particularly healthy place.

As early as 1907 the authorities were fending off criticism in the House of Commons about the 'alleged unhealthy conditions' at Osborne. Though they would not, as requested on 5 March, rebuild the whole College in brick, they did promise that an isolation hospital would be built there.[71] Two years later, in 1909, this was completed, its necessity having arisen from the fact that boys aged thirteen 'are peculiarly susceptible to all kinds of diseases, chicken pox, measles, etc'.[72]

The cadets did suffer from a wide range of illness. In 1910 they were reported to be suffering from measles, German measles and 'pink eye'.[73] A year later Lord Charles Beresford enquired whether there had been an outbreak of scurvy at the College, in addition to the 'mysterious' pink eye infection. Mckenna, the First Lord, denied both claims,[74] but George Lambert, the Civil Lord, could not deny two years later that one boy was currently suffering from typhoid, one from bronchitis and two from pneumonia.[75]

Despite official reluctance to admit to the existence of serious problems, continued outbreaks of diseases of various kinds nevertheless gave the authorities pause for thought. The Fourth Report of the Custance Committee of 1912 noted all the diseases (infectious or otherwise) that had been through the College between 1904 and 1911. The committee did not make it particularly clear what its definitions of these types of illness were. It included influenza, measles, German measles, mumps and chickenpox among the infectious diseases, while conjunctivitis was the most common of diseases categorised (incorrectly) as non-infectious. It is clear from the committee's figures that cases of infectious disease were usually outnumbered by 'non-infectious' ones – the one exception was in 1906, when there were 670 cases of the former type, compared with 359 cases of the latter (when there were about 450 cadets present at the College). The next highest years for infections were: 1911, with 383 cases (among 440 cadets); 1910, with 284 cases (among 420 cadets); and 1908 with 227 cases (among 300 cadets).

Figures for infectious diseases were much lower in other years: 43 cases in 1904 (among only 280 cadets); 67 cases in 1905 (among 440 cadets); a mere 17 cases in 1907 (among 420 cadets); and 72 cases in 1909 (among 410 cadets). Cases of non-infectious disease outnumbered these. In 1903, with the first term of the College only just admitted, there were only 37 cases (among 72 cadets), but thereafter, numbers rocketed: 379 in 1904; 467 in 1905; 607 in 1907; 446 in 1908; 509 in 1909; 413 in 1910; and 590 in 1911.

The committee noted the prevalence of conjunctivitis cases in 1904 (when there had been 95 cases), 1905 (173 cases) and 1911 (121 cases). In 1906, which was the worst year for infectious diseases, there were 61 cases of chicken pox, 118 of measles, 233 of influenza, and 251 of mumps. German measles made its appearance in 1908 (73 cases), influenza reappeared in 1910 (260 cases), and epidemics of measles and German measles both occurred in 1911 (116 and 251 cases respectively).

These figures appear disturbingly high. The committee admitted that the site of the College was damp and that the crowding of cadets in the dormitories might encourage the spread of disease – although it pointed out that the boys at Osborne were as healthy as their contemporaries at public schools. It expressed the hope that conjunctivitis had been stamped out by insistence on regular changing of the plunge-bath water and it noted that improvements had been made to the College accommodation since the influenza epidemic of 1910. Since that time, also, the College hospital had been extended and it now contained sixty beds, together with eighteen beds for non-infectious diseases and another sixteen in the College 'sick-quarters'. The latter, however, was not very suitable for use as a hospital.[76]

But little permanent good seems to have resulted. Even in 1915 Beresford was asking if sickness was still rampant at the College and was not reassured when the Admiralty spokesman declared that there were 136 cadets on the sick list – 106 with influenza, 12 with measles, 10 with conjunctivitis, 5 with pneumonia, 2 with mumps and 1 with tonsilitis – among some 330 cadets present.[77] Two years later further concern was expressed about the state of cadets' health. This climaxed early in 1917, when a boy returned from leave carrying the germs of measles, which, as Mcnamara reported to the Commons, 'was of a severe type, and in a considerable number of cases was followed by bronchopneumonia, causing six deaths'.[78] It is no coincidence that in that year a committee was sent to investigate conditions at the College and it is not, perhaps, surprising, that it was not very impressed with the improvements made since the Custance Committee report of 1912. It argued that, contrary to the views of the Custance Committee, the infections suffered by the boys at Osborne were both severe and often resulted in unusual complications, citing in particular frequent catarrhal infections among the cadets. The Committee recommended that with measles treated as an infectious disease, the number of beds in the hospital should be increased still more to 104. If the College was to remain at its present site, the hospital overall ought to be further extended. The committee also stated the walls of the single-bed sick-bay should be filled in to deaden sound, but it felt nothing realistic could be done to improve the dormitories.[79]

These reports serve to suggest that the public and the Admiralty's perceptions of Osborne do not always coincide with those of the former cadets. As one of these pointed out:

I've heard criticism in later life that Osborne was unhealthy and that the cadets got a lot of diseases but I never thought the place was unhealthy and I don't think our particular lot had any more ailments than you'd get out of a large crowd of small boys. After all, Osborne was a lovely site. I was not ill at Osborne. Whether perhaps the sick-bay facilities weren't all they might have been I simply don't know.[80]

He was not alone in downplaying the significance of outbreaks of illness at the College:

The only time I went sick I think I was knocked out playing rugger once and they sent me off to hospital for one night. And I spent about four days [there] once with tonsilitis, otherwise I was extremely fit.[81]

One former cadet commented that:

We youngsters, we never gave it a thought. There it was, we just accepted what was there. Whether it was unhealthy or not, that I really don't know. I wouldn't say so. I should think the whole of the Isle of Wight was a pretty healthy area really as far as I could remember. But I think all cadets were very fit apart from this bout of Spanish 'flu which no-one could avoid there. That was nobody's fault, it was over the whole country.[82]

Another made the point that

I know one cadet in our term died and I think the College casualty list was five deaths that term. It was very sad. It was very interesting to hear the remarks of the people at home when one went home on leave. The papers were all full of it. 'The College is built on the old Royal stables at Osborne, what can you expect with those dear little boys over the drains,' and things like that. It wasn't until I was a fully grown up man that I could have retorted, 'What do you expect in London practically everybody lives in mews over old stables which were not half so well kept as Queen Victoria's.'[83]

One former cadet, who entered the College in January 1920, summed things up thus: 'Living conditions were hard up to a point but healthy, clean and all that you would expect from the senior service.'[84]

But some other cadets recollected serious health problems at the College. It certainly seems that once an infection took hold at Osborne, it made rapid progress through the ranks and could have serious consequences: 'We had one very bad epidemic indeed of measles while I was there. One of my classmates at school there got pneumonia and died. In the same term there was another who also died.'[85]

Several cadets recollected the great influenza epidemic of late 1918, and the effects it had on them and on the College:

We were there during the big 'flu epidemic . . . just after the war. An awful lot of us went down with 'flu, I went down myself.[86]

We were there in November '18, yes. I remember it because the 'flu went right through the College and all the dormitories were converted to wards, and nurses were introduced.[87]

Some cadets had more intimate reasons for remembering this outbreak. One recalled:

this bout of Spanish 'flu which everybody got: personally I got pneumonia . . . from this. I gather I was fairly ill but I didn't know it at the time, of course. Very efficient nursing staff . . . they looked after us very well. The sick-bay was overflowing, they just used the dormitories, there wasn't enough room when the whole College went down with this 'flu business.[88]

Another believed he:

was about one of the forty last to succumb. Then I remember the surgeon coming into the dormitory and announcing that the armistice had been signed. We hardly knew what this meant and in any case we all felt so ill we all just turned over and groaned.

This former cadet was one of several who also made the point that: 'The College was so badly affected by this epidemic that [it] was closed down and all the cadets sent home.'[89] Another cadet thought that catching 'flu could get you into trouble in more ways than one:

when in the 'flu epidemic I was laid up I had a very high temperature and mentioned this to my mother. The next thing I heard was from my father who said he had had a letter from the Admiralty requesting Mrs Ford in future to make enquiries in the right quarters. My mother thought I was going to die. But [he continued] in the next bed . . . was [Viscount] Borrowdale, who was in our term, son of Lord Beatty, and the great man himself came down and . . . immediately put me at my ease by saying 'Oh, I played cricket, Ford, with your father.' It was very nice.

This cadet wondered 'whether the sequel of what happened to Osborne had anything to do with this epidemic which [Beatty's] son was involved with . . .'.[90] However, since the decision to close the College had already been taken – at least in principle – this seems most unlikely. Besides influenza, it was noted that the cadets 'had out tonsilitis, various bits of mumps and things like that'.[91]

Probably the illness Osborne Naval College was most notorious for is known as pink eye. This certainly appeared among the diseases listed regularly in the House of Commons. In 1910 questions were asked about whether this disease had been caused by the College being built on the site of the stables for Osborne House.[92] In 1915 Beresford again questioned whether the 'prevalency of the complaint called pink eye' was due to the siting of the College.[93]

Former cadets had vivid memories of this complaint: 'We had . . . this one outbreak of pink eye – not serious but it did stop one from doing the ordinary work because your eyes were always running and being bandaged up.'[94] Another agreed that: 'Yes, that was quite a common complaint. . . . I can remember their putting drops in our eyes to get rid of the pink eye.'[95]

A rumour got around at the time that occurrences of this affliction had something to do with the site of the College:

The site of Osborne College had been stables for Osborne House . . . and it was possible to catch an eye disease that horses got. Practically the whole College got it. I got it and it makes your eyes swell up and painful. I got it and was sent home and my father caught it from me. It was a damned nuisance.[96]

But that the site of the College could be blamed for the outbreak of pink eye was not the universal view of former cadets:

There was a rumour which I'm very doubtful about that because of the stables there were remaining infection troubles from that. The only thing I think there was likely to be any truth in, was the fact that the . . . College was subject to pink eye.[97]

At least one ex-cadet thought the whole question of pink eye was exaggerated:

I think that was the sort of thing that was built up in the press when they had nothing else to say. They produced this pink eye . . . there were a number of specialists brought in from London and God knows where . . . into the Isle of Wight to try and discover the root cause of it. But it didn't leave any serious after-effects, nobody lost the sight of an eye or anything like that. . . . I think this pink eye was just built up out of all proportion just by the local Portsmouth press as much as any.[98]

Another cadet was not at all bothered by it:

There was a story about pink eye but it didn't worry me. . . . I don't think it had any permanent effect on anybody, it certainly didn't worry me and I don't remember anybody in our term being in any way incommoded by it.[99]

But pink eye persisted. The first of the ex-cadets to mention it went to the College in 1910, the last in 1917, but it was also apparent there in 1913–15.

The suggestion that the attacks of pink eye were because of the siting of the College received sufficient publicity and appeared so serious that the 1917 Admiralty Committee specifically investigated it. Despite its general reservations about the site of the College, the committee stated categorically that the pink eye epidemics were *not* caused by the College being built on the site of the Osborne House stables, although it did not venture an opinion as to what might be the cause.[100] What seems most likely is that cadets suffered from pink eye for the same reasons that they suffered from other complaints. It was not – solely – the accommodation that was at fault: as the 1917 committee realised, other general factors might also be to blame. In its opinion, these other factors included the too-rigorous routine under which the boys had to live (they needed more sleep), but it also thought infections could be brought in by parents visiting unannounced and by College servants who lived out in the community.

It would appear that the cadets did suffer a lot from ill health. While it is true, as several witnesses agreed, that 'it was a larger concentration than any public school at the age of 13 and 14 and . . . we were particularly vulnerable at that age',[101] the level of disease does seem somewhat high, and this was caused, in part at least, by the factors identified at the time: the standard of accommodation and the routine the cadets followed.

Those cadets who fell ill and who recollected their treatment at the hands of the medical authorities were, however, unanimous in their praise. Doctors were commended:

At the end of 1918 in November there was a terrible outbreak of 'flu, the first 'flu I think that anybody had ever known and practically everybody went down with 'flu. Aspirin had just been invented and one of our really clever naval surgeons who was there insisted we were given aspirin and that did undoubtedly save a lot of lives. . . .[102]

Nurses, too, received their share of the credit:

The nursing was very good, they took great care to see that we were properly looked after whilst we had 'flu and in the post-'flu conditions, too, [they] made quite certain we were rehabilitated. They were very good nursing staff, I think. The surgeons were good, too.[103]

There was additional consolation for those who fell ill:

I was always very fit until my very last term when everybody had left. I got mumps which was rather sad and another very nice chap and I were relegated to the sick-bay right at the end of the passageway where I was nursed by the most delightful dear nurse whom I fell flatly in love with, I don't mind admitting. I can't remember her name now. She was utterly sweet, nursed me through this and I always remember the marvellous porridge I was given the last day there because I was well enough.[104]

Perhaps the last word on this subject should rest with the former cadet who stated, quite bluntly, that 'I was never in the sick-bay.'[105] The vast majority of cadets survived their time at Osborne and most did so with no more than the usual run of childhood illnesses, and perhaps the occasional injury. It seems highly unlikely the College site itself was any more or less healthy than its surroundings.

One final element in the cadets' daily life mattered greatly, both to them and to the College authorities: discipline. In overall charge of the College, and senior to all members of the staff, was the Captain of the College, aided by a Commander. Both of these men were serving naval officers, although the outbreak of the First World War led to sudden – and apparently not always beneficial – changes of personnel at all levels.

> The College was run . . . under the command of an active service Captain. Holmes à Court was his name, and there was a Commander, the executive officer of the College . . . one of the many Boyles . . . most Boyles I've met in the Navy are men of great character and considerable humour. They were not afraid of anybody. . . .[106]

But another former cadet remembered:

> the Commander who was sent to us was really beyond it. For one thing he always had great sores all over his face and that sort of thing, powdered with borassic powder which didn't make him particularly attractive as . . . a disciplinarian.[107]

The Captain, or more usually, the Commander, would make nightly rounds of the dormitories. Precisely who it was, could make a difference to the cadets:

> The first lieutenant was Lieutenant Commander T.B. Curteis. The extraordinary thing was that at round, in the dormitories at night, if it was Commander Curteis' turn to go round, the buzz went round and everybody froze. For some reason he had the most extraordinary effect of instilling reverence for his presence.[108]

The Commander was the senior officer in charge of day-to-day discipline at the College. While most cadets had little recollection of him, Captain the Hon. E.S.H. Boyle, 'Ginger' Boyle, as he was known, had a considerable impact on the College:

Captain Boyle was a seaman of the old school, saltiest of salt horses, with formidable bushy eyebrows. He could inspire awe in officers as well as cadets. . . . Captain Boyle was indeed the key figure of Osborne in the First World War.

 . . . no Term Master ever went midnight rounds as officer of the day without meeting Captain Boyle, muffled up to the eyes and grey as death (for he ought to have been on the sick-list himself), passing noiselessly between the beds of a dormitory or sick-bay, hurrying to fetch a doctor or nurse, or being a nurse himself. . . . He was a man of iron with a heart of gold.[109]

One former cadet remembered Captain Boyle for one reason only, and explained how the Commander operated his system of discipline:

the only thing I do remember about this Commander was that the College was, or great number of us were, sent for and assembled in the hall . . . Nelson . . . some misdemeanour had been committed, I don't know what it was, but they were trying to find out who'd done it. It came to sending for the College or half the College and falling them in the Nelson and it had a gallery running across the end of the building and up into the gallery got Commander Boyle. 'Who did this?' That sort of harangue. 'I want to know who did this. Now any of you boys who did it tell me here and you won't be punished for it, so badly as if I had to find you out,' and a little noise came from the audience and a hand went up. 'Me, sir.' 'I is the correct answer, not me.' That was that little episode that sank in. He had us all right, that chap.[110]

But Captain Boyle also with less compliant cadets:

One evening Captain Boyle, who nothing usually perturbed, entered the ante-room with the air of a man who had seen trouble, ordered a drink, and confessed to a master he needed it. When walking through 'Nelson' he had been passed by a first-termer who did not salute, an omission which had occasioned the following conversation:
  'Young gentleman, come here. What's your name?'
  'Jones.'
  'Do you know the meaning of these four stripes?'

'Yes, they show you're a captain.'

'Don't you think you ought to salute a captain?'

'Yes, I suppose I ought.'

'And don't you think you should call a captain, "Sir"?'

'Yes, I suppose I should.'

Whereupon Captain Boyle told him to carry on, which he had done without saluting.

Notwithstanding these flagrant breaches of discipline, Captain Boyle did not order the boy's term master 'to give him a dozen of the best'.[111]

One of Captain Boyle's successors, Commander Charles F.R. Cowan, was remembered for another reason: 'he was', one cadet recalled, 'very smart and wore stays under his frock coat.'[112]

While the Captain and Commander tended to be somewhat distant figures to most of the cadets, the same cannot be said of their 'Term Lieutenant'. Each of the new terms entering the College came under the overall command of a 'Lieutenant of the Term'. This post had been introduced to *Britannia* by the then Captain, A.W. Moore, in 1894.[113] His many duties were summed up by the Admiralty as responsibility 'for the general discipline and well-being of the cadets of his term . . . he comes to know them intimately, makes his personal influence felt, and continues his charge of the particular group so long as they remain in the College'.[114]

His second-in-command was an Engineer Lieutenant who took responsibility for teaching that subject, as well as disciplinary matters that might arise. Both before and after the First World War, these men were serving Royal Navy officers, although during the conflict they were replaced by civilian masters who took over their functions. Cadets' recollections of their Term Lieutenants varied widely, but it is clear that those who thought most highly of their officers were those whose general memories of their time at Osborne were most favourable. They certainly had an important role to play: '. . . our Term Lieutenants were a much more important factor in our life than the masters . . . really'.[115]

Both civilian and naval term 'officers' had their admirers: 'The term officers were civilians. We had one Mr Bunting . . . he was an ex-England rugger player. Everybody loved him and did what he told them. He was a kind man.'[116]

Before the war, one naval Term Lieutenant was remembered as being 'very normal. I think he was quite popular'. Much the same could be said of at least one post-war officer. 'We couldn't have had a nicer man than Petwell, we were all devoted to him. He didn't spoil us. I don't think he had favourites.'[117] Another, Lieutenant Walter Lucas, was if anything too lenient with the cadets, though he was 'very much liked' by one witness, whose 'Engineer Lieutenant Lionel Wansborough was a somewhat different character, but no less liked. A great rugby player, he was also a very stern disciplinarian.'[118]

One other former cadet had rather more mixed memories:

One or two of the masters in their disciplinary duties were the way schoolmasters are . . . not bullies but . . . rather unreasonable . . . ours was a very nice man but he wasn't easy. He did justice, he beat your bottom if he thought it was necessary, he was entitled to. He oversaw you and did all the sort of things in the way of advice that you knew you could always go and see him. . . .[119]

One famous ex-cadet, who generally had a very bad time at the College, firmly believed that those who went there during the war were fortunate in their Term Lieutenants:

As every officer on the Active List was then required for sea service the functions of Term Lieutenant had been taken over 'for the duration' by selected civilian Masters. Later I was to realise that this was on the whole beneficial to us, since the Masters were generally wise and kindly men, whose devotion to the Navy was tempered by their scholastic interests and their experience of teaching the young. . . . [120]

At the end of the war, the return of serving officers to the role of Term Lieutenant appears to have had unfortunate consequences for those enrolling at that time. Two former cadets, who both entered in September 1918, had very bad memories of their Term Lieutenant. As one put it, 'We didn't like him much. Does it suffice to say that?'[121] The other was more outspoken:

He wasn't a very nice fellow really. He was a bad choice for a Term Lieutenant. He had no sense of humour. He'd been chosen I think by the Commander . . . he was one of [his] pets. . . . He really was a bit of a brute to be quite honest. I was just terrified of him, really I was quite terrified of him. So were a lot of other people, especially the smaller boys. I suppose he had his good side but I can't say that I ever saw it myself.

But, he admitted, there was a reason for this, if not, perhaps, a justification:

During the war all the naval officers were on active service, so Osborne was taken over, was run by academic staff [and] was a much more humane regime while it was being run by the academic staff. Then as soon as the naval staff came back they felt that everything . . . had got very slack so they hardened up on us very hard.[122]

The impact of the Term Lieutenant on the cadets in his term clearly varied, and much depended on his personality and empathy with the young boys under his command. Some boys simply did not get to know them very well: 'We didn't really see very much of him . . . he was a rather distant figure in a way,'[123] but this seems to have been exceptional and most cadets had more direct experience of their Term Lieutenants than this.

The Admiralty was aware that Term Lieutenants needed some help and, on occasion, someone to mediate between them and the boys under their command. For this purpose, each term had two Petty Officers appointed to take care of them in various ways. Captain French recalled that his 'term Petty Officers were PO Stone and PO Swan – who were wonderful advisers and "guiders" . . .' and, he added, 'specially chosen'.[124] Other cadets remembered their term Petty Officers for a number of reasons. One thought, 'They were very carefully selected and they were mostly gymnastics experts,'[125] while another was

taught seamanship badly by old Chief Petty Officers who had their set pieces that they let off [at] us with some splendid mispronunciations which we carried with us into later life. [One of the] markings on the lead line . . . is a Raw Hide Becket but we always thought it was a Row-Eyed Becket because the thing had a hole in it and that's what the Chief Petty Officer called it. The masts of boats were made of Oregon pinewood but we thought they were made of Hurricane pinewood, which is what we called them.[126]

However, the most important duty of the Petty Officers was not tuition, but to introduce the cadets to some of the rigours of naval life, and to help them out if they needed it. They apparently did this very well.

> We had a Petty Officer . . . who was the term Petty Officer. He was a very nice man indeed. He led us into the very strange change of routine from a prep school very gently indeed for 48 hours so that when the rest of the College arrived we weren't just plain ignoramuses about the life we were expected to lead there.[127]

While they were at the College, the cadets found the Petty Officers very useful:

> If your uniform was dirty – boys being what they are and eating in a great hurry would spill food perhaps – . . . the term Chief Petty Officer would be on duty just before divisions in the morning with a little bottle of ammonia and a rag. And if there were any fearful spots on a cadet he would quickly sponge [them] off on a clothes brush.[128]

Sometimes Petty Officer's duties were a little more intimate:

> Generally we were told when we had to change from winter underclothing to summer underclothing, that sort of thing. Our Chief Petty Officer used to come along, in fact, we used to call him Chief Petty Officer Underpants. He was always coming along and saying 'You've got to change your underpants today,' that sort of thing. In other words [this cadet concluded] we were very carefully looked after.[129]

On other occasions, his activities were rather less private:

> We fell in every morning for short prayers and inspection before we were moved off to our various studies and we had a term Petty Officer called Petty Officer Johnson. He was dressed in brown gaiters which was the rig of the day, and the organist, who was the choir master [who] used to teach music, was up in the organ, and no sound came out of the organ, which was hand-blown. So Petty Officer Johnson, who was on duty, who must have weighed about

sixteen stone, slowly and sedately walked up to the gallery, and, as he climbed the wooden staircase, there was a breathless silence from all assembled company, only disturbed by the creaking of the wooden steps as he slowly but steadily climbed to his duty. After he'd pumped a few pumps on the handle the organist could get on with the hymn tune.[130]

The place of the Petty Officer in the College was well summed up by one former cadet. He stated that

The Chief Petty Officers were very much in command of the cadets, though they always called you 'Sir'. If you were called to attention to speak it was 'Stand to attention, Mr Ham, Sir!'. Even no exclusion of royalty. 'Stand to attention, Prince George, Sir!'. Occasionally it was 'Mr Prince George'.[131]

But the Petty Officers were not the only officially appointed mediators between the cadets and their Term Lieutenants. As the 1914 semi-official Admiralty guide (which did not mention the role of the Petty Officers) pointed out, each term had

four 'Cadet Captains', who compared in a general way, to the prefects in a public school. They are selected from among the cadets of the senior terms as boys who show early promise of officer-like qualities. In matters of minor discipline and in keeping up a good tone in the term they are effective aids to the Term Lieutenants. Two 'Chief Captains' are selected from among the cadets of the senior term to see that the cadet captains perform their duties properly. The cadet captains are made responsible for the orderly marching of cadets into study or elsewhere, for good behaviour at mess, and for checking any tendency to bullying. They receive a small weekly allowance and have certain privileges to match their authority.[132]

The place and role of the Cadet Captains was stressed by one former cadet, who eventually became one of their number:

. . . the Cadet Captain was . . . a man of great importance. There were two Cadet Captains in each dormitory. . . . One slept at one end of the dormitory and the other at the other end and woe betide you if you committed any [offences] – or if your uniform wasn't kept clean and spotless . . . the two big men in my term became Chief Cadet Captains because each term had two Cadet Captains. . . . They were really in charge more or less of the Cadet Captains to see they did their job properly. I remember we were all very impressed by them. Before that when we first arrived we had two Chief Captains who were rather magnificent people, one was a big tall good-looking chap and a very husky sort of chap. One was called Walkey and the other was called Norfolk . . . you bowed down if you ever saw them coming. I was terrified of them and they had a little room to themselves, they messed together the two of them. The Cadet Captain always used to say grace in this great room.[133]

The Cadet Captains appear to have carried out their duties efficiently, even if, most of the time, this appears to have involved the imposition of punishments for various offences:

You had, every day, to give what was known as a log, in other words, the Cadet Captain took down what each member of the dormitory did during the day and if you'd done nothing that generally got you into trouble.[134]

What kind of trouble you got into varied, but only in its intensity:

When I was a Cadet Captain I had a little sort of . . . ruler . . . for slapping people's hands. 'Put your hands out', give 'em ten if they didn't come up to scratch. Warned them beforehand of course.[135]

But matters could be a bit more serious:

There was a Cadet Captain's room and if you transgressed you were hauled before the Cadet Captains and given a sort of tribunal and if they considered you'd done wrong you were probably beaten. Not very hard. Three cuts was normal but nobody liked going there because you knew exactly what you were going to expect and it was really rather painful.[136]

Sometimes these beatings were more rigorous still:

. . . there was this chap called Keyhoe and he was a bit insubordinate and he was given a C.C.'s beating in the C.C.'s reading room. In any lot there were two Chief Cadet Captains when I was in the senior term . . . and this chap was beaten in the reading room with all the other Cadet Captains present. I thought it was a fairly severe beating but this chap was one of those daredevils . . . they are very difficult to discipline, they have plenty of spirit. But they have to obey the rules and I thought this chap was being given a pretty severe beating. I think it had some effect. Probably the staff all knew that this was going on, the masters and the headmaster, they all kept their ears to the ground.[137]

Cadet Captains had the power to reward to other cadets for carrying out small tasks for them:

one gave me his British Warm [overcoat] although I think it must have been a warmish day but I suppose we'd been told to carry British Warms. He told me to take his British Warm up to the College, for which he rewarded me with half an extra bath, [and] I spent the rest of the term trying to get the other half – never did.[138]

Given these various recollections, it is, perhaps, not surprising that few memories of these young Cadet Captains were favourable. One former cadet thought

. . . our Cadet Captains were proper little terrors. They were our own lot but from a senior term and they wore a little device on their sleeve to make sure we knew who they were. They used to order us about mercilessly.[139]

Another believed 'We had a great deal of suffering on account of what the Cadet Captains of the senior term did to us.'[140]

One famous ex-cadet went into more detail in his memoirs:

The worst feature of the training system then in force lay in the power accorded to the Cadet Captains. These could be only a few months older than their charges, yet they were allowed to exercise unbridled power over them – including that of summary, severe, and utterly senseless beatings. One of these young tyrants slept at the end of each dormitory and was responsible for its discipline and good order. . . . We were at once taught that everything was done 'at the double', meaning a sort of shambling trot which lay somewhere between a walk and a run. We juniors always had to double the whole length of the corridors past our seniors' dormitories to assemble in 'Nelson' or for any other purpose. The Cadet Captains were always on the watch and their most common opportunity to flog a junior arose from the accusation that he had not been 'doubling' fast enough. The orgies of sadism that resulted were outrageous.[141]

The Cadet Captains thus clearly played a major role in imposing discipline on their juniors. The Admiralty, however, was not anxious to stress publically the disciplinary element of life at its naval colleges:

Small breaches of discipline are usually punished by short periods of extra drill taken from what would otherwise be the cadet's own time, or by confinement to the College grounds. . . . Caning (a punishment for grave offences only) is but rarely resorted to, and by Captain's orders alone.[142]

The 'extra drill' normally 'meant doubling around "Collingwood" for an hour or more with a "wand" held above one's head'.[143] Recollections of former cadets, however, strongly suggest that this picture is not complete. In particular, corporal punishment was involved more often than this suggests, and Captain's orders were only required for the most serious of all punishments that could be meted out by the Osborne College authorities – 'official cuts'.

Most former cadets agreed that discipline at Osborne College was rigorous, and their recollections sometimes provide an indication of the variety of reasons for which punishment, usually corporal, was meted out. One cadet recalled that 'Discipline was very, very strict indeed. . . . There was a great deal of beating went on, of course.' This cadet noted that it was

made quite clear to us that it was a disciplined service we were going into and we had to obey orders without question throughout. We were not encouraged to question anything . . . although it may have been a strict discipline I don't think it did any of us any harm in later life.[144]

Several former cadets remarked on how a combination of 'minor offences' could lead to a beating:

> Discipline was rather strict. For minor offences one got what was called a tick. Three ticks meant a beating. And I got three of the best for my toothbrush pointing east instead of west. . . . It was obviously conspicuous in the line of toothbrushes. I also got beaten for taking two buns on one occasion. . . . At Osborne everything was done to order.[145]

'It was', as another remarked

> a very, very rigid discipline. It was all regarded as part of the hardening process. Virtually everything had to be done at the double. If you didn't you caught it. For any misdemeanour there were various sanctions, there were various kinds of drill that were given, so many days of drill . . . during your spare time. Of course, the cane was used quite liberally one way or the other . . . compared with what I should have thought any ordinary public school, even in those days, it was pretty strict, stricter than almost any public school I should have thought.[146]

A third expressed full agreement with these views:

> Discipline, I think, was pretty acute there. You were kept on your toes all the time. You weren't allowed to walk between dormitories or anything like that. Wherever you went you had to do it at the double. . . . At the end of each bed was a big sea-chest and that sea-chest held everything we'd got. When you went to [bed], at night, everything had to be laid out on the chest . . . all carefully folded, your shirts beautifully folded, your coats folded, trousers creased and everything. If not you used to get a caning.[147]

One veteran of the College summed up the overall place of corporal punishment in Osborne's disciplinary procedures rather well: 'You got four cuts on the backside for almost anything.'[148] The majority of former cadets on the receiving end of this treatment, however, had few complaints about it:

> . . . when you laid out your things for the evening rounds . . . your toothbrush had to be on top of your tooth mug, and if the bristles

were pointing to the left when it had to be pointed to the right, you got a tick. If you got three ticks, you reported to the term officer, and he would interview you, and usually deliver three strokes on the backside with the cane. Beatings were quite frequent and were always done by the term officer himself. You got the word, 'Term officer wants to see you in the oilskin room.' This was a little room outside the entrance to the dormitory, just opposite the officer's own cabin, and there were oilskins all hanging up. 'All right, Bradbury, bend over.' But nobody took the slightest exception to it. You knew the rules and if you hadn't kept to them, well then that was it. But there was no shame in it or anything of that sort. . . .[149]

Another thought that

The discipline was strict but I shouldn't have called it unfair. I know one or two people think we were unnecessarily beaten for silly little things. But the beatings weren't anything to worry about. I wasn't particularly big or burly, as a matter of fact I was one of the smaller ones, but I suppose I was probably beaten at Osborne about, I should think, on average once or twice a term for rather minor things. It never worried me at all.[150]

A third remembered how 'I felt that the Engineer Lieutenant who beat me was much too strong and I turned round and said so on one occasion. He stopped beating me.'[151]

But there were other punishments available to the authorities. One was experienced by Stephen King-Hall, who explained how he had not wished to attend a match and support his term team:

The Term Lieutenant sent for me and asked for an explanation. I looked at this boy of twenty-three who seemed to rank with, but after, God and remained – for once – silent. He decided to teach me a lesson.

The Term Lieutenant did not resort to a beating in this instance: instead, he drew up the term and King-Hall was made to stand in front of it. 'That', said the Term Lieutenant, 'is a pipsqueak.' King-Hall felt that 'it was undoubtedly a cruel and stupid punishment'.[152]

There was, however, one further weapon in the authorities' disciplinary armoury that the cadets remembered well and with trepidation. This was the punishment universally referred to as 'official cuts'.

> There's one thing in one of these I've read, they talk about official cuts and they make an awful lot of it. If anybody had done anything which was particularly bad he was taken along to a gym horse and held over it. He was given six of the best. . . . I saw it happen once while I was there in five terms so it was very rare and then it was very well deserved for whatever anybody had done . . . if you've read in a book or anything that it was always occurring, it's absolute nonsense. I think the five terms I was there were fairly average interpretations of it all.[153]

> There were occasions when, for instance, two cadets behaved themselves rather badly and were bent over and given six official cuts in front of the whole College – but that was very, very rare.[154]

There is no doubt that the imposition of this dreadful punishment was rare: some cadets never witnessed it at all, and others on only one occasion. It was also, usually, administered to only one or two boys at a time, but there was at least one exception to this.

> The incident occurred about half way through one Osborne term when the boys in one of the dormitories . . . were caught in the dormitory at a time when they shouldn't have been. There were about eight of them. I think they were caught by Hartnell himself. Hartnell took them up before the Commander on the grounds that they had mutinied. On the strength of that Commander Cowan gave instructions that they should receive a public thrashing. These eight or ten boys were publicly thrashed in front of the whole of the rest of the term. I think it made an indelible mark on us all because we felt it was totally unjustified . . . most disagreeable.[155]

However, this witness was prepared to admit that his feelings towards the College were, in general, somewhat negative – his brother, a more extrovert character, had had a much better time there. It may also be true that this was not 'official cuts' but a less formal version. The full version of 'official cuts' was even more terrifying. One cadet recollected one of his colleagues being given them for what 'was considered an accumulation of quite petty peccadilloes':

> He was given . . . these official cuts which a Royal Marine administered. He had to get over one of the horses in the gym, which was HMS Nelson rigged as a gym, and he had to lean over the horse and he was given six cuts and we had to witness this sight. We all felt very regretful about it – poor chap, why he ever deserved this no one ever [knew] – he was a very nice bloke indeed, but he was always the butt of everything and I think it was very probably our fault that he got into this trouble. . . . I think it was a very rare punishment fortunately and he took it really stoically. But no one enjoyed it very much. . . . But otherwise we used to have the ordinary normal beatings that the term officer or the Cadet Captain could administer.[156]

This seems to have been unusual. 'Official cuts' were generally reserved for major offences, such as 'desertion' or 'mutiny'. In July 1913 two cadets stole a boat and rowed to the mainland. A large police search eventually found them hiding in the New Forest. The consequences were, of course, serious. One boy was withdrawn by his parents before anything could happen to him. The other – less fortunate – was paraded before the whole College to receive 'official cuts'. At least one witness 'felt very sorry for him'.[157] One cadet recounted his generally bad time at the College, and the events leading up to, and following, the 'official cuts' he received:

> The treatment of us young lads was absolutely abominable. We had a neurotic officer whose one delight was beating. As far as I was concerned the one thing I made quite sure of was that if I was beaten it would be for something that I deserved. To quote one particular example, we had a Cadet Captain we all hotly disliked. There was general discussion and we decided to beat the bloke up. I very much regret to say that I was the person who slapped him and started the riot.
>
> What we didn't realise was that we were under the Naval Disciplinary Act and to strike a senior officer comes under the heading of mutiny which is punishable by death. We were all hauled up in front of the Captain who solemnly pronounced that 'Mutiny is punishable by death.' We were very young and quite a few of us half believed this. However, we were kept waiting for a week and in due

course the sentence was announced – a beating to be delivered publicly in front of the whole College.

There was a box horse and four instructors, one to each arm, one to each leg, and Chief Petty Officer to deliver the blows. This was done with great solemnity: 'Cadet Nelson, three cuts of the cane, Chief Petty Officer Stamper, do your duty.' Then one, then two, then three, and I'm sorry to say, though some guys took it all right, one poor little chap . . . had a nervous breakdown afterwards. . . . As far as I was personally concerned, and I think it shows what a mean sort of chap I am, I earned 6d a time for about a week showing the bruises on my backside.[158]

Another former cadet provided perhaps the best, and certainly most detailed, account of this punishment, on the one occasion he witnessed it:

. . . this was a quite appalling thing that happened and I can only describe it as an absolute disgrace to the Navy and the nation. When you consider this was meted out to a boy who was a potential naval officer. It was supposed to be for serious . . . crimes but one boy who got it in my gunroom, one Picton-Warlow, his offence was nothing worse than making a continual nuisance of himself and the Navy didn't like having the mickey taken out of them much. He used to do stupid things like defacing notices and stupid things of that sort. And egged on, I'm very sorry to say, by a lot of his contemporaries. We've always had it on our consciences. The worst thing about this was the appalling ritual which accompanied it. . . . The boy concerned – the first thing he had to do was to report sick in the morning to see whether he was fit to undergo the punishment. Then at about nine o'clock in the morning he was paraded in special clothes, physical training kit actually, in front of the Captain, the Commander, the staff, his whole term and then his punishment was read out and how many cuts he'd been awarded. He was then thrown over a vaulting horse, his wrist was held by a surgeon, and a beefy Petty Officer then proceeded to give him the ordained number of strokes with a cane about four, five feet long. It was very painful. It was not called cuts for nothing. I believe in the old days the Petty Officer used to get half a crown each time he drew blood – I suppose that's where it got its name. But as you can imagine this was an appalling ordeal for a boy of fifteen. . . . The only good thing that came out of it was that we did have an absolutely exceptionally good senior cadet in the Hawke Term called G.C. Wolfe-Barry . . . as far as we were concerned he said to all the rest of us . . . 'We've got to be there, but you are not to watch this.' So directly the punishment commenced we all just looked down. I hope the fact was not lost on . . . our officers. I have no hesitation in saying this was the most disgraceful and barbaric episode I've ever witnessed.[159]

While these strong words did come from someone who was prepared to admit that he was 'one of the Navy's failures', the fact remains that they suggest quite clearly that 'official cuts' was a most unpleasant punishment. But not everyone thought so. The College doctor on one occasion reported to the young Louis Battenberg that one cadet 'could only stand 7 or so [cuts] the doctor said: I had a splendid view. He squealed and struggled rather like a rabbit when you pick it up by its ears. It was awful fun.'[160] The only 'defence' of this punishment that can be offered was its rarity – but it might have been better had it never happened at all.

In more general terms, most former cadets had a high regard for the discipline they experienced at Osborne: 'The discipline is the thing I remember more than anything else because it's remained with me ever since and it has been of very great value.'[161] Most would have agreed with one of their number in his overall comment: 'The discipline, I think, was very fair.'[162]

The ultimate test for any system of discipline, of course, is whether or not it worked. The disciplinary regime at Osborne certainly appears to have been severe, but its effectiveness must surely be judged by whether or not it did what was intended: did it keep the boys in line? Perhaps one of the best indicators of this is how well the College managed to prevent the rivalry it encouraged between terms from degenerating into bullying between, or even within, those terms. One modern commentator has remarked that 'There was little or no bullying at Osborne,'[163] but the cadets' own responses to enquiries about bullying varied, depending in some measure on a definition of what actually constituted 'bullying'. Some cadets felt there was none at Osborne:

Absolutely none. The terms were strictly segregated. You had nothing to do with any term either above or below you, except for the Cadet Captains, as it were, the prefects. No bullying at all.[164]

While another former cadet agreed – 'I don't think there was any bullying at all as far as I can remember.'[165] – the recollections of others are not so comforting:

> The one thing that they were down on was bullying in theory, but for all that there was a good deal of bullying. . . . I don't think there was as much bullying at Osborne and Dartmouth as there would have been at an ordinary public school. There was a band of big boys in our term. They banded together and used to go searching for the little ones. If they caught a little one alone they set upon him. I know because I was one of the little ones, and we all knew . . . these big ones who were inclined to bully. I won't say there was a great deal of it but woe betide any small one who got caught by them. I got caught two or three times and it wasn't very nice.[166]

Another remarked 'There was a certain amount . . . I got a certain amount and I think it taught me a helluva lot. . . .'[167]

The political situation could also prompt some bullying. Stephen King-Hall, suspected of Liberalism, was on the receiving end of a beating, while Louis Battenberg suffered at least some verbal abuse about his status as a prince.[168] It would also appear that any friendly rivalry between terms sometimes got out of hand and led to what might be described as bullying:

> Generally speaking [there was] practically none but like all small boys there are always one or two who get attacked by the rest but it wasn't very heavy. . . . There was considerable rivalry . . . in sport and everything else . . . but friendly rivalry and generally speaking we got on very well as a term.[169]

But according to another witness

> . . . really it wasn't bullying at all. There was never any physical bullying. If you were wandering round on Sunday afternoon, for example, in the grounds of Osborne House which were open to us and you came across two of the senior term, they would say, 'Ho, you! Stand up there, now sing!'. . . Even though they were quite nice about it, you were terrified of them and yet at the end of it they'd say

'Have a toffee' and they gave you a toffee. You went away realising there was no harm in it.[170]

It was noted that

The cadets had their own simple forms of torture . . . it was largely snobbish. For instance, no cadet would ever address a cadet of a senior term unless he was spoken to . . . if a senior term came up to you, he would say 'Name, number, tutor and cook?' and I think the object of that was purely inquisitive . . . to find out what sort of chap you were.[171]

The disciplinary system did, apparently, cause some restraint to be exercised by senior terms

. . . if anybody did do any bullying it had be done carefully because you went straight to the Captain and he brought him up before the term officer and there was hell to pay. . . . No, I can't remember any bullying except the usual sort, examination of the new boy, sort of thing. When we were the senior term we used to call up a junior cadet who'd just joined and plaster him with awful questions about his forebears and family. One of the questions was, 'What's the name of your cook?' I can never make out why but we always used to ask everybody that.[172]

This 'sort of examination' could, on occasion, take a rather unpleasant form:

We had to double past [the] senior gunroom and we were not allowed to speak to any cadet in the term senior to ours unless spoken to. I remember two boys from a senior term coming to see me whose parents had been with my father and the question they said to me was 'What is your name?' They said 'That's a funny name, sounds like mongrel to me.' I thought it was rather offensive but I couldn't answer back.[173]

Whether or not this could be considered bullying clearly depended on the view of the witness. Several former cadets commented on these examinations, but they tended to see them in terms that did not amount to bullying. One declared that

As far as I know there was no bullying. There was a certain amount of bossing by . . . the people who'd been there for six terms in the recreation grounds and that sort of thing, rather lorded it over the ones who'd just arrived but we kept so much to ourselves in our dormitories and gunrooms that I don't remember any embarrassment at all.[174]

Another remembered how

One kept very much . . . to one's term who went down with you because the senior terms were not bullies really but they tried to keep you in order just rather like boys at a public school. But there wasn't much bullying because you all kept together in your own little gunroom, four gunrooms to my term and we rather supported one another. When we were all together you couldn't touch us much but if we were out walking in Osborne grounds or something we'd perhaps be made to sing or do something by a senior term. . . . [175]

The petty, unofficial restrictions known as 'guff', which were imposed on junior terms by their seniors, do not seem to have been viewed as 'bullying' either:

. . . we had to double past any senior term's reading room and show proper respect for our seniors and we could impose it on our juniors later on so we could get our own back but I wouldn't have said there was any bullying. Don't recollect it. I think you were a bit nervous initially . . . of those senior to you but that was normal apprehension.[176]

One former cadet complained 'of all these ridiculous restrictions imposed upon us by the senior term who made life even more difficult for one'.[177] The senior terms were apparently 'looked upon . . . as a very superior race altogether',[178] but it would seem that as a rule junior terms 'knew their place' and outright physical bullying, both between and within terms, was a relatively rare phenomenon.

Only one former cadet recalled:

. . . a certain amount of scrapping among our gunrooms for some unknown reason . . . when we arrived . . . for some extraordinary reason which was very odd when you think we were a collection of strange little boys not knowing whether we were coming or going, after about three or four days the gunrooms set on each other with the most unparalleled ferocity. This used to happen every single term with a new term. It didn't happen again with us once you'd got it out of your system the first term . . . each first term always did this. . . . Cadet Captains . . . never did anything to stop this at all. I think it was considered necessary to toughen us up or do something but it really was quite the most extraordinary thing. . . .[179]

No other cadet remembered this, although it suggests that at times the College's disciplinary machinery did not function well – or, at least, was not put into operation. On the whole, however, it would seem that discipline was strictly maintained at Osborne, and it is rather unfortunate for the reputation of the College that the most famous incident in its history concerns not only a breakdown in discipline but also an injustice to one of its cadets: the case of George Archer Shee.

On 17 October 1908 the father of George Archer Shee was told to remove his son from Osborne. It was not explained why he had to do so. Only after repeated enquiry did he discover that ten days before a 5 shilling postal order had gone missing at the College and his son had been found guilty by the College authorities of stealing and cashing it. When the father pressed the matter further, the Navy decided the Judge Advocate to the Fleet should investigate the case. He did so, but did not call any witnesses or permit any counsel to be present, and his final report agreed with the findings of the Osborne authorities: Archer Shee was guilty of theft. On receipt of this, the First Lord, Reginald McKenna, confirmed that Archer Shee was to be dismissed from the Navy.

However, Archer Shee's father did not let the matter rest there. He took the case to the Civil Court, accusing the Admiralty of breach of contract. This initial case was dismissed, but the father was advised to appeal, and it was decided that, at this point, a case had to be heard in court. For this case, Mr Archer Shee senior secured the assistance of the formidable Sir Edward Carson. As G. Cave explained to the House of Commons on 6 April 1911:

After all, or nearly all, the evidence had been tested and sifted to the bottom, it was at last apparent to the Admiralty, as it had been apparent to others some months before, that no jury in England could come to a conclusion adverse to this young fellow.[180]

The Admiralty counsel then 'threw up' the case.

On 29 July 1910, an agreement was reached between Carson and the Solicitor General that the former cadet 'did not write the name on the postal order, and did not cash it, and, consequently, that he was innocent of the charge'. The matter became such a *cause célèbre* that it was discussed in the House of Commons on no less than three occasions.[181] On the third of these, McKenna explained at some length why he had acted in the way he did. He had not, he said, been 'vindictive':

> If I came to a conclusion upon the evidence brought before me that a boy is guilty of the charge made against him, it is my duty to have him withdrawn from the College for the sake of the 399 other boys. That is my duty, whatever I know, believe, or am told whether a jury would or would not convict. [If I went against College evidence] I should be undermining the authority of the administration of the College, I should be allowed to remain . . . a canker . . . the suspicion . . . would pervade the whole College . . . and would never be lost sight of, through the whole career of the boy charged.[182]

While he was prepared to pay some of the boy's trial expenses, as well as offer an apology, McKenna refused any further concessions. He was determined that, guilty or not guilty, George Archer Shee's brief career in the Royal Navy was over.

The Admiralty, McKenna and the Osborne authorities do not come out particularly well from this. To give the boy no chance at all to begin with, and then only reluctantly investigate the case and finally decide to insist upon Archer Shee's removal from the service was a very poor exercise in public relations.

To leave the Royal Naval College, Osborne under the shadow of the 'Winslow Boy' is not, however, altogether just. The recollections of former cadets are, generally, more cheerful than this story. Most, if not all, felt the College did a good job and that they were well looked after while they were there, both in sickness and in health. Perhaps those who did not enjoy their time there, or did not prosper at Osborne, simply did not respond to questionnaires. But while the College was clearly out of step with what are considered acceptable ideals in education today, it did do a good deal to prepare the boys for the equally strict or stricter discipline they were to experience at Dartmouth and at sea.

CHAPTER FIVE

The Closure of the College

The outbreak of the First World War marked the busiest time for Osborne Naval College. The number of cadets entered per term had increased from between 60 and 80 to over 100 boys, reaching a peak of 122 in the Grenville term of January 1915, though numbers were reduced from this level before the war reached its end (to about 100 boys in the St Vincent term of January 1918 and to only 77 in the Hawke term of September that year). By May 1919 only 37 cadets entered in the Exmouth term but, by that time, it had already been decided the College was to be closed down and the cadets present transferred to Dartmouth.

By the beginning of 1917 the Admiralty had begun to be convinced that the stories of ill health caused by the condition of the buildings and possibly the site of the College had some basis in reality. In April of that year a circular letter was addressed to the Secretary of the Admiralty, T.J. Macnamara, the First and Second Sea Lords, Admirals Sir John Jellicoe and Sir Wester Wemyss – former Captain of Osborne – and the Civil Lord, E.G. Pretyman, by the First Lord, Sir Edward Carson. He stated the general view was that the site and buildings at Osborne were both unhealthy, but added that up until this time it had only been possible to make temporary improvements and decide to rebuild after the war. The reason for raising the matter now, he declared, was not the 'recent serious epidemic' (he was referring to the outbreak of disease which had resulted in six deaths among the cadets), but the continued deteriorating condition of the buildings. He felt that boys were bound to catch infectious illnesses and the nursing care at Osborne could not be better, but a committee to enquire into the overall situation would be a good idea.

To support his case, Carson enclosed a memorandum detailing some of the changes that had taken place at the College. In particular, he noted that in 1905 Dr Lewis Parkes of the Board of Works had decided that the water in the cadets' plunge baths needed to be changed more often and that in 1910 it had been noted that the site was damp. In April of that year Dr Parkes had suggested tarmacing parts of the grounds to give protection against the damp. The Custance Committee had gone so far as to recommend rebuilding, but Parliamentary approval was needed for this. The increase in numbers because of the war had meant additional temporary buildings had been constructed during the conflict and some other improvements had been made.[1]

Admiral S.C. Colvile, Commander-in-Chief at Portsmouth, agreed with this assessment. He believed many of the buildings at the College were in poor condition, and those dormitories built during the war were especially bad. He disapproved of the need for boys to sleep in beds placed on bare concrete floors and also believed the boys were turned out too early in the morning, at 6.15 a.m. [2]

In response to these communications, the Board of Admiralty decided to appoint a committee to consider the whole future of Osborne Naval College. This was a fairly high-powered body, chaired by Pretyman, the Civil Lord. Other members were two surgeon generals, Sir Arthur May and H.D. Rolleston, Rear Admiral Michael Culme Seymour, T. Sims, the Admiralty Director of Works, C.W.F. Young, the Medical Officer of Health for Middlesex, Miss A.G. Morley, the Matron of Weymouth College and, as Secretary, P.D. Thompson, the First Lord's secretary.[3]

The committee first met on 23 April 1917. Its terms of reference were broad. First, it was to investigate what, if anything, could be done to improve the structure and domestic arrangements at Osborne as a temporary measure. It was to bear in mind that it was the intention of the Admiralty to build a new college as soon as possible. Secondly, the committee was to see whether there was anything inherent in the soil or climate of the Isle of Wight that would render it desirable to build a new college elsewhere.

The committee wasted no time and completed its report within six weeks. The members visited the College and interviewed various witnesses, among them the Captain, H.E. Holmes à Court, and the headmaster, Charles Godfrey, as well as Lady Hood, widow of the former Captain of the College who had been killed at Jutland.

The Report was outspoken in its condemnation of the College in terms of both its construction and the regime under which the boys lived. It noted that the removal of the asbestos packing meant that there were 'only two thin layers of fragile uralite between the dormitories and the open air'. The committee felt that Osborne could not be protected totally from epidemics, but that the severity and frequency of these was unusual and was chiefly a result of the structural defects of the dormitories. The committee believed that, whatever improvements were made to them, the dormitories would never be totally satisfactory. But it went further than this. Crowding in dormitories was seen as another problem, while considerable reservations were expressed about the College's regime. The committee believed that there was much – perhaps too much – competition between terms and dormitories, and that so much work was required of cadets that they did not have sufficient time for relaxation or, indeed, sleep. From now on, it recommended, cadets should rise at 7.00 a.m. and have breakfast at 7.30 a.m. Early morning school should be abolished and the 'unofficial' portion of the day's activities, in particular, should be relaxed. However, marching to and from the workshops at Kingston was not seen as an unnecessarily stressful activity.

To try and reduce the number of infectious diseases entering the College, the committee believed cadets' parents should not visit without giving advance notice. It also thought the College servants who lived out might bring in infections, but it did lay one ghost to rest, stating decisively that the pink eye epidemics were not due to the fact the College buildings were on the site of the Osborne House stables. If measles was to be treated as an infectious disease, the committee argued, the number of beds in the isolation hospital should be increased to 104 – but, in any case, the hospital should be extended if the College was to remain where it was.

The committee stated categorically the College's dampness was because of its overall position. It pointed out that the climate of the Isle of Wight was 'relaxing' and it would therefore be better to build a new College elsewhere. The most significant of the committee's conclusions was that no time ought to be lost in building this new college.

Things moved swiftly after this report was presented to the Board of Admiralty. The committee's recommendations were accepted by the Board on 14 June 1917,[4] and in July it decided on a course of action. It was agreed that all cadets at Osborne should be sent to Dartmouth by Christmas 1917, while cadets currently at Dartmouth should be sent to sea to make room for them. The three senior Dartmouth terms would be sent to sea in September 1917 and at the same time the three senior terms at Osborne would move on to Dartmouth. At the end of the next term – Christmas 1917 – the current Dartmouth first term and Osborne fifth term would be sent to sea, and the remaining Osborne cadets sent to Dartmouth. This, the Board agreed, would close Osborne, which was desirable – indeed, it felt 'the sooner this is done the better' – and it would also provide enough officers for 1919.[5]

However, it also meant that boys as young as fifteen were going to be sent to sea, and this in a time of war. Memories of the losses of Dartmouth cadets on the *Aboukir, Hogue,* and *Cressy* in 1914 were still vivid.

On 17 July 1917 another small committee was set up by the Board of Admiralty to look once more at the conditions of the buildings at Osborne. It was chaired by Lord Selborne, and included the Second Sea Lord, the Civil Lord, the Naval Secretary, Rear Admiral A.F. Everett, and E. Packe as Secretary.[6]

This committee stirred up some strong debate in the Admiralty. Selborne argued that the cadets' training programme should be drastically modified to meet the urgent needs of the fleet in 1918–19. He proposed that the existing nine-term training course be cut to six, all of which were to be at Dartmouth. He accepted that this would mean cadets' training and education would suffer and that those affected would not be trained up to the standard of their pre-war counterparts. This, he suggested, could be made up for by courses held at Greenwich after the war. He pointed out that several naval officers felt lack of training was relatively unimportant and six-term cadets would still be very valuable additions to the fleet.

The committee's response to this was not initially favourable. It felt that Osborne and Dartmouth should not be emptied and it would be better to fill gaps in the fleet with special entrants from public schools and temporary officers. The latter, it felt, would be a good idea, since the number of officers required after the war might well be less than the number taken on during the crisis. The committee therefore pressed for the continuation of a nine-term course, although with some modifications. In particular, it suggested that Osborne should only hold 300 cadets, or they could be accommodated at a larger country house or hydropathic establishment.

The Second Sea Lord, Wemyss, however, did not, agree with the committee. He argued that training had to be cut short to fill the gaps in the fleet and the alternatives suggested by the committee were not viable. Public school entry cadets, for example, would take two years to train and the need for officers was urgent. He pressed for the immediate release of the three senior terms at Dartmouth.[7]

But these comments had no immediate effect on Osborne Naval College, as no definite conclusions were reached. However, over the summer of 1917 the future of Osborne became a matter of some public concern. In August Captain Douglas Hall, MP, put seven questions to the Admiralty spokesman in the House of Commons. Among these, he asked whether the College was to be done away with or 'transformed'. The Parliamentary Secretary to the Admiralty, Dr Macnamara, responded that no decision had yet been taken, but Hall replied that he would raise the matter again.[8]

He did so three months later, on 1 November 1917. On this occasion he complained about the Admiralty decision to move the College from the Isle of Wight – if, he declared, such a decision had been taken. Hall was clear in his mind that closing the College was wrong: it would mean scrapping valuable buildings and workshops. If it had been decided to do so, he declared, it was not because the Isle of Wight was unhealthy – in his opinion it was not – and the site was first class for views of ships and developing a naval spirit. There was, he continued, nothing wrong with the Isle of Wight, but there was with some of the College buildings and it was this that the Admiralty was trying to cover up. They were built of uralite, 'which I have put my umbrella through', but Hall felt that, while rebuilding was necessary, it would be cheaper if it was done on the present site.

Civil Lord Pretyman's reply, on this occasion, made it clear that the Admiralty had been considering the future of Osborne, but had not yet decided very much. He said that if and when the College was rebuilt, it would not necessarily be rebuilt at Osborne, but if nowhere better was found then such a rebuilding was possible. But Pretyman did not express himself strongly in favour of the current site. He felt that it was not especially healthy: the soil was clayey sand and damp, and while he did not blame this for the epidemics the College had suffered, medical opinion believed the soil and climate had made them worse. But the Admiralty would not move the College without a good reason. Pretyman concluded in a less than conciliatory manner: there was little public interest in the question and the Admiralty was not bound to choose the Isle of Wight as the site for a new College if a better one could be found elsewhere.[9]

The Admiralty finally reached a decision by December 1917. In that month a new committee was established to enquire into sites for a new college. Various sites were proposed and in March 1918 one was found at Seaford. That the Admiralty took the possibility of moving seriously is clear from the plans and estimates for a new college that were drawn up at this time.[10] But things did not work out as expected, and Osborne was to stay open for another three years.

It is unfortunate that the historical record at this point is not very full. The decision to close the Naval College was put off some time after March 1918, but the reasons for this have not survived. Clearly the

Admiralty had other things on its minds at this point, and winning the war was obviously its top priority. Sir Herbert Richmond felt strongly that naval education, to which he attached such importance, was not a concern of the naval high command:

> I go to Eton to talk to the masters tonight about the Navy and Education. It is disgusting to be doing this and getting nothing changed in the middle of war. Wemyss [by now the First Sea Lord] pigeonholes every paper I send in . . . he says he has no time to deal with them. He has time to go and make speeches in schools. . . .[11]

Richmond was convinced that the education being offered by the Navy was poor, for reasons he explained to Viscount Haldane, former Secretary for War and Lord Chancellor, in February 1919:

> Enough attention is not paid to the need for general education. . . . There is no attempt to develop the reasoning faculties.
> Technical education is begun too young, and at the same time an attempt is made to teach too much. . . . Instruction in the Colleges becomes a mere cram. Development of the mind is sacrificed to learning technical, or quasi-technical, facts.[12]

Whatever the strength of this argument, Richmond could expect little action during the war. But circumstances soon changed. With victory in the war, the Admiralty found itself with far too many naval cadets for the post-war world. The numbers of cadets taken in to Osborne College fell from 85 in May 1918 to a mere 37 a year later, and thereafter stayed at around 40 per term (up to 42 in the last intake, the Grenville term of January 1921).

In March 1920 Captain Leatham of Dartmouth College told his cadets that the present senior term could pass out at full strength, but the other four large Dartmouth and the three large senior Osborne terms would have to be cut by 40 per cent. While 'the departures seem to have been voluntary and not as great as originally intended',[13] more space was made available at Dartmouth.

In these circumstances, in August 1919, the Admiralty had already felt able to declare publicly that it did 'not anticipate that a new College for naval cadets will be required'.[14] When Commander Viscount Curzon enquired four months later why, in that case, the Admiralty still required

£8,550 to spend on Osborne, he was told that the future of the institution was still 'under recommendation', but the money was needed for the comfort and health of those cadets currently at the College.[15]

By this time, however, the future of Osborne had been decided, at least in the mind of one highly influential figure. This was the First Sea Lord, Admiral Earl Beatty. Richmond had lunch with the Admiral in December 1919 and learned of his plans for naval education:

> His idea is to abolish Osborne, get the boys at 13½, give them 3 years at Dartmouth, then a year in a cruiser . . . 'To do the practical work of the ship, I suppose'. 'Yes', says B., 'but they must keep up their mathematics. They'll have to do them both.' Then to go to the sea-going ships as officers a year and a half at sea, then to a College for 2 years.

Richmond felt the combination of practical and theoretical work on the cruiser was 'a blot', but, he added, 'it is an advance'.[16]

Enough anxiety was felt about the future of the College by March 1920 that questions were raised in the House of Commons about it, even before the year's estimates were discussed.[17] The news of impending closure was officially announced by Walter Long, the First Lord, in his speech on the estimates of 17 March. Long explained that, in future, boys would be taken directly into Dartmouth between the ages of 13½ and 14 years – although a small number would be taken in under the terms of special entry between 17½ and 18½ years. He anticipated that no more than 120 cadets (plus about 15 special entry cadets) would be taken on each year. He continued that parents of cadets who withdrew their boys before July would receive a payment of £300 from the Admiralty, or they could stay on, but they would not necessarily secure a naval commission. He argued that Osborne cadets secured a first-class education at a moderate cost and, if they could not go into the Navy, they could use it to go to university or into any profession.

Long also touched on other matters in this speech. In particular, he stressed that the Admiralty was looking into ways to make it possible for boys from elementary schools to become officers, and also for seamen from the lower deck to secure earlier promotion. The new system, he said, would mean cadets would spend three years and eight months at Dartmouth College, eight months in a training cruiser, and then two and a half years as Midshipmen, before proceeding to Greenwich Staff College (or Cambridge University, in some cases).[18]

However, Osborne was not to be closed immediately, and when Lieutenant Commander H. Kenworthy complained about this 'waste of money' (he preferred, he said, to see later entry for cadets and more promotion from the lower deck), Long explained why. The College would have to remain open another twelve months, he stated, because Dartmouth did not yet have the facilities for the extra teachers required, nor the necessary athletic facilities. This exchange opened a quite sharp debate as the Government's plans were attacked by those opposing the whole idea behind the College either because they favoured later entry, or because they would like to see greater democratisation of the entry process, or, like Kenworthy, because they favoured both of these options.[19]

If, however, Osborne was to close, the college at Dartmouth would have to take all cadets entering. Work on the extension of Dartmouth had already begun, even before Long had made his announcement. As early as the summer of 1914, in order to accommodate the larger numbers of cadets coming up from Osborne, as well as the new Special Entry cadets entering, work had started on a new block at Dartmouth. This included three large new gunrooms, an extra dining hall and dormitories for the new cadets, as well as extra laboratories, classrooms and a Masters' common room.

This new work was delayed somewhat by the war – the studies connecting the new buildings with the old were not completed until May 1917 and the first cadets moved in only at the beginning of the next year. (The headmaster received a new, larger study, taking over the old Masters' common room.)[20] The arrival of all the cadets from Osborne, as was now proposed, nevertheless necessitated some additional work. As Long had indicated in his Parliamentary address, most of this involved extensions to the sporting facilities, but some structural modifications were also made: gunrooms in D block, for example, were partitioned, to make room for two terms instead of one. (The number of terms at the College went up from six to eleven when the transfer of the Osborne cadets was completed.)

While the Admiralty adhered firmly to its plans to close the Royal Naval College, Osborne, it did amend slightly the arrangements for the withdrawal of cadets. Long reported to the Commons in July 1920 that King's Cadets and the sons of officers who had served afloat during the war were to receive special treatment. He declared they would not have to be compulsorily withdrawn at the end of their Dartmouth course but they could pass out wherever they were placed, and enter the Navy. Only a small number of cadets were affected, and he added that parents who fell into the latter category who had withdrawn their boys would be allowed to reconsider their decision. [21]

The serious winding down of the College began at the end of 1920. On 13 December an Admiralty minute noted that preparations should be made to pay off the College at the end of the spring term: 'for estimate purposes it is not desired to keep her going any longer after 1st April than can be helped'.[22]

Some ranks and ratings were to be transferred to Dartmouth, but, as the Commander-in-Chief, Portsmouth, was informed a few days later, 'it has been assumed . . . that it will not be necessary to transfer more than one-half of those now employed at Osborne. Every effort, however, should be made to reduce the number as much as possible below that figure.'[23] The Captain of the College, F.A. Marten, announced that the first two terms were leaving for Dartmouth on 12 January 1921.[24] This, as the Commander at Dartmouth, H. Hext Rogers reported at the beginning of February, left three terms, Rodney, Blake and Duncan, and their Lieutenants, J.G. Aitchison, R.B. Cunliffe and J. Harding, to be transferred. Other personnel needed at Dartmouth included Engineer Lieutenant Commander A.C. Whippell, to instruct the junior cadets in engineering, Mr. E. Smith, Commissioned Gunner, for gunnery instruction, four Chief Petty Officer or Petty Officers, one lorry driver and one civilian printer.[25]

By this time a definite date for closure had been fixed: 20 May 1921. Captain C.W.R. Royds, who had succeeded Marten, reported to the Admiralty that he would actually be leaving on 3 May. He added that Paymaster Captain C.M. Luckham, Paymaster Lieutenant Commander Archer, Engineer Commander G.D. Campbell and Commissioned Shipwright T. Longridge would stay longer to close the College accounts. He pointed out that the premises would need a caretaker, as would the machinery and boilers. He made enquiries about the lathes in the Kingston workshops. He was confident, however, that all the 'gear' earmarked for Dartmouth, with the exception of the 'Sick-bay furniture' would have been shipped out by the 20th. The latter was at Park House, where he was staying, and would need another visit by the steamer *Growler* to collect it.[26]

The last term of cadets had been admitted to the College in January 1921. They did not have an especially good time while they were there. Living conditions, for example, were

. . . inclined to be damp and cold in January . . . my recollection is it was all beginning to be a bit run-down because it was the last term and things we had at the beginning of the term disappeared during the term because they'd been moved to Dartmouth, or they'd been shut down or something.

One thing in particular stood out in this former cadet's recollections

. . . the canteen was shut down . . . towards the end of the term there was a terrible disaster because the canteen had been closed down. [Otherwise] I can't remember anything specific except I have the impression that we used to say 'What about so-and-so?'. They said 'No, no, you've got to wait until you get to Dartmouth for that now!'[27]

The Admiralty had no doubt about what to do with these cadets, but a bigger question soon arose over the future of the College buildings. At the beginning of 1921 the Admiralty had asked the Treasury to approve the retrocession of the buildings to the Office of Works. Unfortunately, no response had been received to this enquiry and neither was there a reply to the Admiralty's reminder to the Treasury, sent in April. Accordingly, by the beginning of May, with less than a fortnight to go to the closure date, the Navy's Civil Engineer-in-Chief, L.C.H. Savile, suggested that the Air Ministry or War Office might be interested in acquiring it.[28]

While this matter was being discussed, further consideration was given to the question of caretakers. Paymaster Captain Luckham put in a word for the 'late' Head Cadet Steward, H. Bullimore: 'Bullimore has been employed as Head Cadet Steward for the whole of the time the College has existed, about twenty years and I am sure no more suitable man could be found for the work.'[29]

When arrangements were finalised, however, Bullimore was not among the four men selected. In the end two 'skilled labourers', G. Street and W. Huxtable, were appointed caretakers for the main College buildings and one, W. Tuck, was appointed to take care of the Infectious Hospital building. Finally, G.W. Sims, a 'hired fitter', was appointed caretaker of the Kingston workshops and their machinery.[30]

Commander C.F.R. Cowan, the Commander and last senior officer of the Royal Naval College, Osborne, had one last request before the College finally closed its doors. On 13 May he requested that Paymaster Captain Luckham should be retained until the end of June, to help close the College accounts. His immediate superior, Admiral Sir Somerset Gough-Calthorpe, the Commander-in-Chief, Portsmouth, agreed, provided that Luckham's services were not required elsewhere. The Admiralty, however, refused this request categorically.[31]

The Royal Naval College, Osborne, was formally 'paid off' on the agreed date, 20 May.[32] The Navy's Accountant General had to remind the Admiralty in mid-June, however, that, since Osborne College had closed in May, it was no longer an educational establishment and therefore should not appear on the naval education vote in the estimates.[33]

The effects of this on naval training were limited. All cadets were transferred to Dartmouth, but the only changes to training regulations were minor. All references to Colleges (in the plural) were amended to the singular, and references to joining arrangements for Osborne were deleted. Dress regulations were also amended somewhat.[34] In essence, though, things remained unchanged. The age of joining for cadets remained at 13½ as it had been since 1913, and the syllabus for education was broadly unaltered, although the emphasis on practical engineering was reduced. It remained so for another twenty-five years. Cadets were now to spend three and three-quarter years at Dartmouth and this remained the norm (although 'special entry' at 17½–18½ years for some boys was retained) until 1947. In that year the age of entry was raised to 16 (and the length of the course cut by half), only to be raised again, to 17½, in 1955–6. Under the latest system, the idea of training boys at the same time as they received general education was finally abandoned.

Meanwhile, all ideas of officer 'interchangeability', as adopted by the Cawdor Memorandum, were abandoned. Following discussions in June 1921, the Admiralty announced that Engineer and Executive Officers would once again be confined to their respective branches. As it explained, 'Each side requires a special study and for this reason final separation of the branches is essential.'[35] Dartmouth College, the senior and surviving partner, carried on into the 1920s training solely Executive Officers.[36]

Osborne Royal Naval College had firmly closed its doors in May 1921, but the College buildings remained. The final decision about what to do with them had not been taken when closure came about. The next seventy years witnessed some surprising developments in their history.

The Admiralty had informed the Treasury as early as January 1921 what buildings were available and their value. They were noted as the St Vincent building, of 13,733 square feet, which was described as being of brick, part of Osborne House and containing class- and dining-rooms and the College library, but it was not valued. The Masters' Quarters, of 6,673 square feet, described as 'temporary' and as being worth £9,682. The lecture rooms were of 2,030 feet, brick-built and worth £2,945. The 'Nelson' gym was of 11,370 square feet, temporary and worth £16,498. There were three dormitories with thirty beds, with a total area of 11,748 feet and worth £17,046, and nine with thirty-six beds, with a total area of 36,609 square feet, and worth £53,121 – both of these groups of buildings were of 'temporary' construction. The hospital, with sisters' quarters, of 43,850 square feet, was brick-built and contained fourteen beds in two isolation rooms. It was deemed to be worth £6,362. There was also a gym additional to Nelson, of 3,834 square feet, brick and worth £5,563. The Officers' Quarters comprised sixteen rooms and servants' quarters, smoking and ante rooms and a large mess room, of 7,209 square feet in total, of temporary construction and worth £19,460. The Captain's house consisted of four reception rooms, a kitchen, offices, nurseries and bedrooms, was built of brick, was 2,550 square feet and worth £3,700. The cold storage and meat store was of 600 square feet and valued at £870. The brick-built lavatories and water tower of 8,730 square feet was worth £1,266. The servants' quarters were made up of two large dormitories, mess rooms, bathroom and lavatories, covered 5,027 square feet, were built of brick and valued at £7,294. There was a cricket pavilion of 1,548 square feet, which was temporary, and a large tuck-shop and refreshment rooms, visitors' room and lavatories, worth £2,246. Petty Officers' quarters consisted of one large dormitory, twelve bedrooms, two dining halls, a kitchen and offices. These were built of brick, covered 32,860 square feet and were worth £4,768. Seamen and marines' barracks comprised three blocks, each of 17,300 square feet and providing accommodation for twenty-four men, corporals' rooms, stores, lavatories, etc. These were 'temporary' and worth £2,510. Finally, a canteen for these servicemen, made up of a tap room and bar, cookhouse, stores etc., recreation and writing rooms, bathrooms and several small rooms, was provided. This was of 1,840 square feet, 'temporary' and worth £2,669.

In all, the College buildings were valued at £147,000 (although in fact these figures add up to £156,000). The 'temporary' buildings were somewhat optimistically described as 'substantial' timber-framed rooms of uralite and extra concrete blocks. The Admiralty informed the Treasury that this valuation was based on pre-war figures. To it should be added £15,000 for the larger Infectious Hospital and Sewerage Works, and £31,000 for the workshops at Kingston. This, again, was at pre-war values: all three figures, the Admiralty contended, should be doubled to get their true 1921 worth.[37]

The Treasury tried to get things moving. It asked the Office of Works whether the Air Ministry would be interested in the property. The Office of Works declared itself at a loss: 'I have no idea what the Government intend to do with the Naval College buildings,' but it thought they were of no use to the Air Ministry. After an inspection, the Air Ministry agreed with this: the site was 'entirely unsuitable' for the RAF.[38]

There matters appear to have rested until after the closure of the College. In October, basing its work on a long survey of the College drawn up by a local estate agent the month before, the Office of Works submitted an extensive report on the College to the Treasury. The report listed the permanent buildings of the College and declared that options for the future were limited. It stated that it would cost 'not less than £10,000' to destroy the temporary buildings and noted that the buildings could be disposed of by adding them to the Barton Manor estate – though no purchaser was likely to want them. It might be possible to dispose of the playing fields and the buildings as separate lots – but, again, the market appeared limited, so perhaps a holiday camp could be set up. In the report's opinion 'undoubtedly the most desirable solution' would be to hold on to the buildings and let a Government department make use of them: 'it seems incredible' that no use could be made of these complete and equipped buildings. But, the report went on, the Captain's house should comprise a separate lot (it would be a good Preparatory School or similar) and 'at present I cannot see what possible use can be made of the St Vincent building or other permanent buildings'.[39]

In response to this report, Sir John Oakley of the Crown Lands Department, submitted his own views on the future of the buildings. He believed they should be kept in repair, but should also be made to produce income (such as letting the racquet court). He felt the Isolation Hospital should be handed over to the Local Authority, in which case the sewerage farm could also be given up. Most importantly, he suggested that there was 'no reason' to retain the Kingston workshops: 'It appears the best thing to do is to try and dispose of them as soon as possible for some commercial purpose.'[40] The Office of Works agreed with this summary in January 1922 and two months later the Admiralty agreed that it would hand over the control of the property to the Office of Works from 1 April 1922.[41] On that date, therefore, the direct involvement of the Royal Navy with the Osborne Estate came to an end.

However, the rather sorry story of the remaining Royal Naval College buildings does not finish then. Various ideas circulated in 1923 and 1924, including proposals for their use as a College or as a convalescent camp (though the latter idea was 'definitely . . . abandoned' by December 1924).[42] By summer 1925 the Office of Works proposed the demolition of all buildings except for the St Vincent building. Lecture rooms, the Captain's house and adjoining furniture store, two water towers, the racquets court and the cricket pavilion should all be demolished, at a cost of £7,400.[43] While the Office requested Treasury permission to go ahead, in the last quarter of 1925, further proposals were received to use the buildings as a convalescent home for elementary school children or as a hospital for paraplegic soldiers, though the Ministry of Pensions declared it was 'absolutely unsuitable' for this purpose.[44]

But the Treasury did not want to spend money demolishing the College if it could make money by letting it. Accordingly, in February 1926, it agreed to the 'Allnatt plan'. By this, Messrs Allnatt Ltd would lease the College buildings as a holiday camp. It would cost them nothing in the first year, £250 in the second year, £500 in the third year and £750 p.a. thereafter. The negotiations were carefully carried out in the summer and autumn of 1926, but by November some doubts were being expressed about whether Allnatts really did intend to set up their camp.

During 1927, however, Allnatts did lease the old Isolation Hospital, but by the end of the year the Board of Works had decided that unless the other buildings could be let, the 'temporary structures' would have to be demolished. In May 1928 three dormitory buildings were let to Allnatts for use in the summer of 1929 as a holiday camp. In that year, too, the British Red Cross Society leased some of these buildings. In the summer of 1930 Allnatts went so far as to offer to buy the whole site, but only if they had direct access to the sea. In 1931 various parties declared an interest in Osborne. They include Allnatts, who wanted by this date to use the site as a college for foreign university students (especially Austrian and German); the Ministry of Agriculture; the Prisons Commission (for use as a borstal); the War Office (for use as an army educational centre) and the training ship *Arethusa*. Unfortunately, all of these proposals came to nothing.[45] The British Red Cross Society maintained a lease on some of the College buildings until 1934, when the Crown Lands Department agreed that they should be demolished.[46]

By the end of 1933, however, the Office of Works had already decided the time had come for the temporary College buildings to go. According to the Office, the buildings had been:

derelict ever since they were vacated by the Admiralty in 1922.

Continuous efforts have been made to find a use for them . . . their condition has gradually deteriorated and for some years now they have been a blot on the Osborne Estate. What is more, so long as the buildings remain, they form a steady temptation to anybody who is out to house some quasi-public concern . . . and the sooner that risk is out of the way, the better.

The Public Accounts Committee of the House of Commons had twice proposed demolition and in January the Treasury had agreed. The Captain's house, it was decided 'from a letting point of view . . . is a hopeless proposition', and it would be best to demolish this as soon as possible '& so be rid of what . . . can only be described as a white elephant'.[47] Demolition began on 6 October 1933.[48] The King, George V, agreed to the demolition of the Captain's house, four days later, on 10 October.[49] By March 1935 all demolition contracts had been 'completed'.[50]

All of the College that remained by this date was the former stable block (the 'St Vincent' building of the College) and the foundations to the temporary dormitories. Two years later, however, the Governor of Osborne House reported that something had to be done about the latter. Some shrubs had been planted to hide them, but, he stated, the foundations remained visible, a 'blot on the landscape'. A year later, the situation was little better and no improvement was reported by January 1939.[51] At this point, however, with the renewed likelihood of war, new ideas were put forward for the use of this site. It was suggested in May 1939 that a 'hutted camp' for the Royal Naval Special Reserve could be built at Osborne – presumably on the foundations of the dormitories – but within a month, this proposal was reported dead.[52]

But the surviving buildings were put to use in the war. In June 1940 the aircraft manufacturers Saunders Roe requested the use of the old stable block to help their production. In September they moved in, beginning a rather troubled association with the convalescent home in Osborne House and (until they moved out in mid-1942) the Royal Army Medical Corps. On 5 May 1942 the buildings were damaged in an air raid, but the company remained at the College, despite some persistent doubts about the healthiness or otherwise of the site. The Saunders Roe lease was renewed for five years in November 1944.[53]

In 1944–5 further attempts to destroy the foundations of the temporary buildings were made but this, too, was not properly carried out because of the expense. A further use for this part of the site was found in July 1945 when 100 German prisoners of war were housed there (until 1948). In August 1946 the foundations were again being discussed and proposals made for planting trees on the site.[54]

In 1947 Saunders Roe secured a lease on the stable block for twenty-one years.[55] This led to a series of disputes in the mid-1950s, when it became apparent that Saunders Roe had been encroaching on the Osborne Estate and the land was needed for new car-parking facilities.[56] It emerged that the Crown could not lease this land to the company, and in any case the 1947 lease was not legally valid. After discussion, it was agreed, in 1956, that Saunders Roe could be granted a new lease for twenty-two years. They and their successor companies, Westland Aircraft Ltd and the British Hovercraft Corporation Ltd, then remained in possession until 1987. In this year the entrance block to the stables was listed as a Grade II structure. Between 1988 and 1991 a furniture manufacturer occupied the building, which is currently under-utilised.[57]

Seventy years before this, in the summer of 1921, it was deemed that Osborne Royal Naval College had served its purpose. Now that the new buildings at Dartmouth were complete and the number of officer cadets had fallen so much that there was room for them all there, there was no need for the junior – temporary – establishment. Quite why closure had been decided on in 1917 and then delayed is not clear; perhaps it can be best put down to the heavier demands of the war. By the time consideration of the future could be resumed, the realities of the situation had changed, and this was appreciated in good time by the Admiralty. Closure of Osborne was the only sensible decision to take.

What to do with the Osborne buildings thereafter was another matter, but one which was soon taken off the Admiralty's hands. At the time of writing, the future of the surviving College feature on the estate – the stable block – remains uncertain.

But, if the College had served its purpose, the question of whether or not it was a success – whether or not it achieved the aims of its founders – remains to be answered.

Conclusion

After a brief life of less than eighteen years, the Royal Naval College, Osborne, formally closed its doors on 20 May 1921. Had it achieved the aims of its founders?

The closure in itself does not, of course, indicate that it had 'failed'. The terms for the recruitment of junior officers remained unchanged by the closure, as did the form of cadets' training. This is as clear an indication as possible that the Admiralty considered Osborne College was a success and it fitted boys well for their future as naval officers. The abandonment of the 'interchangeability' of officers for another generation might suggest, however, that the new educational and training scheme as a whole was not viewed as a total success in many influential circles in the Navy.

More recent opinion has also tended to view the College as a success, particularly when taken in context with the course at Dartmouth. Messrs Davies and Grove offer this assessment of the course at Dartmouth after Cyril Ashford had moved there, which might be applied to Osborne:

> mathematics and science, supplemented by considerable practical engineering instruction, added together to create a grounding in applied science unique in contemporary secondary education. . . . The humanities were not forgotten, however. Indeed, the attempt to develop the intellects of the boys through the medium of Modern Languages, History and English rather than the Classics was as novel as the technological implications of the Royal Naval College course.[1]

Looking solely at the junior college, E.A. Hughes offers another opinion. He argues that:

> within two years Osborne had its full complement [and they] had achieved the aims of its founders – to make it a naval public school. From the outset [he continues] one of the main aims of Osborne was clearly defined and constantly borne in mind – the *education* of cadets.[2]

But these high opinions were not shared by all those who attended the College. Indeed, one former cadet, who went there in 1917, has gone on record to express very negative feelings about his time at Osborne:

> I always feel completely uneducated in the presence of public school men . . . and bitterly regret that I was diverted at the very last moment from Eton, for which I was destined, to that horrible collection of cardboard huts known as Royal Naval College, Osborne. The educational system was the worst that could possibly have been devised. It was not a good preparation for a naval career, while as an introduction to everyday life it was utterly useless.[3]

This, of course, is in large measure a reflection of his obvious and lasting disappointment at being sent to Osborne rather than Eton.

Those former cadets whose experiences form the main part of this work had some mixed views about the College. Most of them clearly had some affection for the institution. Whether or not they thoroughly enjoyed their time there, they had all stayed in contact with term-mates. Most had attended a ceremony to mark the unveiling of a memorial plaque by the Countess Mountbatten on 14 August 1985.

It is, therefore, not unexpected that the majority of their recollections should be of a more or less positive nature. Some, even if their careers did not prosper in the Navy, felt that the College served its purpose

> Very well indeed. Mainly I think from the disciplinary side, and if one took the trouble to observe how other senior people controlled those under them, it was bound to be beneficial. It resulted in helping me for instance to run a factory, 'cos I was in the aircraft industry and . . . I put down the success that I had to my original initial training.[4]

Another former cadet thought that:

> . . . I think that it gave us the background . . . we were trained I think possibly to be much more ingenious than the present day requires . . . they did a very good job. Take off my hat to the lot of them.[5]

A third believed that:

> in the circumstances, it was fine – you've got to go back to what it had been in the *Britannia*, where the conditions were awful. . . .

Everything moved so far. But it served its purpose at the time. . . . At the time it was excellent.[6]

A number of cadets believed that it was this combination of the initial two years' training at Osborne with the next two years at Dartmouth, as well as later experience, that made the time spent at Osborne of particular value. One noted that the College equipped him for his later career in the Navy 'very well', but he went on to point out that

> it had to be followed up by Dartmouth. You couldn't have . . . gone to sea from Osborne, but by the time you'd finished at Dartmouth you had quite a good knowledge of navigation, astronomical navigation and trigonometry, all the things you needed for that and quite a lot really to prepare you. The next step was to get to sea and try it out but I'm sure that Osborne was in many ways more valuable than, you might say, than Dartmouth certainly was for me. It got you onto the rails, onto the lines which you had to pursue from then onwards, you saw the point.[7]

This was reiterated by another former cadet, who believed that 'altogether it served very well indeed – linked with Dartmouth – because it was almost a continuous movement just from one to the other . . . the training was very good indeed,'[8] and by a third who felt that

> it was a good general education and it was followed up by Dartmouth, of course, and then followed up at Greenwich later on in all the courses that we did as sub-lieutenant. I think Osborne was extremely good. . . .[9]

One cadet thought, however, that while Osborne served well 'As a prep school, yes, you got more when you went to Dartmouth and when you went to sea at the age of fifteen as I did. . . .'[10] Another stressed the point that

> it would be wrong to try and consider the education at either Osborne alone or Dartmouth in isolation because so much of our technical training came later at the gunnery school, HMS *Excellent*, the torpedo school, HMS *Vernon*. If you take all these together I think they were very suitable but if you try and take Osborne in isolation it's not a very fair picture.[11]

One former cadet remarked that in his view Osborne had served its purpose well, but he perceived this in a somewhat different way to his contemporaries:

. . . this I must say and I do remember very clearly, I was utterly filled with tremendous pride about the whole thing. We were in the middle of a war, training to go and fight the enemy. This is a little boy's thoughts after all and I was wearing this magnificent uniform, the King's uniform, and the traditions of the Navy were being explained to us. We were learning all the tricks of the trade. I was filled with awe, yes, but pride as well, enormous pride. I'm quite sure that ever since I've felt exactly the same. It must have fitted us well because it enthused us all the time.[12]

Several cadets believed the main aim of the College was to introduce them to the rigours of naval discipline and the true ambience of naval life:

I've no doubt it broke the ice and it certainly taught one discipline and I think it was, one was always struggling to make good: probably a lot of the glamour had worn off by the time one got to Dartmouth. No, I think I was very grateful for the opportunity of being there and the interest that was taken in one.[13]

There was no doubt that in this sense, Osborne succeeded, especially – ironically enough – during the years of the First World War, when the naval Term Lieutenants were temporarily replaced in this capacity by civilian masters. One cadet, who entered in September 1917, felt Osborne fitted him well for a naval career, but

in a very pleasant and friendly fashion. It was rather quietly and gently into what was a pretty strict discipline in the Navy at sea. It was a strict discipline and fairly heavily enforced, certainly when you were a Midshipman.[14]

Another cadet, who spent all his time at Osborne while the war was on, noted:

It really did fit you into a naval atmosphere as the masters there were very good at that. They'd been at Osborne for quite a long time so they also knew the naval atmosphere because they'd been there when there were naval officers as term masters so they drilled it into us.[15]

But, even if this introduction to naval life was viewed with favour by some cadets, others still had reservations about it:

> I think Osborne was a very good training for a service career because one needed strict obedience. 'Their's not to reason why, their's but to do and die.' That is the ethic in naval life. The Commander-in-Chief in charge of a fleet was the only man . . . who decided what to do. . . . I think looking back on the training we were turned out rather like a lot of sausages out of a machine because in my day when Britannia ruled the waves . . . until a person became a Commander, which was a very high rank to attain . . . you really couldn't think for yourself very much. . . .[16]

and another believed the training had a particular and rather negative effect on the boys:

> The discipline was admirable but it was a limited outlook on life and I think one effect was that when we left Osborne and later Dartmouth we were younger for our age than many other boys from schools which had a wider outlook. I think that was rather marked. We were rather young for our age, matured later.[17]

The general tenor of views about the value of the training provided at Osborne, however, was a cautious one among the former cadets. Even some of those who saw the College, overall, as a success, had some criticisms to make of it. One commented that

> there were one or two things that were a bit out of date. Some of those bends and hitches and messing around with dummy models and laying out anchors and that sort of thing, they were all a little bit outdated by the time we got to sea.[18]

Another thought that

> generally speaking . . . it fitted one very well for a service career. I think perhaps my main criticism might be that it tended to suppress initiative and possibly desirably. I think perhaps it built up a very strong fear of doing anything wrong which I think was not very good

for one in many ways but this again must very much depend on the personality of the cadet concerned. . . .[19]

A third remarked how it was necessary to remember that

in those days it's very different from these days, you were being brought up to be a naval officer and nothing else. You had one language, you had seamanship, in those days they were thinking about mixing up the whole engineering department with the executive department and we did a third of our time in engineering. You've got to remember we were only thirteen years old when we started and I suppose it is true to say we were brought up . . ., in the language of those days, in a rather narrow groove with the object of being naval officers and officers in ships with engines.[20]

These two criticisms – of the narrow outlook that was being instilled into future naval officers and of the suppression of initiative – were commented on by others, too. One former cadet declared that

in my opinion . . . by and large the Osborne-Dartmouth experiment was a failure . . . because they were trying to do something which was incompatible with the British character really. They were trying to form a caste, a rigid, inward-looking caste of naval officers of a particular type . . . the kind of questions they asked in order to decide who was to be selected to enter depended upon questions about their fathers as much as anything. . . . In other words they were drawing from the gentry class and then creating a narrower caste within that caste which was to be the naval officer. . . .[21]

Another, whose naval career did not prosper, was even more outspoken about the rigidity being instilled into the young cadets:

This is only my own idea, I may be quite wrong, that I couldn't help getting. I have always had the impression that while one was at Osborne and Dartmouth [the] Royal Navy were absolutely determined to turn out a sealed pattern of naval officer. That was undoubtedly, quite appallingly one might say, efficient, but on the other hand it did not encourage initiative and I would say the initiative was . . . as far as I was concerned . . . almost stamped out of me at Osborne. . . .[22]

This view was more or less repeated by another cadet, who did, however, follow a successful career in the Royal Navy:

I couldn't criticise the tuition at Osborne but taking Osborne and Dartmouth together as a whole it was terribly specialised for the Navy and the humanities, as the Admiralty called them, weren't much bothered with. There was no drawing class. You weren't taught a lot about English and literature. It was a crash course for making you suitable to be a midshipman at sea at the end of it. When you got to sea you did two and half years as a midshipman and that is when you really became a professional naval officer at a very young age compared to other navies. I'm sure you could say that naval officers of that period were narrowly educated, the system was designed to produce a standard article which wasn't likely to fail, nor did it, in the war afterwards. But of course you could also say that it didn't encourage the brilliant and . . . it was discouraging on original thought. I think that would be a fairly generally accepted criticism of the standard naval product of my generation which was always adequate but perhaps lacked, didn't encourage, the more brilliant.[23]

One more criticism expressed by several cadets concerned the age at which boys began their career at Osborne, and the consequences of this. As one noted:

I think we were all much too young in the first place and I think much more time was devoted to general education which you could have got anywhere rather than to grounding in naval things. One would have been better off if one had had a bit more boat work or lived on board a ship, for example, for a few weeks. No, I don't think the grounding was particularly good there. Much better at Dartmouth. But I think you were really too young to appreciate the whole thing. You went straight on from a prep school to Osborne and it was from the educational point of view very much the same, just a slightly higher standard in everything, I suppose, a bit broader. But there wasn't a great deal of naval training in it, I don't think.[24]

Another cadet criticised the whole notion of recruiting boys at such an early age:

Of course, they abandoned the whole thing in the end, this whole
business of an early intake . . . it was an experiment and I think it was
not a good experiment. I think they'd have done much better never
to have started this system of taking boys at thirteen but taken them
out of secondary school, public school or otherwise, grammar school
or whatever at the age of eighteen as they finally did.[25]

Perhaps it is not surprising that not all of the former cadets had
particularly vivid recollections of their time at Osborne or the value – or
otherwise – of it to them in their naval careers. More than one of them
did not spend much time in the service: 'Of course I decided to leave the
Navy [at] the end of our time at Dartmouth but . . . I can't blame the
training at Osborne for my decision.'[26]

Others found it difficult to comment on the value of the overall
experience. One thought that it was

very difficult to say. One got used to doing what one was told . . . but
how it affected my future I don't really know. It must have had a
deep down effect somewhere . . . but I don't think one's future was
really very much motivated by what one did as a cadet. . . .[27]

Another was more cautious still: '. . . on the whole I think Osborne was
quite good training for a naval officer as far as I could see.'[28] One cadet,
however, who only spent one term at Osborne before its closure, expressed
well some views on the significance of the College in his naval experience:

It was a beginning. It was the beginning of 34 years in the Navy. One
has to start somewhere and it was the beginning and it didn't appear
to change very much when one went to Dartmouth. . . . I can't think
of anything in particular worth mentioning as the end of an era in
naval training.[29]

Did Osborne Naval College do its job successfully and does it deserve this
rather negative obituary? The criticisms of the College, raised at the time
and repeated in the recollections of the survivors over sixty-five years
later, were various. Perhaps the most significant was that concerning the
age at which cadets were recruited. By bringing in cadets at the age of
thirteen and three-quarters or even younger, the College was landed with
two distinct tasks. The most important of these, at least in the eyes of the

naval authorities, was training them in the ways and duties of Royal Navy officers. But this, in large measure, was incompatible with the second task, which was the wider education of the boys. This difficulty was compounded by the desire under the Selborne and Cawdor schemes to train all potential officers in all subjects, including elements of engineering. Trying to cope with all of these duties in two years was not at all easy and something had to be sacrificed: this, it seems, was general education. But this difficulty could have been avoided by recruiting cadets from among older boys, and abandoning some elements in the College syllabus. Taking them at such an early age did not solve the problem of 'crowding' in the curriculum. As was suggested at the time, it surely would have been preferable to wait until boys had completed their schooling (or, indeed, university undergraduate studies) before teaching them naval discipline and some of the intricacies of engineering.

One other issue that was never satisfactorily tackled by the College – despite the effort devoted to it in both the Osborne and Dartmouth curricula – was the question of recruiting sufficient numbers of Engineer Officers. With the closure of the Keyham Engineering College and concentration of all officer cadet training on the Osborne/Dartmouth sites, it became a matter of urgency to fill the Engineering Officer vacancies in the fleet with cadets from these institutions. Fisher had hoped, of course, that the new common-entry scheme of officer recruitment, combined with the reduction in the numbers of Engineer Officers needed because of the improvements in the training of engineer artificers and their increasing use in the fleet engine-rooms, would solve this long-standing problem.

The Osborne curriculum was therefore designed to include considerable amounts of practical engineering work, the intention being to entice cadets from the College into this branch of the service. But the fact remained that, whatever the authorities did to encourage the boys at Osborne, too few of them volunteered for the Engineering Branch. The early age of recruitment and the practical engineering work undertaken – whatever Wemyss and others may have hoped – simply did not have the desired effect. In the end, the Admiralty was forced to recognise this. With the First World War concluded and drastic reductions in the size of the fleet, it became possible to revise the officer training scheme once again. The decision to return to separate entry for the majority of engineering cadets – signalled by the reopening of the Engineering College at Keyham – marked the albeit temporary end of one of the key elements in the Fisher/Selborne scheme and in the *raison d'être* of the Royal Naval

College, Osborne. This was the entry and training of all future naval officers – Executive and Engineer – under one common system. As the hoped-for source of all the Engineer Officers needed for the Royal Navy, therefore, it has to be said that Osborne was not really a success.

Introducing the boys to naval discipline would appear to have been the primary aim of the Osborne authorities. Recollections tend to suggest that, in this, they were successful: perhaps, indeed, they were too successful. The extent to which the inculcation of discipline stymied the development of initiative in the young cadets was – and is – of course, a matter for debate, but the general opinion is that it did do this to an undesirable degree. Some of the more general issues of command and control would presumably remain ingrained in the cadets' minds and later in their career might hinder the adoption of independent ideas when urgent and serious decisions were called for.

It is perhaps going a little too far to suggest that the authorities sought to create a 'caste' of naval officer, but they did seek to create a uniformly recognisable one and in this they were successful. The Osborne cadets, recruited from a particular type of boy, usually from a particular background, were moulded, eventually, into a particular type of naval officer. Osborne, of course, did not achieve this unaided, it served as a beginning and was rounded off by two more years at Dartmouth and then time spent on the training cruisers.

The Osborne naval cadets performed well in two world wars, and in the many other duties required of them. They were trained to carry out particular duties and they did so in an efficient and, sometimes, exceptional manner. Not all rose to become Admirals of the Fleet, or First Naval Lords, but more than one achieved these distinctions. The training at Osborne Naval College had its weaknesses, as did the education provided. But the Admiralty believed it was a success and most of the former cadets held to this opinion, to a greater or lesser extent. Given the limitations of time and place, the Osborne experiment might be counted as a qualified success. It deserves to be remembered, as do the numerous boys who attended it and who went on from it to a variety of successful careers and tasks, one of which was to help in the completion of this history.

Notes

Chapter One

1 Full details of these early days are to be found in H.W. Dickinson, 'Britannia at Portsmouth and Portland', Mariner's Mirror, 84 (1998), pp. 434–43.

2 E.L. Davies and E.J. Grove, The Royal Naval College, Dartmouth: Seventy-five Years in Pictures (Portsmouth, 1980), pp. 9–10.

3 S.W.C. Pack, Britannia at Dartmouth (London, 1966), p. 135.

4 Davies and Grove, Dartmouth, p. 10.

5 Pack, Britannia, pp. 135–6.

6 Davies and Grove, Dartmouth, p. 10.

7 Pack, Britannia, pp. 42–3, 60.

8 'Preliminary and final reports of the Committee appointed by the Lords Commissioners of the Admiralty, to inquire into and report on the education of naval executive officers', Aug. 1885; 23 June 1886. P[ublic] R[ecord] O[ffice], ADM 116/863.

9 Davies and Grove, Dartmouth, p. 10.

10 Life on Board HMS Britannia (London, c. 1904), pp. 19–21.

11 Pack, Britannia, p. 135.

12 Memorandum, enclosed in Fisher to Selborne, letter, 25 Feb. 1902, copy in Fisher papers, Churchill Archive, Churchill College, Cambridge, FISR 1/3, 90, ff. 45–50.

13 Earl of Selborne, 'Memorandum dealing with the entry, training, and employment of officers and men of the Royal Navy and Royal Marines', 16 Dec. 1902, issued as a P[arliamentary] P[aper], 1902 [Cd 1385] LXI, p. 675.

14 See [A.W. Ewing], Director of Naval Education, The Entry and Training of Naval Officers (HMSO, London, 1914), pp. 32–7.

15 Selborne, 'Memorandum', 16 Dec. 1902, p. 5.

16 Capt. J.A. Grindle, interview, 17 Dec. 1987, I[mperial] W[ar] M[usuem], S[ound] A[rchive], 10055/1/1/; Capt. K.L. Harkness, interview, 15 Sept. 1987, ibid., 9933/1/1; Capt. D.M.L. Neame, interview, 12 Aug. 1987, ibid., 9872/2/1.

17 Capt. G.A. French, interview, 19 Aug. 1987, ibid., 9899/1/1.

18 Adm. J.D.N. Ham, interview, 14 Dec. 1987, ibid., 10053/2/1.

19 Cdr. L. Gowlland, interview, 11 Aug. 1987, ibid., 9871/1/1; Cdr. H.L. Jenkins, interview, 25 Aug. 1987, ibid., 9896/2/1.

20 Earl of Selborne, Report, 23 July 1917; Board of Admiralty, memorandum, July 1917, PRO ADM 1/8520/98.

21 Cadets who entered in 1918 reported spending up to six terms at Osborne,(Lt. Cdr. J. Cobb, interview, 18 Aug. 1987, IWM SA 9900/2/1). This was reduced to five as terms were progressively moved out to go to Dartmouth (Brig. C.W.P. Richardson, interview, 13 Aug. 1987, ibid., 9873/1/1). Interestingly, the Gieves publication How to Become a Naval Officer makes no mention of any of these changes whatsoever (see, for example, 1916 edition).

22 Earl of Selborne, memorandum, 16 Dec. 1902, pp. 3–5.

23 Capt. H.W. Richmond to Adm. W.H. Henderson, letter, copy, 7 June 1902, Richmond papers, N[ational] M[aritime] M[useum], NMM/RIC/14/2; Richmond to Julian Corbett, letter, copy, 31 Dec. 1902, ibid.

24 Adm. Sir Reginald Bacon, From 1900 Onward (London, 1940), p. 90.

25 Hansard's Parliamentary Debates, fourth series, vol. 119, 16 Mar. 1903, cols. 865–939.

26 Ibid., vol. 122, 8 May 1903, cols. 168–91.

27 See, for example, speeches by C. Robertson, Sir Edward Grey, Sir John Gorst, *ibid.*, vol. 130, 1, 2 Mar. 1904, cols. 1382–5, 1407, 1501–3.

28 E.G. Pretyman, 1 Mar. 1905, *ibid.*, vol. 142, cols. 442–3.

29 [Sir John Fisher], Memorandum on 'The Extension of the New Scheme of Entry and the Training of Naval Officers', [*c.* 1905] Fisher papers, FISR 8/29.

30 Sir John Fisher, Memorandum, 'State Education in the Navy', strictly private and secret, [*c.* 1905], pp. 1, 3, 4. Fisher papers, P 3/06.

31 A letter giving Selborne's views to an unnamed correspondent dated 9 Jan. 1903, is preserved among Fisher's papers, P/206.

32 Fisher, Memorandum, 'The Extension of the New Scheme', [*c.* Sept. 1905], Fisher papers, P3/06.

33 Capt. R.E. Wemyss, 'Remarks', [*c.* Sept. 1905], Appendix A to *ibid.*

34 Capt. W.E. Goodenough, 'Remarks', [*c.* Sept. 1905], Appendix B to *ibid.*

35 Engineer-Commander H.W. Metcalfe, 'Remarks', [*c.* Sept. 1905], Appendix C to *ibid.*

36 Engineer-Commander C.J. Taylor, 'Remarks', [*c.* Sept. 1905], Appendix D to *ibid.*

37 C. Ashford, 'Remarks', [*c.* Sept. 1905], Appendix E to *ibid.*

38 Fisher, Memorandum, 'Extension of the New Scheme', [*c.* Sept. 1905], p. 3 *ibid.*

39 Fisher, Memorandum, 'Entry and Training of Officers of the Navy', n.d., Fisher papers, FISR P4/08.

40 Fisher, Memorandum, 'State Education in the Navy', pp. 5–7, *ibid.*, P 3/06.

41 Bellairs spoke against the changes four times in 1906, on 1, 5, 21 Mar. and 24 May, *Hansard*, fourth series, vol. 152, cols. 1345–52; vol. 153, cols. 48–9; vol. 154, cols. 352, 361 and vol. 157, cols. 1461–71. He also spoke on 14 Mar. 1907, *ibid.*, vol. 171, cols. 261–2 and on 8 July 1908, *ibid.*, vol. 191, cols. 1694–1703.

42 In the Navy Estimates debate on 7 Mar. 1907, *ibid.*, vol. 170, esp. cols. 1015–82 and 8 July 1908, *ibid.*, vol. 191, cols. 1683–1739.

43 22 July 1912, *ibid.*, fifth series, vol. 41, col. 853.

44 See, for example, Churchill's written reply to Hall, 28 Nov. 1912, *ibid.*, vol. 44, col. 1496; and oral answer of 19 Dec. 1912, *ibid.*, vol. 45, col. 1685.

45 Adm. Lord Charles Beresford, 27 Mar. 1913, *ibid.*, vol. 50, col. 1925.

46 W.S. Churchill, 26 Mar., 10 Apr. 1913, *ibid.*, vol. 50, cols. 1925–6; vol. 51, col. 1361.

47 E.A. Hughes, *The Royal Naval College, Dartmouth* (London, 1950), pp. 41–3.

48 J.A. Ewing, 'The new scheme of naval training' in Gieves' *How to Become a Naval Officer* (1907 edn), pp. 54–5.

49 Pack, *Britannia*, pp. 142–3.

50 Davies and Grove, *Dartmouth*, pp. 12–13.

51 *Ibid.*

52 *Ibid.*, pp. 11, 13.

53 Sir Sidney Lee, *King Edward the Seventh: a biography* (2 vols., London, 1925–7), II, 20.

54 Osborne Note Book, PRO WORK 15/2.

55 *Hansard*, fourth series, vol. 120, cols. 590–2, 30 Mar. 1903.

56 Osborne Note Book, PRO WORK 15/2.

57 Lady Wester Wemyss, ed., *The Life and Letters of Lord Wester Wemyss, GCB, CMG, MVO, Admiral of the Fleet* (London, 1935), p. 67.

58 Details can be found in a volume entitled 'Lighting at Osborne', PRO WORK 15/29.

59 Hughes, *Dartmouth*, pp. 26–7.

60 *Illustrated London News*, No. 3362, p. 444.

61 Pack, *Britannia*, p. 149.

62 Wemyss to ?, letter, 9 Sept. 1903, Lady Wester Wemyss, *Wemyss*, p. 72; Wemyss to Fisher, letter, 16 Sept. 1903, inclosure in report on visit to Portsmouth Dockyard, and Royal Naval College, Osborne, 12 Sept. 1903, Fisher papers, FISR 8/14, p. 9.

63 C.E. Ashford to Fisher, letter, 22 Sept. 1903, in *ibid.*, pp. 10–11.

64   A Retired Naval Officer, 'Life at Osborne' in *How to Become a Naval Officer* (London, rev. edn 1916), pp. 29–30.

65   [Ewing], *Entry and Training*, p. 19.

66   *Ibid.*, p. 20.

67   Fisher, Memorandum, 'Visit to Portsmouth Dockyard and Royal Naval College, Osborne, 12 Sept. 1903', Fisher papers, FISR 8/14.

68   Office of Works to Admiralty, letter, 5 Jan. 1906, PRO WORK 15/1.

69   Correspondence on all of this is to be found in PRO WORK 15/15.

70   G. Lambert, 1 July 1909, *Hansard,* fifth series, vol. 7, col. 618.

71   [Ewing], *Entry and Training*, p. 17.

72   *How to Become a Naval Officer* (London, rev. edn 1916), p. 36.

73   J.R.P. Newman, 28 June 1910, *Hansard,* fifth series, vol. 18, col. 160.

74   J.R.P. Newman, R. McKenna, 11 July 1910, *ibid.*, cols. 18–19.

75   D. Hall, R. McKenna, 5 July 1911, *ibid.*, vol. 26, col. 1113.

76   D. Hall, W.S. Churchill, 5 Nov. 1912, *ibid.*, vol. 43, col. 1045.

77   D. Hall, Sir Henry Craik, 5 May 1913, *ibid.*, vol. 52, cols. 1660–1.

78   As Hall had pointed out on 5 Nov. 1912, *ibid.*, vol. 43, col. 1045.

79   A. Lee, 5 Mar. 1907, *ibid.*, fourth series, vol. 170, col. 672.

80   G. Lambert, 25 Apr. 1907, *ibid.*, vol. 173, col. 297.

81   Adm. Lord Charles Beresford, R. McKenna, 28 Feb. 1910, *ibid.*, fifth series, vol. 14, cols. 569–70.

82   See A. Lee, R. McKenna, 21 Mar. 1911, *ibid.*, fifth series, vol. 23, col. 383–4.

83   Sir Herbert Richmond, diary, 8 Aug. 1911, quoted in A.J. Marder, *Portrait of an Admiral: the Life and Papers of Sir Herbert Richmond* (London, 1952), p. 82.

84   D. Hall, Adm. Lord Charles Beresford, G. Lambert, 1 Nov. 1911, *Hansard,* fifth series, vol. 30, cols. 848–9.

85   Adm. Lord Charles Beresford, G. Lambert, 25 Apr. 1912, *ibid.*, vol. 37, cols. 1380–1.

86   D. Hall, W.S. Churchill, 28 Nov. 1912, *ibid.*, vol. 44, col. 1496.

87   Fourth Report of the Custance Committee, 20 Sept. 1912, PRO ADM 116/1288.

88   See W.J. Macnamara's response to Adm. Lord Charles Beresford, 28 Nov. 1912; also questions by D. Hall, 19 Dec. 1911, 3 Feb 1912, Beresford, 17 Mar. 1912, *Hansard,* fifth series, vol. 44, col. 1473; vol. 45, col. 1685; vol. 50, col. 718.

89   *Ibid.*, vol. 50, col. 1301.

90   Lord H. Cavendish-Bentinck, 14 Mar. 1916, *ibid.*, vol. 80, col. 1927.

Chapter Two

1   [Ewing], *Entry and Training*, p. 1.

2   *Ibid.*, pp. 5–6.

3   *How to Become a Naval Officer* (London, rev. edn 1906), p. 8; [Ewing], *Entry and Training*, p. 5; *How to Become a Naval Officer* (London, rev. edn 1916), p. 7.

4   *How to Become a Naval Officer* (London, rev. edn 1906), pp. 14–15.

5   Estimates varied between £35 in the 1906 edition of *How to Become a Naval Officer* to £45–£50 in [Ewing], *Entry and Training*, p. 11. The 1916 edition of *How to Become a Naval Officer* has the figure of £35 crossed out.

6   *How to Become a Naval Officer* (London, rev. edn 1916) has an extra page pasted in, opposite p. 20, with these details.

7   See correspondence in PRO ADM 1/8465/190. The proposal for the remission of fees for the sons of fallen officers has first been made in Oct. 1914.

8   *How to Become a Naval Officer* (London, rev. edn 1907), p. 17.

9   *Ibid.*, pp. 16–17.

10   [Ewing], *Entry and Training*, p. 12.

11   *Ibid.*, p. 7.

12   *Ibid.*, pp. 6, 7, 9–10.
13   R. McKenna, 27 June 1910, *Hansard*, fifth series, vol. 15, col. 665; McKenna had to repeat his denial on 25 July 1910, *ibid.*, vol. 19, col. 1905. W. Long, 6 June 1919, *ibid.*, vol. 116, col. 1982.
14   The list of interviewees for 1903 and 1905 is preserved among papers held at the Royal Naval Museum, Portsmouth. That for 1915 is at the PRO, ADM 1/8417/88.
15   Capt. D.M.L. Neame, interview, 12 Aug. 1987, IWM, SA, 9872/2/1.
16   Cdr. L. Gowlland, interview, 11 Aug. 1987, *ibid.*, 9871/1/1.
17   Adm. Sir Charles Madden, interview, 5 Aug. 1987, *ibid.*, 9869/1/1.
18   M. Sherwood, *Coston Gun* (London, 1946), p. 5.
19   Rev. R.G. Bliss, interview, 26 Nov. 1987, IWM SA, 10052/2/1.
20   J.F. Worthington, interview, 2 Sept. 1987, *ibid.*, 9907/1/1.
21   J.R. Bryans, interview, 24 Aug. 1987, *ibid.*, 9897/1/1.
22   Capt. J.R. Grindle, interview, 17 Dec. 1987, *ibid.*, 10055/1/1.
23   Capt. G. French, interview, 19 Aug. 1987, *ibid.*, 9899/1/1.
24   Lt. Cdr. P. Barlow, interview, 17 Sept. 1987, *ibid.*, 9934/1/1.
25   Vice Adm. Sir Arthur Pedder, interview, 16 Dec. 1987, *ibid.*, 10054/2/1.
26   Rev. A.E. Ford, interview, 2 Sept. 1987, *ibid.*, 9908/1/1.
27   Cdr. H.G.D. de Chair, interview, 27 Aug. 1987, *ibid.*, 9905/1/1.
28   Cdr. H. Jenkins, interview, 25 Aug. 1987, *ibid.*, 9896/2/1.
29   Cdr. W.O. Bradbury, interview, 21 Aug. 1987, *ibid.*, 9982/2/1.
30   Brig. C. Richardson, interview, 13 Aug. 1987, *ibid.*, 9873/1/1.
31   Completed examples of both of these forms may be found at the PRO in ADM 1/8417/88.
32   Copies (uncompleted) of the original and proposed amended versions of this form are included among the papers collected by the Custance Committee in 1912. PRO ADM 116/1288.
33   Capt. G.A. French, interview, 19 Aug. 1987, IWM SA 9899/1/1.
34   Cdr. R.H. Barrett, interview, 17 Sept. 1987, *ibid.*, 9934/1/1.
35   Capt. E. Hale, interview, 26 Aug. 1987, *ibid.*, 9895/2/1.
36   [Ewing], *Entry and Training*, p. 9.
37   R. McKenna, 25 Nov. 1909, *Hansard*, fifth series, vol. 7, col. 464.
38   Lt. Cdr. P. Barlow, interview, 17 Sept. 1987, IWM SA, 9934/1/1.
39   Adm. J.D.N. Ham, interview, 14 Dec. 1987, *ibid.*, 10053/2/1.
40   Rev. R.G. Bliss, interview, 26 Nov. 1987, *ibid.*, 10052/2/1.
41   Cdr. H.G.D. de Chair, interview, 27 Aug. 1987, *ibid.*, 9905/1/1; Cdr. E. A. Morrison, interview, 17 Aug. 1987, *ibid.*, 9901/1/1.
42   Cdr. H.L. Jenkins, interview, 25 Aug. 1987, *ibid.*, 9862/2/1.
43   Sherwood, *Coston Gun*, p. 7–10.
44   Capt. F. Hale, interview, 26 Aug. 1987, IWM SA, 9895/2/1.
45   [Ewing], *Entry and Training*, p. 9.
46   Rev. A.E. Ford, interview, 2 Sept. 1987, IWM SA, 9908/1/1.
47   L. Hamilton, Memorandum, undated, Hamilton papers, National Maritime Museum, HTN 347.
48   Lt. Cdr. P. Barlow, interview, 17 Sept. 1987, IWM SA 9934/1/1.
49   Cdr. H.W. Barry, interview, 14 Sept. 1987, *ibid.*, 9932/2/1.
50   Cdr. H.G. D. de Chair, interview, 27 Aug. 1987, *ibid.*, 9905/1/1.
51   Cdr. R.H. Barrett, interview, 4 Aug. 1987, *ibid.*, 9868/1/1.
52   J.R. Bryans, interview, 24 Aug. 1987, *ibid.*, 9897/1/1.
53   Adm. J.D.N. Ham, interview, 14 Dec. 1987, *ibid.*, 10053/2/1.
54   Cdr. H.L. Jenkins, interview, 25 Aug. 1987, *ibid.*, 9862/2/1.
55   Cdr. L. Gowlland, interview, 11 Aug. 1987, *ibid.*, 9871/1/1.
56   Brig. C.W.P. Richardson, interview, 13 Aug. 1987, *ibid.*, 9873/1/1.
57   Vice Adm. Sir Arthur Pedder, interview, 16 Dec. 1987, *ibid.*, 10054/2/1.
58   Capt. G.A. French, interview, 19 Aug. 1987, *ibid.*, 9899/1/1.

59 Details from the Interview List, Nov. 1903, Royal Naval Museum, Portsmouth.
60 Lt. Cdr. P. Barlow, interview, 17 Sept. 1987, IWM SA 9934/1/1.
61 Sherwood, *Coston Gun*, p. 7–10.
62 Cdr. H.G.D. de Chair, interview, 27 Aug. 1987, IWM SA 9905/1/1.
63 Capt. K. L. Harkness, interview, 15 Sept. 1987, *ibid.*, 9933/1/1.
64 Cdr. J. Cobb, interview, 18 Aug. 1987, *ibid.*, 9900/2/1.
65 Interview List, Nov. 1903, Royal Naval Museum, Portsmouth.
66 [Ewing], *Entry and Training*, p. 10.
67 *Ibid.*, pp.4–5.
68 Cdr. H.L. Jenkins, interview, 25 Aug. 1987, IWM SA 9896/2/1.
69 Cdr. W.O. Bradbury, interview, 21 Aug. 1987, *ibid.*, 9898/2/1.
70 Cdr. R. Barrett, interview, 4 Aug. 1987, *ibid.*, 9868/1/1.
71 Cdr. L. Gowlland, interview, 11 Aug. 1987, *ibid.*, 9871/1/1.
72 J.R. Bryans, interview, 24 Aug. 1987, *ibid.*, 9897/1/1.
73 Cdr. E.A. Morrison, interview, 17 Aug. 1987, *ibid.*, 9901/1/1.
74 Rev. A.E. Ford, interview, 2 Sept. 1987, *ibid.*, 9908/1/1.
75 Details from the 'Regulations and Training of Cadets at the Royal Naval Colleges, effective from Sept. 1913, sect. 9', printed in [Ewing], *Entry and Training*, pp. 53–4.
76 J. McVeagh, R. McKenna, 22 July 1908, *Hansard*, fourth series, vol. 193, cols. 76–7. McKenna had to fend off further criticisms on 21 Oct. *ibid.* vol. 194, cols. 1134–5.
77 Cdr. R.H. Barrett, interview, 4 Aug. 1987, IWM SA 9868/1/1.
78 Vice Adm. Sir Arthur Pedder, interview, 16 Dec. 1987, *ibid.*, 10054/2/1; Brig. C.W.P. Richardson, interview, 13 Aug. 1987, *ibid.*, 9873/1/1.
79 Vice Adm. J.E.S. Salter, interview, 21 Sept. 1987, *ibid.*, 9935/1/1.
80 Lt. Cdr. P. Barlow, interview, 17 Sept. 1987, *ibid.*, 9934/1/1.
81 Regulations, 1913, in [Ewing], *Entry and Training*, pp. 60–1. This was reprinted more clearly in Gieves' *How to Become a Naval Officer* (London, 1916 edn), pp. 91–2.
82 Adm. Sir Charles Madden, interview, 5 Aug. 1987, IWM SA 9869/1/1.
83 Cdr. W.O. Bradbury, interview, 21 Aug. 1987, *ibid.*, 9898/2/1.
84 Vice Adm. J.C.S. Salter, interview, 21 Sept. 1987, *ibid.*, 9935/1/1.
85 Capt. J.A. Grindle, interview, 17 Dec. 1987, *ibid.*, 10055/1/1; Capt. E. Hale, interview, 26 Aug. 1987, *ibid.*, 9895/2/1; Rev. A.E. Ford, interview, 2 Sept. 1987, *ibid.*, 9908/1/1.
86 Capt. E. Hale, interview, 26 Aug. 1987, *ibid.*, 9895/2/1.
87 Cdr. W.O. Bradbury, interview, 21 Aug. 1987, *ibid.*, 9898/2/1.
88 Lt. Cdr. P. Barlow, interview, 17 Sept. 1987, *ibid.*, 9934/1/1.
89 Cdr. W.O. Bradbury, interview, 21 Aug. 1987, *ibid.*, 9898/2/1.
90 Cdr. H.L. Jenkins, interview, 25 Aug. 1987, *ibid.*, 9896/2/1.
91 Capt. H. Gairdner, 'Recollections' undated, published in J. Wells, *The Royal Navy: An Illustrated Social History, 1870-1981* (Portsmouth, 1994), pp. 133–4.

Chapter Three

1 [Ewing], *Entry and Training*, pp. 21–2.
2 Quoted in *ibid.*, p. 22. A full copy of the report is to be found in the appendices to the Fourth Report of the Custance Committee, 20 Sept. 1912, ADM 116/1288, inclosures 8 and 9.
3 [Ewing], *Entry and Training*, pp. 22–3.
4 *Ibid.*, p. 24.
5 *Ibid.*, p. 25.
6 *Ibid.*, p. 26.
7 *Ibid.*, p. 26, 28.
8 *Ibid.*, p. 29.
9 Adm. J.D.N. Ham, interview, 14 Dec. 1987, IWM SA, 10053/2/1.

10   Cdr. R.H. Barrett, interview, 4 Aug. 1987, *ibid.*, 9868/1/1.
11   Adm. Sir Charles Madden, interview, 5 Aug. 1987, *ibid.*, 9869/1/1; also Cdr. E.A. Morrison, interview, 17 Aug. 1987, *ibid.*, 9901/1/1.
12   J.R. Bryans, interview, 24 Aug. 1987, *ibid.*, 9897/1/1.
13   Rev. A.E. Ford, interview, 2 Sept. 1987, *ibid.*, 9908/1/1.
14   J. Worthington, interview, 2 Sept. 1987, *ibid.*, 9907/1/1.
15   [Ewing], *Entry and Training*, p. 14.
16   Capt. J.R. Grindle, interview, 17 Dec. 1987, IWM SA 10055/1/1.
17   J. Worthington, interview, 2 Sept. 1987, *ibid.*, 9907/1/1.
18   Cdr. J. Bradbury, interview, 21 Aug. 1987, *ibid.*, 9892/2/1.
19   Capt. S.W. Roskill, memorandum, 'Naval Cadet, 1917–1920'. Typescript in Roskill papers, Churchill Archive, Churchill College, Cambridge, ROSK 24/1, pp. 8–9.
20   'Report of the Director of Naval Education for the year 1905', Jan. 1906, ADM 268/39.
21   'Report of the Director of Naval Education for the year 1906', [Jan. 1907], *ibid.*
22   'Reports of the Director of Naval Education for the year 1907' [Jan. 1908] and '1908' [Jan. 1909], *ibid.*
23   The reports of the Director of Naval Education for 1909 and 1911 are unfortunately missing at the Public Record Office: that for 1910 makes no specific reference to the Osborne curriculum, *ibid.* The Department of Education Inspectors' Report is inclosure 9 in the Fourth Report of the Custance Committee, 20 Sept. 1912, ADM 116/1288.
24   'Report of the Director of Naval Education for the year 1912', [Jan. 1913], ADM 268/39.
25   Enclosure in Adm. Sir David Beatty to Admiralty, 29 Sept. 1917, in 'Junior Officers: courses and examinations: correspondence 1916/17', ADM 116/1707.
26   Capt. E. Hale, interview, 26 Aug. 1987, IWM SA, 9895/2/1.
27   Lt. Cdr. P. Barlow, interview, 17 Sept. 1987, *ibid.*, 9934/1/1.
28   Cdr. R.H. Barrett, interview, 4 Aug. 1987, *ibid.*, 9868/1/1.
29   S. King-Hall, *My Naval Life, 1906–1929* (London, 1952), p. 67.
30   Capt. G.A. French, 'To which I had the honour to belong', 'Memories', p. 12.
31   Cdr. H.W. Barry, interview, 14 Sept. 1987, IWM SA, 9932/1/1.
32   Vice Adm. J.C.S. Salter, interview, 21 Sept. 1987, *ibid.*, 9935/1/1.
33   Rev. A.E. Ford, interview, 2 Sept. 1987, *ibid.*, 9908/1/1.
34   Cdr. W.O. Bradbury, interview, 21 Aug. 1987, *ibid.*, 9892/2/1.
35   Capt. E. Hale, interview, 26 Aug. 1987, *ibid.*, 9895/2/1.
36   Cdr. L. Gowlland, interview, 11 Aug. 1987, *ibid.*, 9871/1/1.
37   Cdr. W.O. Bradbury, interview, 21 Aug. 1987, *ibid.*, 9892/1/1.
38   Capt. K.L. Harkness, interview, 15 Sept. 1987, *ibid.*, 9933/1/1.
39   Capt. G.A. French, interview, 19 Aug. 1987, *ibid.*, 9899/1/1.
40   Cdr. W.O. Bradbury, interview, 21 Aug. 1987, *ibid.*, 9889/2/1.
41   Capt. E.H. Thomas, interview, 6 Aug. 1987, *ibid.*, 9870/2/1.
42   Capt. K.L. Harkness, interview, 15 Sept. 1987, *ibid.*, 9933/1/1; Capt. E. H. Thomas, interview, 6 Aug. 1987, *ibid.*, 9870/2/1.
43   Cdr. H.L. Jenkins, interview, 25 Aug. 1987, *ibid.*, 9896/2/1.
44   Capt. G.A. French, interview, 19 Aug. 1987, *ibid.*, 9899/1/1.
45   J.F. Worthington, interview, 2 Sept. 1987, *ibid.*, 9907/1/1.
46   Cdr. E.A. Morrison, interview, 17 Aug. 1987, *ibid.*, 9901/1/1.
47   Cdr. H.L. Jenkins, interview, 25 Aug. 1987, *ibid.*, 9896/2/1.
48   Adm. J.D.N. Ham, interview, 14 Dec. 1987, *ibid.*, 10053/2/1.
49   Capt. G.A. French, 'Memories', p. 12.
50   Lt. Cdr. P. Barlow, interview, 17 Sept. 1987, IWM SA, 9934/1/1. This procedure was also emphasised by Cdr. W.O. Bradbury, interview, 21 Aug. 1987, *ibid.*, 9898/2/2.
51   Capt. E.H. Thomas, interview, 6 Aug. 1987, *ibid.*, 9870/2/1.

52   Cdr. R.H. Barrett, interview, 4 Aug. 1987, *ibid.*, 9868/1/1.
53   Vice Adm. J.C.S. Salter, interview, 21 Sept. 1987, *ibid.*, 9935/1/1.
54   Brig. C.W.P. Richardson, interview, 13 Aug. 1987, *ibid.*, 9873/1/1.
55   Capt. H. Gairdner, 'Naval Cradle, Osborne Memories', quoted in Wells, *Royal Navy*, p. 134.
56   Adm. J.D.N. Ham, interview, 14 Dec. 1987, IWM SA, 10053/2/1.
57   Vice Adm. Sir Arthur Pedder, interview, 16 Dec. 1987, *ibid.*, 10054/2/2.
58   Capt. E. Hale, interview, 26 Aug. 1987, *ibid.*, 9895/2/1.
59   Rev. R.G. Bliss, interview, 26 Nov. 1987, *ibid.*, 10052/2/1.
60   Cdr. H.L. Jenkins, interview, 25 Aug. 1987, *ibid.*, 9896/2/1.
61   Cdr. E.A. Morrison, interview, 17 Aug. 1987, *ibid.*, 9901/1/1.
62   Capt. H. Gairdner 'Memories', quoted in Wells, *Royal Navy*, p. 134.
63   Cdr. W.O. Bradbury, interview, 21 Aug. 1987, IWM SA, 9898/2/2.
64   Rev. R.G. Bliss, interview, 26 Nov. 1987, *ibid.*, 10052/2/1,
65   *Osborne Magazine*, Dec. 1905, quoted in J. Matson, *Dear Osborne: Queen Victoria's Family Life in the Isle of Wight* (London, 1978), p. 142.
66   Capt. E. Hale, interview, 26 Aug. 1987, IWM SA, 9895/2/1.
67   Capt. E.H. Thomas, interview, 6 Aug. 1987, *ibid.*, 9870/2/1.
68   Cdr. L. Gowlland, interview, 11 Aug. 1987, *ibid.*, 9871/1/1.
69   This rather unlikely story is recounted in Pack, *Britannia*, p. 147, but has not been verified from other sources.
70   Brig. C.W.P. Richardson, interview, 13 Aug. 1987, IWM SA, 9873/1/1.
71   Cdr. E.A. Morrison, interview, 17 Aug. 1987, *ibid.*, 9901/1/1.
72   Vice Adm. J.C.S. Salter, interview, 21 Sept. 1987, *ibid.*, 9935/1/1.
73   Capt. J.A. Grindle, interview, 17 Dec. 1987, *ibid.*, 10055/1/1.
74   Capt. D.M.L. Neame, interview, 12 Aug. 1987, *ibid.*, 9872/2/1.
75   Capt. E. Hale, interview, 26 Aug. 1987, *ibid.*, 9895/2/1.
76   Rev. R.G. Bliss, interview, 26 Nov. 1987, *ibid.*, 10052/2/1.
77   Cdr. H.G.D. de Chair, interview, 27 Aug. 1987, *ibid.*, 9905/1/1.
78   Lt. Cdr. P. Barlow, interview, 17 Sept. 1987, *ibid.*, 9934/1/1.
79   Capt. E.H. Thomas, interview, 6 Aug. 1987, *ibid.*, 9870/2/1.
80   Cdr. E.A. Morrison, interview, 17 Aug. 1987, *ibid.*, 9901/1/1.
81   J.F.Worthington, interview, 2 Sept. 1987, *ibid.*, 9907/1/1.
82   Adm. J.D.N. Ham, interview, 14 Dec. 1987, *ibid.*, 10053/2/1.
83   Capt. D.M.L. Neame, interview, 12 Aug. 1987, *ibid.*, 9872/2/1.
84   Brig. C.W.P. Richardson, interview, 13 Aug. 1987, *ibid.*, 9873/1/1.
85   Rev. R.G. Bliss, interview, 26 Nov. 1987, *ibid.*, 10052/2/1.
86   Cdr. H.G.D. de Chair, interview, 27 Aug. 1987, *ibid.*, 9905/1/1.
87   Capt. D.M.L. Neame, interview, 12 Aug. 1987, *ibid.*, 9872/1/1.
88   Cdr. E.A. Morrison, interview, 17 Aug. 1987, *ibid.*, 9901/1/1.
89   Brig. C.W.P. Richardson, interview, 13 Aug. 1987, *ibid.*, 9873/1/1.
90   Lt. Cdr. J. Cobb, interview, 18 Aug. 1987, *ibid.*, 9900/2/1.
91   Cdr. L. Gowlland, interview, 11 Aug. 1987, *ibid.*, 9871/1/1.
92   Capt. E. Hale, interview, 26 Aug. 1987, *ibid.*, 9895/2/1.
93   Cdr. E.A. Morrison, interview, 17 Aug. 1987, *ibid.*, 9901/1/1.
94   Cdr. W.O. Bradbury, interview, 21 Aug. 1987, *ibid.*, 9898/2/1.
95   Vice Adm. Sir Arthur Pedder, interview, 16 Dec. 1987, *ibid.*, 10054/2/2.
96   Lt. Cdr. J. Cobb, interview, 18 Aug. 1987, *ibid.*, 9900/2/1.
97   Cdr. W.O. Bradbury, interview, 21 Aug. 1987, *ibid.*, 9898/2/1.
98   Cdr. H.L. Jenkins, interview, 25 Aug. 1987, *ibid.*, 9896/2/1.
99   Brig. C.W.P. Richardson, interview, 13 Aug. 1987, *ibid.*, 9873/1/1.
100 Cdr. L. Gowlland, interview, 11 Aug. 1987, *ibid.*, 9871/1/1.

101 Lt. Cdr. P. Barlow, interview, 17 Sept. 1987, *ibid.*, 9934/1/1.
102 Adm. Sir Charles Madden, interview, 5 Aug. 1987, *ibid.*, 9869/1/1.
103 Rev. R.G. Bliss, interview, 26 Nov. 1987, *ibid.*, 10052/2/1.
104 Cdr. R.H. Barrett, interview, 4 Aug. 1987, *ibid.*, 9868/1/1.
105 Cdr. H.L. Jenkins, interview, 25 Aug. 1987, *ibid.*, 9896/2/1.
106 Custance Committee, Fourth Report, 20 Sept. 1912, Inclosure 9, ADM 116/1288.
107 Capt. G.A. French, interview, 19 Aug. 1987, IWM SA, 9899/1/1.
108 Cdr. E.A. Morrison, interview, 17 Aug. 1987, *ibid.*, 9901/1/1.
109 J.F. Worthington, interview, 2 Sept. 1987, *ibid.*, 9907/1/1.
110 Rev. R.G. Bliss, interview, 26 Nov. 1987, *ibid.*, 10052/1/1.
111 J.R. Bryans, interview, 24 Aug. 1987, *ibid.*, 9897/1/1.
112 Capt. E.H. Thomas, interview, 6 Aug. 1987, *ibid.*, 9870/2/1.
113 Capt. K.L. Harkness, interview, 15 Sept. 1987, *ibid.*, 9933/1/1.
114 Rev. A.E. Ford, interview, 2 Sept. 1987, *ibid.*, 9908/1/1.
115 Capt. J.A. Grindle, interview, 17 Dec. 1987, *ibid.*, 10055/1/1.
116 Lt. Cdr. P. Barlow, interview, 17 Sept. 1987, *ibid.*, 9934/1/1.
117 Roskill, 'Naval Cadet', p. 9.
118 Capt. C.H. Drake, interview, 28 Aug. 1987, IWM SA, 9906/1/1.
119 Brig. C.W.P. Richardson, interview, 13 Aug. 1987, *ibid.*, 9873/1/1.
120 Capt. C.H. Drake, interview, 28 Aug. 1987, *ibid.*, 9906/1/1.
121 Lt. Cdr. P. Barlow, interview, 17 Sept. 1987, *ibid.*, 9934/1/1.
122 Cdr. H.L. Jenkins, interview, 25 Aug. 1987, *ibid.*, 9896/2/1.
123 Capt. C.H. Drake, interview, 28 Aug. 1987, *ibid.*, 9906/1/1.
124 Vice Adm. J.C.S. Salter, interview, 21 Sept. 1987, *ibid.*, 9935/1/1.
125 Roskill, 'Naval Cadet', p. 10.
126 Rev. R.G. Bliss, interview, 26 Nov. 1987, IWM SA 10052/2/1.
127 Capt. D.M.L. Neame, interview, 12 Aug. 1987, *ibid.*, 9872/2/1.
128 J.R. Bryans, interview, 24 Aug. 1987, *ibid.*, 9897/1/1.
129 Capt. K.L. Harkness, interview, 15 Sept. 1987, *ibid.*, 9933/1/1.
130 Capt. C.H. Drake, interview, 28 Aug. 1987, *ibid.*, 9906/1/1.
131 Lt. Cdr. J. Cobb, interview, 19 Aug. 1987, *ibid.*, 9900/2/1.
132 Cdr. W.O. Bradbury, interview, 21 Aug. 1987, *ibid.*, 9898/2/1.
133 King-Hall, *Naval Life*, pp. 46–7.
134 Capt. C.H. Drake, interview, 28 Aug. 1987, *ibid.*, 9906/1/1.
135 Cdr. E.A. Morrison, interview, 17 Aug. 1987, *ibid.*, 9901/1/1.
136 A. Cunninghame Graham, *Random Naval Recollections, 1905–1951* (1979), p. 89.
137 R.H. Barrett, interview, 4 Aug. 1987, IWM SA 9869/1/1.
138 Cdr. W.O. Bradbury, interview, 21 Aug. 1987, *ibid.*, 9898/2/1.
139 Capt. E. Hale, interview, 26 Aug. 1987, *ibid.*, 9895/2/1.
140 Vice Adm. J.C.S. Salter, interview, 21 Sept. 1987, *ibid.*, 9935/1/1.
141 Capt. E. Hale, interview, 26 Aug. 1987, *ibid.*, 9895/2/1.
142 J.F. Worthington, interview, 2 Sept. 1987, *ibid.*, 9907/1/1. These two masters were also remembered by Capt. D.M.L. Neame, interview, 12 Aug. 1987, *ibid.*, 9872/2/1.
143 J.F. Worthington, interview, 2 Sept. 1987, *ibid.*, 9907/1/1.
144 Capt. E. Hale, interview, 26 Aug. 1987, *ibid.*, 9895/2/1.
145 Cdr. W.O. Bradbury, interview, 21 Aug. 1987, *ibid.*, 9892/2/1.
146 Quoted in Pack, *Britannia*, p. 199.
147 Cdr. W.O. Bradbury, interview, 21 Aug. 1987, IWM SA, 9892/2/1.
148 Capt. E.H. Thomas, interview, 6 Aug. 1987, *ibid.*, 9870/2/1.
149 Cdr. W.O. Bradbury, interview, 21 Aug. 1987, *ibid.*, 9892/2/1.
150 Cdr. R.H. Barrett, interview, 4 Aug. 1987, *ibid.*, 9868/1/1.

151 Vice Adm. J.C.S. Salter, interview, 21 Sept. 1987, *ibid.*, 9935/1/1.
152 Capt. E.H. Thomas, interview, 6 Aug. 1987, *ibid.*, 9870/2/1.
153 Capt. C.H. Drake, interview, 28 Aug. 1987, *ibid.*, 9906/1/1.

Chapter Four

1   Adm. Sir Charles Madden, interview, 5 Aug. 1987, IWM SA 9869/1/1.
2   Cdr. R. Barrett, interview, 4 Aug. 1987, *ibid.*, 9868/1/1; Capt. J.A. Grindle, interview, 17 Dec. 1987, *ibid.*, 10055/1/1.
3   Capt. E.H. Thomas, interview, 6 Aug. 1987, *ibid.*, 9870/2/1.
4   Adm. J.D.N. Ham, interview, 14 Dec. 1987, *ibid.*, 10053/2/1.
5   Cdr. H.L. Jenkins, interview, 25 Aug. 1987, *ibid.*, 9896/2/1.
6   Vice Adm. J.C.S. Salter, interview, 21 Sept. 1987, *ibid.*, 9935/1/1.
7   Capt. E. Hale, interview, 26 Aug. 1987, *ibid.*, 9895/2/1; Lt. Cdr. P. Barlow, interview, 17 Sept. 1987, *ibid.*, 9934/1/1.
8   Cdr. L. Gowlland, interview, 11 Aug. 1987, *ibid.*, 9871/1/1.
9   Cdr. H.W. Barry, interview, 14 Sept. 1987, *ibid.*, 9932/2/1; Vice Adm. Sir Arthur Pedder, interview, 16 Dec. 1987, *ibid.*, 10054/2/2.
10 Cdr. H. Jenkins, interview, 25 Aug. 1987, *ibid.*, 9871/1/1.
11 J.F. Worthington, interview, 2 Sept. 1987, *ibid.*, 9907/1/1.
12 Adm. Sir Charles Madden, interview, 5 Aug. 1987, *ibid.*, 9869/1/1.
13 Custance Committee, Fourth report, 20 Sept. 1912, PRO ADM 116/1288.
14 Royal Naval College, Osborne, Committee Report, April 1917, PRO ADM 1/8520/98.
15 [Ewing], *Entry and Training*, pp. 15–16.
16 Lt. Cdr. P. Barlow, interview, 17 Sept. 1987, IWM SA, 9934/1/1.
17 Brig. C.W.P. Richardson, interview, 13 Aug. 1987, *ibid.*, 9873/1/1.
18 Rev. R.G. Bliss, interview, 26 Nov. 1987, *ibid.*, 10052/2/1.
19 Lt. Cdr. J. Cobb, interview, 18 Aug. 1987, *ibid.*, 9900/2/1.
20 Capt. G.A. French, 'Memories', pp. 12–13.
21 Cdr. L. Gowlland, interview, 11 Aug. 1987, IWM SA, 9871/1/1.
22 Cdr. H.L. Jenkins, interview, 25 Aug. 1987, *ibid.*, 9896/2/1.
23 Capt. E.H. Thomas, interview, 6 Aug. 1987, *ibid.*, 9870/2/1.
24 Osborne, Committee Report, April 1917, PRO ADM 1/8520/98.
25 Capt. D.M.L. Neame, interview, 12 Aug. 1987, IWM SA, 9872/2/1.
26 Cdr. W. Bradbury, interview, 21 Aug. 1987, *ibid.*, 9898/2/2.
27 Brig. C.W.P. Richardson, interview, 13 Aug. 1987, *ibid.*, 9873/1/1.
28 Cdr. L. Gowlland, interview, 11 Aug. 1987, *ibid.*, 9871/1/1.
29 Report of the Osborne & Dartmouth Committee, May 1905, PRO ADM 268/38.
30 Cdr. L. Gowlland, interview, 11 Aug. 1987, IWM SA, 9871/1/1.
31 Capt. D.M.L. Neame, interview, 12 Aug. 1987, *ibid.*, 9872/2/1.
32 Adm. Sir Charles Madden, interview, 5 Aug. 1987, *ibid.*, 9869/1/1.
33 Cdr. E.A. Morrison, interview, 17 Aug. 1987, *ibid.*, 9901/1/1.
34 Capt. G.A. French, interview, 19 Aug. 1987, *ibid.*, 9899/1/1.
35 Vice Adm. Sir Arthur Pedder, interview, 16 Dec. 1987, *ibid.*, 10054/2/2.
36 Cdr. H.L. Jenkins, interview, 25 Aug. 1987, *ibid.*, 9896/2/2.
37 J.R. Bryans, interview, 24 Aug. 1987, *ibid.*, 9897/1/1.
38 Vice Adm. J.C.S. Salter, interview, 21 Sept. 1987, *ibid.*, 9935/1/1.
39 Cdr. W.O. Bradbury, interview, 21 Aug. 1987, *ibid.*, 9898/2/1.
40 Cdr. H.G.D. de Chair, interview, 27 Aug. 1987, *ibid.*, 9905/1/1.
41 Rev. A.E. Ford, interview, 2 Sept. 1987, *ibid.*, 9908/1/1.
42 Cdr. E.A. Morrison, interview, 17 Aug. 1987, *ibid.*, 9901/1/1.
43 J.R. Bryans, interview, 24 Aug. 1987, *ibid.*, 9897/1/1.

44   Capt. E.H. Thomas, interview, 6 Aug. 1987, *ibid.*, 9870/2/2.
45   Vice Adm. J.C.S. Salter, interview, 21 Sept. 1987, *ibid.*, 9935/1/1.
46   Cdr. H.G.D. de Chair, interview, 27 Aug. 1987, *ibid.*, 9905/1/1.
47   Cdr. W.O. Bradbury, interview, 21 Aug. 1987, *ibid.*, 9898/2/2.
48   Lt. Cdr. J. Cobb, interview, 18 Aug. 1987, *ibid.*, 9900/2/1.
49   Roskill, 'Naval Cadet', p. 10.
50   Cdr. L. Gowlland, interview, 11 Aug. 1987, IWM SA 9871/1/1.
51   *Osborne Magazine*, VII, no. 38 (Easter, 1916), pp. 8–11; 4–5.
52   *Ibid.*, VII, no. 39 (Summer, 1916), pp. 18–19.
53   *Ibid.*, VII, no. 41 (Easter, 1917), p. 8.
54   Prince Louis of Battenberg to Princess Louise of Battenberg, letter, 19 Oct. 1913, Broadlands papers, cited in Matson, *Dear Osborne*, p. 141.
55   J.R. Bryans, interview, 24 Aug. 1987, IWM SA, 9897/1/1.
56   Cdr. W. Bradbury, interview, 21 Aug. 1987, *ibid.*, 9898/2/2.
57   Rev. R.G. Bliss, interview, 26 Nov. 1987, *ibid.*, 10052/2/1.
58   J.R. Bryans, interview, 24 Aug. 1987, *ibid.*, 9897/1/1.
59   *Osborne Magazine*, VII, no. 42 (Summer 1917), p. 10.
60   Cdr. H.L. Jenkins, interview, 25 Aug. 1987, IWM SA, 9896/2/2.
61   Lt. Cdr. P. Barlow, interview, 17 Sept. 1987, *ibid.*, 9934/1/1.
62   Adm. J.D.N. Ham, interview, 14 Dec. 1987, *ibid.*, 10053/2/1.
63   Cdr. H.G.D. de Chair, interview, 27 Aug. 1987, *ibid.*, 9905/1/1.
64   Vice Adm. J.C.S. Salter, interview, 21 Sept. 1987, *ibid.*, 9935/1/1.
65   Cdr. W.O. Bradbury, interview, 21 Aug. 1987, *ibid.*, 9898/2/2.
66   Capt. K.L. Harkness, interview, 15 Sept. 1987, *ibid.*, 9933/1/1.
67   Cdr. H.W. Barry, interview, 14 Sept. 1987, *ibid.*, 9932/2/1.
68   Cdr. W.O. Bradbury, interview, 21 Aug. 1987, *ibid.*, 9898/2/2.
69   Bacon, *From 1900 Onward*, p. 26.
70   W.S. Chalmers, *The Life and Letters of David, Earl Beatty, Admiral of the Fleet* (London, 1951), p. 345; R.H. Bacon, *The Life of Lord Fisher of Kilverstone, Admiral of the Fleet* (2 vols., London, 1929), I, 190.
71   The first attack on health conditions at the College was made by A. Lee who specifically criticised the uralite construction. G. Lambert of the Admiralty responded on 25 Apr. 1907. *Hansard*, fourth series, vol. 170, col. 672; vol. 173, col. 297.
72   G. Lambert, 1 July 1909, *Hansard*, fifth series, vol. 7, col. 618.
73   Maj. Gastrell, 21 Mar. 1911, *ibid.*, vol. 23, cols. 383–4.
74   Adm. Lord Charles Beresford, R. McKenna, 15 Nov. 1911, *ibid.*, vol. 31, cols. 244–5.
75   G. Lambert, 21 Feb. 1912, *ibid.*, vol. 34, cols. 699–700.
76   Custance Committee, Fourth Report, 20 Sept. 1912, and enclosures 2 & 3, PRO ADM 116/1288.
77   Adm. Lord Charles Beresford, Dr Macnamara, 1 Mar. 1915, *Hansard*, fifth series, vol. 14, col. 547.
78   L. Benn, Dr Macnamara, 5 Apr. 1917, *ibid.*, vol. 92, cols. 1483–4.
79   Osborne Committee, Report, Apr. 1917, PRO ADM 1/8520/98.
80   Adm. Sir Charles Madden, interview, 5 Aug. 1987, IWM SA, 9869/1/1.
81   Lt. Cdr. J. Cobb, interview, 18 Aug. 1987, *ibid.*, 9900/2/1.
82   Lt. Cdr. P. Barlow, interview, 17 Sept. 1987, *ibid.*, 9934/1/1.
83   Cdr. H.L. Jenkins, interview, 25 Nov. 1987, *ibid.*, 9896/2/1.
84   J.R. Bryans, interview, 24 Aug. 1987, *ibid.*, 9897/1/1.
85   Adm. J.D.N. Ham, interview, 14 Dec. 1987, *ibid.*, 10053/2/1.
86   Rev. R.G. Bliss, interview, 26 Nov. 1987, *ibid.*, 10052/2/1.
87   Cdr. R.H. Barrett, interview, 4 Aug. 1987, *ibid.*, 9868/1/1.
88   Lt. Cdr. P. Barlow, interview, 17 Sept. 1987, *ibid.*, 9934/1/1.
89   Lt. Cdr. J. Cobb, interview, 18 Aug. 1987, *ibid.*, 9900/2/1.
90   Rev. A.E. Ford, interview, 2 Sept. 1987, *ibid.*, 9908/1/1.

91   Cdr. H.L. Jenkins, interview, 25 Aug. 1987, *ibid.*, 9896/2/1.
92   See Debate of 28 Feb. 1910 in *Hansard*, fifth series, vol. 14, cols. 569–70.
93   Adm. Lord Charles Beresford, 9 Mar. 1915, *ibid.*, vol. 70, cols. 1261.
94   Capt. C.H. Drake, interview, 28 Aug. 1987, IWM SA, 9906/1/1.
95   Rev. R.G. Bliss, interview, 26 Nov. 1987, *ibid.*, 10052/2/1.
96   Cdr. H.W. Barry, interview, 14 Sept. 1987, *ibid.*, 9932/2/1.
97   Adm. J.D.N. Ham, interview, 14 Dec. 1987, *ibid.*, 10053/2/1.
98   Capt. C.H. Drake, interview, 28 Aug. 1987, *ibid.*, 9906/1/1.
99   Capt. J.A. Grindle, interview, 17 Dec. 1987, *ibid.*, 10055/1/1.
100 Osborne Committee, Report, Apr. 1917, PRO ADM 1/8520/98.
101 Capt. K.L. Harkness, interview, 15 Sept. 1987, IWM SA, 9933/1/1.
102 Capt. E.H. Thomas, interview, 6 Aug. 1987, *ibid.*, 9870/2/1.
103 Rev. R.G. Bliss, interview, 26 Nov. 1987, *ibid.*, 10052/2/1.
104 Cdr. L. Gowlland, interview, 11 Aug. 1987, *ibid.*, 9871/1/1.
105 Cdr. W.O. Bradbury, interview, 21 Aug. 1987, *ibid.*, 9898/2/2.
106 Cdr. H.L. Jenkins, interview, 25 Aug. 1987, *ibid.*, 9896/2/1.
107 Capt. C.H. Drake, interview, 28 Aug. 1987, *ibid.*, 9906/1/1.
108 Lt. Cdr. J. Cobb, interview, 18 Aug. 1987, *ibid.*, 9900/2/1.
109 Hughes, *Dartmouth*, pp. 83–4.
110 Cdr. H.L. Jenkins, interview, 25 Aug. 1987, *ibid.*, 9896/2/1.
111 Hughes, *Dartmouth*, p. 83.
112 Cdr. H.D.G. de Chair, interview, 27 Aug. 1987, IWM SA 9905/1/1.
113 Pack, *Britannia*, p. 50.
114 [Ewing], *Entry and Training*, p. 13.
115 Cdr. E.A. Morrison, interview, 17 Aug. 1987, IWM SA 9901/1/1.
116 Cdr. H.L. Jenkins, interview, 25 Aug. 1987, *ibid.*, 9896/2/1.
117 Cdr. H.W. Barry, interview, 14 Sept. 1987, *ibid.*, 9932/2/1; Rev. A.E. Ford, interview, 2 Sept. 1987, *ibid*, 9908/1/1.
118 E. Wheler Bush, *Bless our Ship* (London, 1958), p. 15.
119 Vice Adm. Sir Arthur Pedder, interview, 16 Dec. 1987, IWM SA 10054/2/2.
120 Roskill, 'Naval Cadet', p. 7.
121 Cdr. E.A. Morrison, interview, 17 Aug. 1987, IWM SA 9901/1/1.
122 Rev. R.G. Bliss, interview, 26 Nov. 1987, *ibid.*, 10052/2/1.
123 Lt. Cdr. P. Barlow, interview, 17 Sept. 1987, *ibid.*, 9934/1/1.
124 Capt. G.A. French, 'Memories', p.10.
125 Capt. C. Drake, interview, 28 Aug. 1987, IWM SA 9906/1/1.
126 Adm. Sir Charles Madden, interview, 5 Aug. 1987, *ibid.*, 9869/1/1.
127 Adm. J.D.N. Ham, interview, 14 Dec. 1987, *ibid.*, 10053/2/1.
128 Cdr. W.O. Bradbury, interview, 21 Aug. 1987, *ibid.*, 9898/2/2.
129 Cdr. E. Morrison, interview, 17 Aug. 1987, *ibid.*, 9901/1/1.
130 Lt. Cdr. J. Cobb, interview, 18 Aug. 1987, *ibid.*, 9900/2/1.
131 Adm. J.D.N. Ham, interview, 14 Dec. 1987, *ibid.*, 10053/2/1.
132 [Ewing], *Entry and Training*, p. 14.
133 Capt. D.M.L. Neame, interview, 12 Aug. 1987, IWM SA, 9872/2/1.
134 J.R. Bryans, interview, 24 Aug. 1987, *ibid.*, 9897/1/1.
135 Capt. D.M.L. Neame, interview, 12 Aug. 1987, *ibid.*, 9872/2/1.
136 Lt. Cdr. P. Barlow, interview, 17 Sept. 1987, *ibid.*, 9934/1/1.
137 Lt. Cdr. J. Cobb, interview, 18 Aug. 1987, *ibid.*, 9900/2/2.
138 J.F. Worthington, interview, 2 Sept. 1987, *ibid.*, 9907/1/1.
139 Cdr. L. Gowlland, interview, 11 Aug. 1987, *ibid.*, 9871/1/1.
140 Brig. C.W.P. Richardson, interview, 13 Aug. 1987, *ibid.*, 9873/1/1.

141 Roskill, 'Naval Cadet', pp. 6–7.
142 [Ewing], *Entry and Training*, p. 28.
143 D. Fairbairn, *The Narrative of a Naval Nobody* (London, 1929), p. 7.
144 Cdr. E.A. Morrison, interview, 17 Aug. 1987, IWM SA 9901/1/1.
145 Cdr. H.G.D. de Chair, interview, 27 Aug. 1987, *ibid.*, 9905/1/1.
146 Rev. R.G. Bliss, interview, 26 Nov. 1987, *ibid.*, 10052/2/1.
147 Capt. D.M.L. Neame, interview, 12 Aug. 1987, *ibid.*, 9872/2/1.
148 J.R. Bryans, interview, 24 Aug. 1987, *ibid.*, 9897/1/1.
149 Cdr. W.O. Bradbury, interview, 21 Aug. 1987, *ibid.*, 9898/2/2.
150 Capt. C.H. Drake, interview, 28 Aug. 1987, *ibid.*, 9906/1/1.
151 Capt. K.L. Harkness, interview, 15 Sept. 1987, *ibid.*, 9933/1/1.
152 King-Hall, *Naval Life*, p. 44.
153 Vice Adm. J.C.S. Salter, interview, 21 Sept. 1987, IWM SA, 9935/1/1.
154 Capt. G.A. French, interview, 19 Aug. 1987, *ibid.*, 9899/1/1.
155 Rev. R.G. Bliss, interview, 26 Nov. 1987, *ibid.*, 10052/2/2.
156 J.F. Worthington, interview, 2 Sept. 1987, *ibid.*, 9907/1/1.
157 Bush, *Bless our Ship*, p. 18.
158 Cdr. J.C.H. Nelson, 'Memoirs' typescript in Churchill Archive, Churchill College, Cambridge, MISC 27.
159 Brig. C.W.P. Richardson, interview, 13 Aug. 1987, IWM SA 9873/1/1.
160 P. Ziegler, *Mountbatten: the Official Biography* (London, 1978), p. 34.
161 J.R. Bryans, interview, 24 Aug. 1987, IWM SA 9897/1/1.
162 Lt. Cdr. P. Barlow, interview, 17 Sept. 1987, *ibid.*, 9934/1/1.
163 Matson, *Dear Osborne*, p. 137.
164 Cdr. W.O. Bradbury, interview, 21 Aug. 1987, IWM SA, 9898/2/2.
165 Lt. Cdr. P. Barlow, interview, 17 Sept. 1987, *ibid.*, 9934/1/1.
166 Rev. R.G. Bliss, interview, 26 Nov. 1987, *ibid.*, 10052/2/1.
167 J.R. Bryans, interview, 24 Aug. 1987, *ibid.*, 9897/1/1.
168 King-Hall, *Naval Life*, p. 42; Ziegler, *Mountbatten*, p. 33.
169 Cdr. E.A. Morrison, interview, 17 Aug. 1987, IWM SA 9901/1/1.
170 Adm. J.D.N. Ham, interview, 14 Dec. 1987, *ibid.*, 10053/2/1.
171 Capt. G.A. French, interview, 19 Aug. 1987, *ibid.*, 9899/1/1.
172 Cdr. L. Gowlland, interview, 11 Aug. 1987, *ibid.*, 9871/1/1.
173 Cdr. H.G.D. de Chair, interview, 27 Aug. 1987, *ibid.*, 9905/1/1.
174 Capt. J.A. Grindle, interview, 17 Dec. 1987, *ibid.*, 10055/1/1.
175 Capt. E.H. Thomas, interview, 6 Aug. 1987, *ibid.*, 9870/2/1.
176 J.F. Worthington, interview, 2 Sept. 1987, *ibid.*, 9907/1/1.
177 Brig. C.W.P. Richardson, interview, 13 Aug. 1987, *ibid.*, 9873/1/1.
178 Capt. D.M.L. Neame, interview, 12 Aug. 1987, *ibid.*, 9872/1/1.
179 Brig. C.W.P. Richardson, interview, 13 Aug. 1987, *ibid.*, 9873/1/1.
180 *Hansard*, fifth series, vol. 23, cols. 2441–2.
181 On 29 July 1910, 16 Mar. and 6 Apr. 1911, *ibid.*, vol. 19, cols. 2609–20; vol. 22, cols. 2454–5, and vol. 23, cols. 2433–88.
182 R. McKenna, 6 Apr. 1911, *ibid.*, vol. 23, 2447.

Chapter Five

1 [Sir] E[dward] C[arson] to Admiralty, letter, 'immediate', 10 Apr. 1917, and enclosed memorandum, Apr. 1917, PRO ADM 1/8520/98.
2 Adm. S.C. Colvile to Admiralty, letter, [*c.* Apr. 1917], *ibid.*
3 Full details of the Committee, and its report of *c.* June 1917, are to be found in *ibid.*
4 Minute, 14 June 1917, *ibid.*

5   Board of Admiralty, memorandum, July 1917, *ibid.*

6   Board of Admiralty, minute, 17 July 1917, *ibid.*

7   Earl of Selborne, report, 23 July 1917; Second Sea Lord, minute [July 1917], *ibid.*

8   Capt. D. Hall, T.J. Macnamara, 7 Aug. 1917, *Hansard,* fifth series, vol. 97, cols. 214–15.

9   Capt. D. Hall, E.G. Pretyman, 1 Nov. 1917, *ibid.*, vol. 98, cols. 1742–9.

10   This site was favoured over ones in Cheshire and elsewhere. See correspondence in PRO ADM 1/8520/98.

11   Diary, 24 Oct. 1918, Marder, *Portrait of an Admiral* (London, 1952), p. 324.

12   Adm. Sir Herbert Richmond to R.B. Haldane, letter, 15 Feb. 1919, *ibid.*, p. 324.

13   Davies and Grove, *Dartmouth*, p. 15.

14   W. Long, 13 Aug. 1919, *Hansard,* fifth series, vol. 119.

15   Viscount Milner; Dr Macnamara, 11 Dec. 1919, *ibid.*, vol. 122, col. 1749.

16   Diary, 13 Dec. 1919, Marder, *Portrait of an Admiral,* p. 361.

17   See Lt. Cdr. H. Kenworthy, C. Wilson, 2, 12 Mar. 1920, *Hansard,* fifth series, vol. 126, cols. 299–300, 1688–9.

18   W. Long, 17 Mar. 1920, *ibid.*, cols. 2308–9, 2310–30.

19   Lt. Cdr. H. Kenworthy, W. Long, 17 May 1920, *ibid.*, vol. 129, cols. 1135–42. Rear Adm. Adair favoured slightly later entry (*ibid.*, col. 1156), W. Benn a wider field of entry (*ibid.*, col. 1152), and Dr Murray, both of these options (*ibid.*, cols. 1152–3).

20   Davies and Grove, *Dartmouth*, pp. 14–15.

21   W. Long, 28 July 1920, *ibid.*, vol. 132, cols. 1402–3.

22   Minute, H.F.O., 13 Dec. 1920, PRO ADM 1/8607/101.

23   A. Flint to C-in-C, Portsmouth, 22 Dec. 1920, *ibid.*

24   Capt. F.A. Marten to C-in-C, Portsmouth, 7 Jan. 1921, *ibid.*

25   Commanding Officer, Dartmouth to C-in-C, Portsmouth, 2 Feb. 1921, *ibid.*

26   Capt. C. Royds, memorandum, [Feb. 1921] in Royds to C-in-C, Portsmouth, 22 Feb. 1921, *ibid.*

27   Capt. E. Hale, interview, 26 Aug. 1987, IWM SA, 9895/2/1.

28   Civil Engineer-in-Chief, minute, 9 May 1921, PRO ADM 1/8607/101.

29   Paymaster Capt. C.W. Luckham to Jewell (Admiralty), 5 May 1921, *ibid.*

30   Memorandum, 19 May 1921, *ibid.*

31   Cowan to C-in-C, Portsmouth, 13 May 1921; C-in-C, Portsmouth to Admiralty, 18 May [1921]; Admiralty minute, 1 June 1921, *ibid.*

32   C-in-C, Portsmouth to Admiralty, 20 May 1921, *ibid.*

33   Accountant General, minute, 23 June 1921, *ibid.*

34   An amended copy of the Regulations for Entry and Training at Royal Naval Colleges, Osborne and Dartmouth, and comments on dress regulations are to be found in *ibid.*

35   Wells, *Royal Navy*, pp. 135–6.

36   Davies and Grove, *Dartmouth*, p.15.

37   Memorandum, enclosed in Admiralty to Treasury, letter, 3 Jan. 1921, PRO WORK 15/60.

38   Treasury to Office of Works, 8 Feb. 1921; Office of Works to Treasury, 14 Feb. 1921; Air Ministry to Treasury, 28 Feb. 1921, *ibid.*

39   Office of Works, report, 4 Oct. 1921, *ibid.*

40   Sir John H. Oakley, 'Report on the Osborne Estate', Nov. 1921, *ibid.*

41   Board of Works, minute, 26 Jan. 1922; Admiralty to Office of Works, 22 Mar. 1922, *ibid.*

42   United Service College to Board of Works, 17 Apr. 1924; Office of Works, minute, 20 Dec. 1924, PRO WORK 15/75.

43   Office of Works, memorandum, 30 July 1925, *ibid.*

44   Office of Works to Treasury, 9 Sept. 1925, *ibid.*; (Royal Naval College: proposed lettings: college transferred to Commissioners of Crown Lands, 25 Mar. 1926) PRO WORK 15/81.

45   Details can be found in *ibid.* and PRO WORK 15/82.

46   See Crown Lands Commissioners to Office of Works, 3 June 1932, PRO WORK 15/75.

47 Office of Works to Col. Wigram, draft, 9 Oct. 1933, *ibid.*

48 *Hampshire Telegraph & Post*, report dated 6 Oct. 1933, *ibid.*

49 D.A. Mitchell (King's Private Secretary) to Sir Patrick Duff (Office of Works), 10 Oct. 1933, *ibid.*

50 Office of Works, minute, 15 Mar. 1935, *ibid.*

51 Governor, Osborne House, reports for 31 Mar. 1937, 31 Mar. 1938 and 17 Jan. 1939, *ibid.*

52 Admiralty to Board of Works, 25 May 1939 and Board of Works, minute, 24 June 1939, *ibid.*

53 Details can be found in PRO WORK 15/134.

54 Details can be found in PRO WORK 15/150.

55 PRO WORK 15/134.

56 Details can be found in PRO WORK 15/157.

57 Details provided in a personal communication from the Crown Estates, Urban Estates Business Group, 8 Jan. 1999.

Conclusion

1   Davies and Grove, *Dartmouth*, p. 13.

2   Hughes, *Dartmouth*, pp. 41, 47.

3   Pack, *Britannia*, p. 198.

4   J.R. Bryans, interview, 24 Aug. 1987, IWM SA, 9897/1/1.

5   Cdr. H.L. Jenkins, interview, 25 Aug. 1987, *ibid.*, 9896/2/2.

6   Capt. G.A. French, interview, 19 Aug. 1987, *ibid.*, 9899/1/1.

7   Cdr. W.O. Bradbury, interview, 21 Aug. 1987, *ibid.*, 9898/2/2.

8   Capt. C.H. Drake, interview, 28 Aug. 1987, *ibid.*, 9906/1/1.

9   Capt. E.H. Thomas, interview, 6 Aug. 1987, *ibid.*, 9870/2/2.

10 Vice Adm. J.C.S. Salter, interview, 21 Sept. 1987, *ibid.*, 9935/1/1.

11 Capt. K.L. Harkness, interview, 15 Sept. 1987, *ibid.*, 9933/1/1.

12 Cdr. L. Gowlland, interview, 11 Aug. 1987, *ibid.*, 9871/1/1.

13 Cdr. H.G.D. de Chair, interview, 27 Aug. 1987, *ibid.*, 9905/1/1.

14 Cdr. R.H. Barrett, interview, 4 Aug. 1987, *ibid.*, 9869/1/1.

15 Adm. J.D.N. Ham, interview, 14 Dec. 1987, *ibid.*, 10053/2/1.

16 Lt. Cdr. J. Cobb, interview, 18 Aug. 1987, *ibid.*, 9900/2/1.

17 Rev. A.E. Ford, interview, 2 Sept. 1987, *ibid.*, 9908/1/1.

18 Adm. J.D.N. Ham, interview, 14 Dec. 1987, *ibid.*, 10053/2/1.

19 Cdr. E.A. Morrison, interview, 17 Aug. 1987, *ibid.*, 9901/1/1.

20 Capt. J.A. Grindle, interview, 17 Dec. 1987, *ibid.*, 10055/1/1.

21 Rev. R.G. Bliss, interview, 26 Nov. 1987, *ibid.*, 10052/2/2.

22 Brig. C.W.P. Richardson, interview, 13 Aug. 1987, *ibid.*, 9873/1/1.

23 Adm. Sir Charles Madden, interview, 5 Aug. 1987, *ibid.*, 9869/1/1.

24 Lt. Cdr. P. Barlow, interview, 17 Sept. 1987, *ibid.*, 9934/1/1.

25 Rev. R.G. Bliss, interview, 26 Nov. 1987, *ibid.*, 10052/2/2.

26 J.F. Worthington, interview, 2 Sept. 1987, *ibid.*, 9907/1/1.

27 Capt. D.M.L. Neame, interview, 12 Aug. 1987, *ibid.*, 9872/2/1.

28 Cdr. H.W. Barry, interview, 14 Sept. 1987, *ibid.*, 9932/2/1.

29 Capt. E. Hale, interview, 26 Aug. 1987, *ibid.*, 9895/2/2.

Bibliography

Primary Sources

Sound Archive, Imperial War Museum, London
Transcripts and tape recordings of interviews between the author and the following former Osborne Naval College cadets (date of interview) (IWM Reference)
Barlow, Lt. Cdr. P. (Drake Term, Jan. 1918) (17 Sept. 1987) (9934/1/1)
Barrett, Cdr. R.H. (St Vincent Term, Sept. 1917) (4 Aug. 1987) (9868/1/1)
Barry, Cdr. H.W. (St Vincent Term, Sept. 1911) (14 Sept. 1987) (9932/1/1)
Bliss, Rev. R.G. (Grenville Term, Jan. 1919) (26 Nov. 1987) (10052/2/1–2/2)
Bradbury, Cdr. W.O. (Drake Term, Jan. 1920) (21 Aug. 1987) (989/2/1–2/2)
Bryans, Mr. J.R. (Drake Term, Jan. 1920) (24 Aug. 1987) (9897/1/1)
Cobb, Lt. Cdr. J. (Blake Term, May 1918) (18 Aug. 1987) (9900/2/1–2/2/)
de Chair, Cdr. H.G.D. (Exmouth Term, May 1919) (27 Aug. 1987) (9905/1/1)
Drake, Capt. C.H. (Exmouth Term, May 1913) (28 Aug. 1987) (9906/1/1)
Ford, Rev. A.E. (Hawke Term, Sept. 1919) (2 Sept. 1987) (9908/1/1)
French, Capt. G.A. (Exmouth Term, May 1913) (19 Aug. 1987) (9899/1/1)
Gowlland, Cdr. L. (Hawke Term, Sept. 1916) (11 Aug. 1987) (9871/1/1)
Grindle, Capt. J.A. (St Vincent Term, Sept. 1913) (17 Dec. 1987) (10055/1/1)
Hale, Capt. E. (Grenville Term, Jan. 1921) (26 Aug. 1997) (9895/2/1–2/2)
Ham, Adm. J.D.N. (Blake Term, May 1916) (14 Dec. 1987) (10053/2/1–2/2)
Harkness, Capt. K.L. (Blake Term, May 1914) (15 Sept. 1987) (9933/1/1)
Jenkins, Cdr. H.L. (Grenville Term, Jan. 1917) (25 Aug. 1987) (9896/2/1–2/2)
Madden, Adm. Sir Charles (Drake Term, Jan. 1920) (5 Aug. 1987) (9869/1/1)
Morrison, Cdr. E.A. (Grenville Term, Jan. 1919) (17 Aug. 1987) (9901/1/1)
Neame, Capt. D.M.L. (Exmouth Term, May 1915) (12 Aug. 1987) (9872/2/1)
Pedder, Vice Adm. Sir Arthur (Drake Term, Jan. 1918) (16 Dec. 1987) (10054/2/1–2/2)
Richardson, Brig. C.W.P. (Hawke Term, Sept. 1918) (13 Aug. 1987) (9873/1/1)
Salter, Vice Adm. J.C.S. (Exmouth Term, May 1915) (21 Sept. 1987) (9935/1/1)
Thomas, Capt. E.H. (Drake Term, Jan. 1918) (6 Aug. 1987) (9870/2/1–2/2)
Worthington, Mr. J.F. (Hawke Term, Sept. 1918) (2 Sept. 1987) (9907/1/1)

Churchill Archive Centre, Churchill College, Cambridge
Fisher papers (Papers of Admiral of the Fleet Lord Fisher of Kilverstone)
Nelson papers (Papers of Cdr. J.C.H. Nelson) (MISC 27)
Roskill papers (Papers of Capt. S. Roskill) (ROSK 24)

National Maritime Museum, Greenwich
Hamilton papers (Papers of Admiral Sir Louis Hamilton) (HTN 247)
Richmond papers (Papers of Admiral Sir Herbert Richmond) (RIC 14)

Public Record Office, Kew
Admiralty Papers
ADM 1 (Admiralty Secretariat – In letters):
8520/98   Royal Naval College, Osborne: Committee Reports. 1917
8607/101 Osborne College: Closing Down. 1921
8375/106 Director of Naval Education: Report. 1913
8645/190 King's Cadetships at Osborne and Dartmouth. Amended Regulations. August 1916.

8417/88   Naval Cadets. 1915 Examinations. List of Candidates.

ADM 116 (Admiralty Secretariat: Cases):

413   Case F279. Junior Naval Officers – training and education. Amendment of Regulations, 1897–9.
862   Case 10793. Volume 1. Reports of Committee on Naval Education, 1905–7.
863   Case 10793. Volume 2. Reports of Committees on Naval Education, 1870–1913.
1287   Case 379. Volume 1. New Scheme for Entry and Training of Officers (Marines) Committee. 1910.
1288   Case 379. Volume 2. Custance Committee on the Education and Training of Naval Officers. 1912.

ADM 268 (Ad Hoc Committee Reports):

38   Report of the Committee on Administration of Training Establishments at Osborne and Dartmouth. May 1905. Osborne Staffing 1905–8.
39   Reports of Director of Naval Education, 1905/6, 1907, 1908, 1910, 1912.

WORK 15 (Osborne Estate):

1   Royal Naval College: erection of additional buildings and execution of works on behalf of Adm. by H.M. Office of Works. Estimates, statements of expenditure, etc. 1905–6.
2   Osborne Note Book. 1902–5.
15   Royal Naval College and other Admiralty buildings: maintenance of buildings. 1908–11.
29   Royal Naval College buildings: lighting, Isle of Wight Light & Power Co.: erection of transformer house.
56   Royal Naval College: gift of ship models by H.M. King George V. 1912.
60   Royal Naval College: transfer from Admiralty to Office of Works. 1920–3.
69   Royal Naval College: lighting agreement with Isle of Wight Light & Power Co. (site of transformer house)1922–6.
75   Royal Naval College: demolition works following transfer of buildings from Crown Lands to Office of Works. 1923–39.
81   Royal Naval College: proposed lettings. 1925–7. College transferred to Commissioners of Crown Lands, 25 Mar.1926.
82   Royal Naval College: proposed lettings: 1927–33.
119   Royal Naval College: demolition works following transfer of buildings from Crown Lands to Office of Works, 1949–51.
134   Royal Naval College: use of accommodation in old stable block: lease to Saunders Roe Ltd. 1939–47.
150   Royal Naval College: demolition works following transfer from Crown Lands to Office of Works. 1945–8.
157   Royal Naval College site: use of accommodation in old stable: lease to Saunders Roe Ltd. 1951–60.

Hansard's Parliamentary Debates

Fourth series, volumes 118–20; 122; 123; 125; 130; 131; 142; 143; 145; 146; 150–8; 160; 170–3; 177; 186; 190–5; 198. (Feb. 1903–Dec. 1908).
Fifth series, volumes 2; 6; 7; 14; 15; 17–19; 22–31; 34; 35; 37; 39; 41–6; 50–4; 68–71; 80; 92; 93; 95–8; 116; 119; 122; 126; 129; 130; 132; 142; 152; 154. (Jan. 1909–May 1922).

Illustrated London News

Nos. 3355; 3358; 3362 (8, 29 Aug., 26 Sept. 1903).

Printed Primary Sources
Collections of Documents

Boyce, D.G., ed., *The Crisis of British Power: the Imperial and Naval Papers of the Second Earl of Selborne* (London, 1990).

Brett, M.V., ed., *Journals and Letters of Reginald, Viscount Esher, vols. 1–2* (London, 1934).
Kemp, P.K., ed., *The Papers of Admiral Sir John Fisher, vol. 2* (Navy Records Society, vol. 106, London, 1964).

Autobiographies and Memoirs
Bacon, Adm. Sir Reginald, *From 1900 Onward* (London, 1940).
Bush, E.W., *Bless our Ship* (London, 1958).
Fairbairn, D., *The Narrative of a Naval Nobody* (London, 1929).
Cunninghame Graham, A., *Random Naval Recollections, 1905–1951* (London, 1979).
King-Hall, S., *My Naval Life, 1906–1929* (London, 1952).
Sherwood, M., *Coston Gun* (London, 1946).

Guides to Entry and Training
The Entry and Training of Naval Cadets. Prepared by the Director of Naval Education under the authority of the Lords Commissioners of the Admiralty. (London, 1914).
Life on Board H.M.S. 'Britannia'. Gieves, Matthews & Seagrove Ltd (Portsmouth, *c.* 1904).
How to Become a Naval Officer and Life at the Royal Naval Colleges at Osborne and Dartmouth. Gieves, Matthews & Seagrove Ltd (Portsmouth, rev. edn, 1907, rev. edn, 1916, rev. edn, 1920).

Biographies
Bacon, Admiral Sir R.H., *The Life of Lord Fisher of Kilverstone* (2 vols., London, 1929).
Hunt, B.D., *Sailor-scholar: Admiral Sir Herbert Richmond* (Waterloo, Ont., 1982).
Lee, Sir Sidney, *King Edward the Seventh: a biography – vol. II* (London, 1927).
Mackay, R.F., *Fisher of Kilverstone* (Oxford, 1973).
Marder, A.J., *Portrait of an Admiral: the Life and Papers of Sir Herbert Richmond* (London, 1952).
Wester Wemyss, Lady, *The Life and Letters of Lord Wester Wemyss, GCB, CMG, MVO, Admiral of the Fleet* (London, 1935).
Ziegler, P., *Mountbatten: the Official Biography* (London, 1985).

Printed Secondary Sources
Davies, E.L., and Grove, E.J., *The Royal Naval College, Dartmouth: Seventy-five Years in Pictures* (Portsmouth, 1980).
Dickinson, H.W., '*Britannia* at Portsmouth and Portland', *Mariner's Mirror*, 84 (1998), pp. 434–43.
Hughes, E.A., *The Royal Naval College, Dartmouth* (London, 1950).
Marder, A.J., *From the Dreadnought to Scapa Flow. Vol. 1* (Oxford, 1961).
Matson, J., *Dear Osborne: Queen Victoria's Family Life in the Isle of Wight* (London, 1978).
Pack, S.W.C., *Britannia at Dartmouth* (London, 1966).
Wells, J., *The Royal Navy: An Illustrated Social History, 1870–1982* (Portsmouth, 1994).

Index

183